300 Pounds of Attitude

300 POUNDS of ATTITUDE

The Wildest Stories and Craziest Characters the NFL Has Ever Seen

JONATHAN RAND

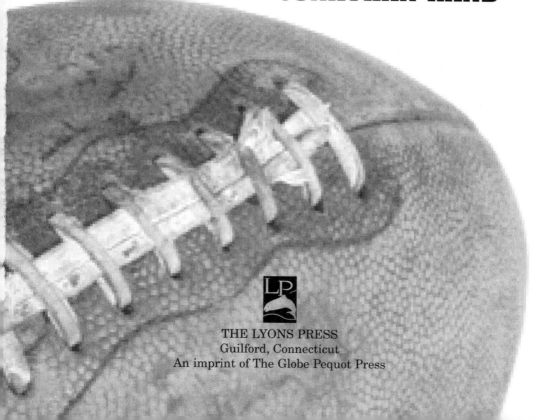

THE LYONS PRESS
Guilford, Connecticut
An imprint of The Globe Pequot Press

To buy books in quantity for corporate use
or incentives, call **(800) 962–0973**
or e-mail **premiums@GlobePequot.com.**

The Lyons Press is an imprint of The Globe Pequot Press.

10 9 8 7 6 5 4 3 2

Printed in the United States of America

ISBN 978-1-59921-176-3

Library of Congress Cataloging-in-Publication Data is available on file.

Contents

Introduction

America takes pro football much too seriously. The game makes us yell, vent, celebrate, and cry. Why shouldn't it make us laugh, too? Of all our major professional sports, pro football is the most pretentious and uptight. You'd never guess it can also be one of the funniest.

Maybe the helmets are to blame. Why is big league baseball considered the temple of chatter and clubhouse clowning while football is supposed to be a war? Because baseball players don't wear face masks, that's why. NFL fans don't get to see the laughs forming and mouths moving between tackles and touchdowns. And if a player dares take off his helmet and show his face on the field, he's looking at a 15-yard penalty. They don't refer to the NFL as the "No-Fun League" for nothing.

So we seldom get to hear what Mike Ditka said to Buddy Ryan, what Warren Sapp said to Brett Favre, what Shannon Sharpe said to Derrick Thomas, or what John Randle said to anybody and everybody. That's why this book is devoted to telling some of the best pro-football stories you've never heard. They're funny, offbeat, sometimes sad, and at the core of the game that has evolved into a national obsession.

If you ask any NFL player what he likes best about his job, besides game day and his paycheck, he'll tell you he loves the camaraderie. Every player is a kid at heart until he takes off his jersey for the last time, and much of what goes on in an NFL locker room and on the field is kid's stuff—funny, outrageous, and highly emotional.

Pro football always has been filled with loose cannons, rebels, and trash talkers. From Terrell Owens to Hollywood Henderson to Joe Don Looney, the NFL has had high-profile characters who speak their mind and march to the beat of a different drummer. Some have been more likeable than others, while all have made the game more interesting. Some players might even be certifiably half-crazy—yet what perfectly sane athlete signs up to get belted around by 300-pound behemoths for three hours every Sunday?

Pro football is a wonderful show for people watchers. Lou Saban, former coach of the Denver Broncos and Buffalo Bills, once grinned sadistically and said, "The fascinating part about this business is what it does to people under pressure."

Now, Lou was a fine one to talk. He once tried to cut Floyd Little, the Broncos' star running back, on the field after a fumble. But Saban's point was well taken. The pressure cooker of the NFL routinely produces explosions—the punches thrown and tempers that flare on the sidelines, for instance. These episodes may not be funny to those involved, but for the rest of us, they're remarkable scenes in a great human comedy.

I've spent thirty-five years covering pro football and have enjoyed what happens off the field and after the whistle as much as I've enjoyed the greatest games. Watching Baltimore Ravens tackle Tony Siragusa plant a big kiss on the cheek of a Japanese reporter during a pre-Super Bowl interview is as memorable as anything that happened in the game. It was also a whole lot funnier.

If that sounds screwy, just ask any longtime fan what he remembers most about the third Super Bowl—Joe Namath's prediction of an upset victory by the Jets over the Colts, or any play during the game? (You won't see any Roman numerals identifying Super Bowls in this book because those numerals are so pretentious, and this book is intended to be anything but.)

A great play or a great game makes me ooh and ah. But Sharpe's one-liners and anecdotes made me laugh all the way from the locker room back to the press box. The games make sportswriting interesting. But the people make it fun.

When the great players of yesteryear get together, they don't talk about X's and O's. They swap stories about the wonderful characters they played with and against.

Joe Montana may be the greatest quarterback who ever lived, but Steve DeBerg was the funniest quarterback you'd ever want to meet. Lawrence Taylor may have been a revolutionary linebacker, but pyromaniac Tim Rossovich was just plain revolutionary.

Johnny Unitas knew how to pick a defense apart, but Jack "Hacksaw" Reynolds knew how to cut apart an automobile.

Jerry Rice or John Taylor could make catches that changed the course of Super Bowls, but so could Max McGee—and he'd been up all night. Walter Payton could run to daylight, but so could Jim Marshall—while running the wrong way, to boot!

This book is confined mainly to the Super Bowl era, but not just to the NFL. You'll also read about the upstart leagues that came and went and all the chaos and laughs they generated. You'll read about the AFL-NFL wars, in which both leagues would stoop to anything—even kidnapping—to sign the best college players.

Forget about football breeding character. Football breeds *characters*, and this book is all about them.

Chapter 1
300 Pounds of Attitude:
Warren Sapp

Warren Sapp seemed larger than life as he was named to seven consecutive Pro Bowls from 1997 to 2003. He was at the heart of a defense that helped the Tampa Bay Buccaneers win the Super Bowl in January 2003. Sapp never backed down from a battle in the trenches or from a war of words. He signed with the Oakland Raiders in 2004.

THE BUCCANEERS LOST for twelve straight seasons before Sapp arrived in 1995. His arrogance and aggressiveness were contagious, and the Bucs became a play-off team in 1997.

"When Warren got here, everything changed," said Rich McKay, then the Bucs' general manager. "He brought an attitude."

You can imagine Sapp's indignation when he and linebacker Derrick Brooks were watching television in San Diego before a 1996 game and an announcer belittled their team as "The Yucks." Brooks and Sapp agreed they had to stop such insults. After the Buccaneers defeated the Eagles 27–10 for the 2002

NFC championship, Sapp reminded everybody, "They called us the Yucks!"

NFL commissioner Paul Tagliabue was explaining a $50,000 fine given to Sapp in 2003. Sapp had bumped an official while entering the field against the Washington Redskins, and the league said he spoke abusively to officials in two other games.

"I think his conduct over a three-week period, which was the basis for the fine, was substantially over the line, to put it mildly," Tagliabue said.

Some would say that Sapp's behavior has been over the line since he broke into the league. Before the bumping incident, the six-foot-two, 300-pound Sapp was told by the league to stop running through opponents in pregame warm-ups. Sapp called the league a "slave system," and added, "Make no mistake about it, slave master say you can't do it, don't do it. They'll make an example out of you. I guess I've become larger than life."

Sapp left Tampa Bay in March 2004 for a six-year, $36.6 million contract with the Raiders. He did not leave quietly.

"I had nine great seasons in Tampa," Sapp said. "There's no animosity. The only thing that sets me on edge is that for all the time me and [coach Jon] Gruden spent face-to-face, he didn't have the nuts to say, 'Warren, you just ain't in our plans anymore.' I would've took that a lot better than no call at all."

The Bucs' decision to not re-sign Sapp begged the question whether they considered him over the hill. "How can I be?" he asked. "Any O-line that's playing the Raiders, I guarantee they put ninety-nine on the board and say this is the man we must block. That's why I play. [For] the respect of my peers. Whether I'll get into the Hall of Fame is for someone else to decide. I'm just going to keep laying the bricks in the road and hope the road leads to Canton."

Before the NFL realigned its divisions in 2003, Sapp's twice-a-year confrontations with Packers quarterback Brett Favre were among the league's liveliest. Their rivalry began with a 21–7 Packers play-off win in 1997 in which Sapp recorded seven tackles, three sacks, two forced fumbles, and one recovery. Favre got up woozy after one hit and was concerned that his nose might be broken.

"Hey, pretty boy!" Sapp yelled. "What's wrong?"

When Sapp started trotting off the field to rest, Favre countered, "Where you going, fat boy?"

Sapp, angered, stayed on the field and replied, "I ain't going nowhere, playboy."

After the game, Sapp said, "He's wearing green and gold and I'm red and pewter. We're going to be fighting for a very long time."

Over the next several years, Sapp would put a lick on Favre, who would then jump up and slap Sapp's helmet and crack wise. Sometimes, they would get in each other's face and butt helmets.

"He won't talk to me no more," Sapp complained in 2003. "'Cause when he talks to me, I play better, so they won't let him talk to me no more. Only going off the field or back on the field. That's the only time he'll talk to me now."

Sapp was a loud, powerful presence in the Bucs' locker room and sometimes rubbed teammates the wrong way. Teammates also rubbed him the wrong way, especially malcontent wide receiver Keyshawn Johnson.

"The thing that I'll always say is that there's never been the real deal," Sapp said. "I want to see the wideout who's supposed to strike fear in a defense. Show me that guy."

Sapp was also irritated by Johnson's spotty attendance at off-season workouts, saying in 2001, "We've changed quarterbacks, we've changed coordinators, we've changed systems. We've changed almost everything—everything but the way our receiver comes to work."

Sapp recorded 16.5 sacks in 2000, a stunning total for a tackle. He didn't seem to believe anybody else worked as hard for his sacks. When New York Giants defensive end Mike Strahan set an NFL record of 22.5 sacks in 2001, Sapp joined critics who claimed Strahan's last sack was tainted because Brett Favre fell down for him in the closing minutes of a 34–25 Packers victory.

Strahan pointed out that to get near Mark Gastineau's record of 22 sacks, he had to record three and a half sacks against the Eagles the week before.

Sapp retorted: "Oh, yeah, your whipping boy, Jon Runyan. I forgot. I don't have one. They won't give me one guy that will go one-on-one with me for four quarters twice a year so I can whoop the hell outta him for eight sacks."

Strahan told Sapp he rarely saw one-on-one blocking and said, "But when it comes to getting to the quarterback, I'm good. I'm sorry. I can't help it."

Sapp replied: "Oh, no, I've never said that you wasn't good. But what I want you to admit to all of America is that [the final sack] was a gimme."

Seldom do you see a head coach go after an opposing player after a game. But that's what Packers coach Mike Sherman did in 2002 after Sapp nailed tackle Chad Clifton about twenty yards from the play. Cornerback Brian Kelly had intercepted a Favre pass and Clifton wasn't prepared for Sapp's hit. He suffered a broken pelvis and spent three nights in a Tampa hospital.

Sherman confronted Sapp on the field and accused him of hurting Clifton with a cheap shot. The league ruled the hit legal and Sapp said, "I can count the number of personal fouls I've had in my career on two fingers. I don't play that way. I know what a clean shot is. Front is front, back is back. I hit him right in the mouth."

Before a game against Minnesota in 2001, Sapp was holding a conference call with Twin Cities reporters when Vikings wide receiver Randy Moss unexpectedly joined the interview. Pretending to be a reporter, Moss obnoxiously yelled into the speakerphone, "Mr. Sapp, Mr. Sapp . . . how are you going to stop Randy Moss?"

Sapp, irritated, barked, "We're not concentrating on Randy Moss. He's part of the team we want to stop."

Moss and some ten reporters began laughing. "Hey, Dawg, it's me," Moss said.

Sapp laughed, too, and said, "That boy is crazy."

Sapp seldom is stumped for an answer. Here's some instant Sapp:

On why he decided to live in San Francisco instead of Oakland after switching teams: "Why would I not live in the city? It's like New York instead of New Jersey. It's a reverse commute, too. The best part is the food. There's a sushi spot in the Castro I like. I want to be treated like every other customer. It's why I go to sushi restaurants. They don't care who I am."

On why Sapp would make a horrible head coach: "You've got to be a politician and a dictator, a capitalist and a communist all at the same time. You have to be all those things, then deal with scouts who may or may not agree with you, twenty assistant coaches, all sorts of things. I don't know how they deal with it."

Sapp, on the NFL rule he'd most like to change: "The celebration rule. It's bad enough they make us run around with our helmet on all the time. That takes away our marketability because fans can't see our faces. There are only about ten guys in the league who the average fan can identify in street clothes. People only know most guys in helmets and with numbers. They wanted me [and several other Buccaneers] to do a Wheaties box after the Super Bowl, but they wanted our helmets on. Forget it."

Chapter 2
Look at Me:
Terrell Owens & Co.

Wide receivers became the NFL's foremost prima
donnas once Terrell Owens, Keyshawn Johnson, and
Joe Horn came into the NFL in 1996. They soon
started grabbing passes, Sharpies, cell phones,
and headlines wherever they went. They became
the poster children for the NFL's "look-at-me"
generation.

For the look-at-me-player, the gridiron isn't
just a playing field—it's a stage for some of the
NFL's most outrageous, commercial, and heavily
fined acts ever.

TERRELL OWENS PROVED he could show Madison Avenue a trick
or two during a Monday-night game at Seattle in 2002. He caught
a touchdown pass for the 49ers, then pulled a Sharpie marker out
of his sock to autograph the ball before handing it to a friend in
the stands. Owens, of course, had a contract with Sharpie, and
what better time for a free plug than during a prime-time telecast?

Owens's Sharpie received more attention than the outcome, a
28–21 San Francisco victory. Owens had shown his audacity in
Dallas three years earlier when, after each of two touchdowns, he
sprinted to midfield and spiked the ball on the Cowboys' star logo.

The second time, safety George Teague chased Owens and knocked him down. The NFL fined Owens $24,294 and suspended him for a game.

"I've learned that everyone is not going to like everything you do," he said. "After the Sharpie incident, I had people tell me they enjoyed it, lots more than those who didn't. Looking at the Dallas thing, maybe it was a little excessive, but at the time you don't think about that.

"I was just out there having fun. But I don't regret it. I know now whatever I do comes with a microscope. I will handle things better because you get wiser as you get older. You learn from your mistakes."

Owens couldn't even get through free agency in 2004 without causing a commotion.

He wanted to leave the 49ers and simply had to notify the NFL office that he was executing his option to void the last three years of his contract. But his agent, David Joseph, missed the filing deadline, so Owens still belonged to the 49ers. They promptly traded him to the Baltimore Ravens. This stunned the Philadelphia Eagles, who'd also been negotiating a trade with the 49ers, as well as a new contract for Owens.

Owens then announced he'd never play for the Ravens, which forced a deal between the 49ers, Ravens, and Eagles that sent Owens to Philadelphia. That was a lot of trouble to move one player. But then again, Owens had always been a lot of trouble.

Eagles coach Andy Reid didn't sound worried about Owens's antics, which included flexing his biceps and dancing the "dirty bird" after scoring. "I hope that I see T.O. do a lot of touchdown celebrations," Reid said.

Owens finally figured out how to stomp on the Cowboys' star without getting in trouble. On his second of three touchdown catches in a 49–21 victory at Texas Stadium in 2004, he made a point to stand on a star logo in the end zone. He pretended to ice skate after his first touchdown, and dunked the ball over the cross-bar after the third.

That same night, Owens became a party to controversy because he joined actress Nicollette Sheridan for the *Monday Night Football* introduction. In a spoof of Sheridan's ABC show, *Desperate Housewives*, Sheridan wore only a towel and flirtatiously asked Owens if he would skip the game and stay with her. She dropped her towel and they hugged, though viewers only saw her back above the waist. Fans and the NFL complained that the skit was inappropriate, and the Walt Disney Co., which owns ABC, apologized.

Owens apologized, too. But he may have found a second career. "I don't know how my acting skills were," he said, "but I can't play football forever."

As it turned out, Owens didn't even play the entire 2005 season. Fresh off a brilliant nine-catch performance in a Super Bowl loss to New England, Owens switched agents and demanded a new contract, though he'd played just one season of a seven-year, $49 million deal. Owens brought a bad attitude to training camp and was sent home for a week by coach Andy Reid. Owens then conducted a circus-like, impromptu press conference while working out in the driveway of his Morristown, New Jersey, home.

When Owens came back, he and the Eagles coexisted, despite his constant sniping at quarterback Donovan McNabb. There were still flashes of his showmanship, as when Owens caught a touchdown pass, then draped a towel over his arm, as if he were a waiter serving up a touchdown on a tray.

Owens should've stuck with pantomime. He complained that the Eagles showed "a lack of class" for not announcing his hundredth career catch during a late-October home game. Then he claimed the Eagles would be better off at quarterback with Green Bay's Brett Favre instead of McNabb. Reid said that was the last straw after "a large number of situations that accumulated over a long period of time."

The Eagles suspended Owens for four games without pay, then deactivated him for the rest of the 2005 season. Owens issued an apology, but it was too little, too late. When the Eagles released him the next spring, he wound up in Dallas, of all places.

Cincinnati Bengals wide receiver Chad Johnson proved there's a fine line between being entertaining and offensive. Johnson's antics weren't much different from those of T.O., yet Johnson was perceived as a fun guy while Owens was seen as obnoxious and selfish. "I think for the most part, [Johnson] is not an in-your-face-guy," Browns cornerback Daylon McCutcheon said. Before a 2004 game against the Browns, Johnson sent a bottle of Pepto-Bismol to each of Cleveland's starting defensive backs. This implied they'd be sick to their stomachs after trying to cover Johnson. But the Browns held him to three catches and beat the Bengals, 34–17.

Johnson was much bolder the year before when he guaranteed the Bengals, then 4-5, would defeat the 9-0 Kansas City Chiefs. The Bengals won, 24–19.

Johnson's fun often comes with a price tag. He made a 10-yard touchdown catch in a 41–38 victory over the 49ers in 2003, then went behind a snowdrift and pulled out a sign that read: DEAR NFL: PLEASE DON'T FINE ME AGAIN.

The NFL did not oblige. Johnson, who'd been fined twice earlier in the season for touchdown celebrations, was fined another $10,000.

He was fined another $5,000 in 2005 after he celebrated a 66-yard touchdown catch by using an end-zone pylon to putt the football. Imitating Tiger Woods sinking a putt, Johnson triumphantly pumped his fist.

Johnson's most famous celebration came a week earlier when he caught a 68-yard touchdown pass against the Colts, dropped to one knee, and pretended to propose marriage to a Bengals cheerleader on the sideline. She pretended to accept and they hugged. Then he picked up a sign that read T.O.—I GOT YOU, BABY. Johnson was trying to support the embattled Owens, whose celebrations had already been shut down for the season. The NFL hoped to shut them down for good by toughening the anti-celebration rules in 2006.

Joe Horn picked up the nickname "Hollywood" in 1996 when Kansas City teammate Derrick Thomas noted the rookie's flashy suits. Horn was also chatty. So it should have come as no surprise when, late in the 2003 season, Horn pulled out a cell phone after scoring for the Saints. With his helmet still on, he made a phone call from the end zone.

Horn had just caught his second of four touchdown passes in a 45–7 Sunday-night win over the New York Giants when teammate Michael Lewis handed Horn the phone. It had been stashed under the goalpost padding.

Horn explained, "I had told my kids to be at home, watching the game, and I told my momma, 'Mom, if I score the second one, I'm going to get my cell phone out.'"

New Orleans coach Jim Haslett wasn't amused. He'd already criticized Horn's touchdown celebration against the Atlanta Falcons that season. Horn had pretended to shoot two teammates, who dutifully dropped in the end zone. "He'll learn," Haslett said. "He's only thirty-two."

Giants defensive end Michael Strahan didn't appreciate Horn's phone call, either. "I have great respect for Joe Horn, but that's not original," he said. "Terrell Owens already beat everybody to that stuff. That's bush league."

Horn's phone call cost him $30,000, and Lewis was fined $5,000 for his part in the stunt. So Horn was quick to notice when, two years later, Falcons coach Jim Mora was spotted using a cell phone in Tampa during overtime. Mora was asking team officials how a tie would affect the Falcons' play-off chances, and Horn publicly asked why Mora wasn't fined. Nobody knew better than Horn that the use of cell phones on the sidelines is prohibited. The league fined Mora $25,000, which prompted him to say, "Expensive phone call. Consider that a lesson learned."

Before the Sharpie, the cell phone, and the proposal, there was Keyshawn Johnson's book. A year after he was the first overall pick in the 1996 NFL draft, he alienated most New York Jets teammates with the publication of *Just Give Me the Damn Ball!*

Johnson wrote that coach Rich Kotite, fired after the 1996 season, "can't coach." He claimed that quarterback Neil O'Donnell "didn't know what the hell he was doing." He demeaned fellow wide receiver Wayne Chrebet as a "team mascot."

Johnson was traded to the Buccaneers in 2000. His old grudges and fresh criticism of Jets coach Al Groh made for juicy pregame stories when the Jets visited Tampa Bay that September. The Buccaneers led 17–6 in the fourth quarter when the Jets scored two late touchdowns, the second on an 18-yard pass from running back Curtis Martin to Chrebet with fifty-two seconds left. Chrebet declined to gloat. The win was good enough.

Johnson wore out his welcome in Tampa once Tony Dungy was replaced by Jon Gruden in 2002. Though the Buccaneers won the Super Bowl that season, Johnson was unhappy that he wasn't a bigger part of the offense.

A 4-6 start in 2003 didn't make Johnson any happier. He missed a mandatory team meeting, a couple of pregame curfews, and the team flight after a road game. Finally, the Bucs deactivated Johnson for the last six games, even though he was midway through an eight-year, $56 million contract.

"For whatever reason he didn't want to be here," Gruden said. "He let me know that sometime after one of our early games."

Johnson said he didn't want to play for Gruden or any of his coaching friends, including Mike Holmgren, Andy Reid, and Mike Sherman. That eliminated much of the league. Johnson was reunited with former Jets coach Bill Parcells when he was traded to Dallas in April 2004 for wide receiver Joey Galloway. He was released two years later to make room for Owens, and Johnson became a Carolina Panther.

Wide receiver Randy Moss has always known how to grab the spotlight, though he's usually been more crass than clever. He celebrated a 34-yard touchdown catch in the Vikings' 31–17 play-off win at Green Bay in January 2005 by pretending to pull down his pants and moon Packer fans.

"It wasn't mean," insisted Moss, who signed with the Oakland Raiders the next season. "It was more a fun thing than a hatred thing. My teammates loved it. I'm probably gonna catch hell, but the Green Bay fans know I don't forget stuff."

Fox play-by-play announcer Joe Buck wasn't amused. "This is a disgusting act by Randy Moss," he said. "And it's unfortunate we had that on our air live."

Indianapolis Colts coach Tony Dungy, who made annual visits to Lambeau Field during his ten years at Tampa Bay, suggested Moss was getting even with a group of Packer fans who moon the visiting team's bus after games. "Anyone who has played in the [same division] knows what that's about," Dungy said. "It's kind of a unique send-off."

The NFL, which fined Moss $25,000 in 1999 for squirting an official with a water bottle, fined him $10,000 for his celebration in Green Bay. Moss, who earned $5.75 million in 2004, laughed off the fine. "Ain't nothing but ten grand," he said. "What's ten grand to me?"

Chapter 3
Homeless:
The Wandering Saints

Hurricane Katrina mauled New Orleans on August 29, 2005, and became the most destructive and costly natural disaster in United States history. It also badly damaged the Louisiana Superdome, home of the New Orleans Saints. Left without their home stadium or a livable city, the Saints spent their season as the NFL's vagabonds.

THE PLIGHT OF the Saints shouldn't seriously be compared with the plight of victims who lost their homes or lives to Hurricane Katrina. In the context of pro football, however, the Saints' 2005 season qualified as an unprecedented disaster.

In a league that prides itself on first-class facilities and unparalleled competitive balance, the Saints enjoyed neither. They practiced under bush-league conditions in San Antonio, their temporary home, and played "home" games in three different stadiums. Upheaval took its toll, and the Saints finished 3-13. "You take however difficult you think it has been—and then multiply that times ten," said Saints coach Jim Haslett.

You could argue for hours over which indignity was the worst. The Saints were kicked out of their Alamodome practice facility in December for the NCAA women's volleyball tournament. The Saints then moved their locker room to a high school baseball complex, and used a tent for a weight room. Coaches and front-office staffers had to move to a mostly vacant city waterworks building.

"We've been doing this—moving around—all year," guard Kendyl Jacox said. "So at this point, nothing surprises me. This would be acceptable if I was in high school. As far as a professional team, no, it's not."

The Saints lost their practice field for almost a week in October because of a home builders' exposition. Several buildings, including a large house, were temporarily built in the Alamodome. The Saints came to work one day and heard a loud pounding. They watched in astonishment as a building was constructed in one end zone.

The Saints even got thrown off some high school fields. Before facing the Green Bay Packers in the fifth game, they couldn't practice because the field they expected to use was reserved for a Special Olympics event. The next day, they arrived at the same field only to find it reserved for an ROTC group. On one of the days they could practice in the Alamodome, workers forgot to put down the padding between the cement and artificial turf. The players practiced, anyway, rather than bus to another high school field.

"NFL standards, huh?" kicker John Carney said. "We just know we're operating on a different playing field than our opponents. It's a challenge for us to overcome it."

Plush locker rooms and modern training facilities, which are common to NFL teams, became distant memories for the Saints. They used a trash can as an ice-water tub, which revives sore and tired legs.

"The hurricane was just the beginning of it," running back Fred McAfee said. "You never know what to expect. You expect the unexpected. And then, after that, the next thing tops the un-expected. A new precedent seems to be set every week."

Only two Saints players and two coaches moved their families to San Antonio. Four front-office staffers quit. For many in the organization, the working conditions proved stressful. One player was ticketed for driving while intoxicated in San Antonio.

"I asked him why and what happened," Haslett recalled. "He said he was so stressed here that he just lost his judgment. How could you fine someone like you normally would when they are under this kind of stress?"

The Saints opened their season at Carolina on September 11, just thirteen days after the destruction of New Orleans. Then came their first so-called home game, against the Giants, and that should've given the Saints a pretty good idea of the disaster awaiting them. The game was rescheduled for a Monday night, switched to Giants Stadium, and telecast nationally.

The game became a showcase for the NFL's fund-raising to help Katrina's victims. But it forced the Saints to play a strong team in its home stadium, and they lost. They evened their record at 2-2 before their season spiraled out of control with a six-game losing streak. It was snapped, ironically, when the Saints came back to Giants Stadium and beat the Jets in late November. They played their last seven home games in the Alamodome and at LSU's stadium in Baton Rouge. For the Saints, no place felt like home.

"It's been crazy," safety Mel Mitchell said. "Just because we play here and there and they put up banners that say 'Saints' does not mean it is home. Any time you get on a plane for a home game, you are not at home. We've been at a big disadvantage in this league since the hurricane. We don't see an end to it."

The Saints suffered so much that they were awarded the NFL version of hazard pay. The league and the NFL Players Association agreed to pay each Saint an extra $40,000 from a fund usually used to give merit bonuses to low-salaried players. According to the Saints, the bonuses were paid because the team "played the 2005 season under unanticipated conditions that included residences and practice facilities, personal and family travel between homes in New Orleans and San Antonio, and home games in three different stadiums."

Nobody complained that any of the Saints were overpaid.

Haslett finally was put out of his misery, and his firing was one of the few predictable developments for the 2005 Saints. Several reports claimed that he was so frustrated by his team's doomed season that he would resign, with a year left on his contract, if he wasn't fired. He quickly was hired as the St. Louis Rams' defensive coordinator.

"It was tough under these conditions for Jim and the team to win games," wide receiver Donté Stallworth said. "But this business is about wins and losses."

The Saints might've questioned the wisdom of settling for any port in a storm.

Chapter 4
Norman Einsteins:
Pigskin Geniuses

Anybody who knows there's a world beyond football would scoff at the notion that someone teaching eleven players to slam into eleven other players could be considered a genius. X's and O's should never be confused with the theory of relativity. Still, fans and media experts insist on anointing the latest Super Bowl–winning coach as some kind of genius.

"Nobody in football should be called a genius," quarterback-turned-commentator Joe Theismann famously insisted. "A genius is a guy like Norman Einstein."

PAUL BROWN OF the Cleveland Browns was the first modern coach accorded "genius" status. Al Davis probably was the first coach to cultivate it, and, granted, he performed an amazing job while lifting the Oakland Raiders out of the basement. Davis's coaching career ended when he became American Football League commissioner in April 1966.

He was elected by AFL owners, who were battling the established NFL, at a meeting in Houston. The Oilers' Bud Adams said, "What we need is some ruthless bastard who won't have any compunction about taking the war right to them."

Raiders owner Wayne Valley had just the man. "Take my genius!" he shouted. Valley's fellow owners took him up on the offer. One of Davis's first acts as commissioner was to have AFL publicity director Jack Horrigan insert "dynamic young genius" before Davis's name in the press release announcing his election.

Bill Walsh was the most celebrated genius of the Super Bowl era, and if anyone deserved the title, he did. He coached the hapless San Francisco 49ers to a Super Bowl title in three years by developing the West Coast offense, drafting superbly, and wheeling and dealing.

Before Walsh became a genius, he was sometimes a gagster. He didn't arrive at the January 1982 Super Bowl in Pontiac, Michigan, with his players because he'd attended a dinner in Washington, D.C. When the 49ers arrived at their hotel in Detroit, a white-haired bellman ran out to the bus to get their bags. The bellman was Walsh. He'd borrowed the uniform to loosen up a team playing in its first Super Bowl.

Playing the fool would become undignified for Walsh once he was labeled a genius. Because he didn't discourage that label, some rival coaches resented him.

But Walsh sure loved his X's and O's. He once absentmindedly drew a play on the bare shoulder of his wife, Geri, at a dinner. When California coach Bruce Snyder asked Walsh about a play over dinner, he diagrammed it on the tablecloth.

Joe Gibbs knew it would be a trap to get recognized as a genius. While he coached the Washington Redskins to four Super Bowls, Gibbs did everything in his power to avoid letting the so-called experts put him on a pedestal.

"Genius is a very embarrassing concept to me," he said. "Some people might think I'm supporting that theory. People might think I'm furthering it along."

Before his first of three Super Bowl wins, against the Miami Dolphins in January, 1983, Gibbs acknowledged there might be geniuses in the NFL. He just wasn't one of them.

"There does seem to be a number of people dubbed geniuses who have jumped up and maybe had a year here and a year there," Gibbs said. "They're not the geniuses. The geniuses are the ones who have done it for ten years."

Joe Bugel, Gibbs's offensive coordinator, explained, "Joe really doesn't like the word, 'genius.' We can't even mention it."

As if to reiterate that he was no genius, Gibbs told reporters at a Super Bowl: "I don't know why all of you are here asking me questions. I'm not that interesting."

Ah, but he is that interesting. Gibbs returned to the Redskins in 2004, after an eleven-year absence, and went through just his second losing NFL season before coaching the Redskins back to the play-offs in 2005.

Being known as a genius does have some advantages. Hall of Fame coach Marv Levy, who was labeled as too conservative when he was fired in Kansas City, sarcastically claimed he might have survived longer had he promoted himself as a genius.

"Talk about offense," Levy advises coaches. "Talk about your aerial circus. Give it a signature name. Call it—if your last name is Kappelmeier—by the appellation 'Air Kappelmeier.' Talk about how innovative you are. Tell them you invented the spiral. Tell them that you like to roll the dice, that punting is for sissies, and that defense is for criminal lawyers. Don't talk about reverses; talk about *triple* reverses and *fake* reverses. Say something catchy, such as, 'Our offense will take no prisoners.' And then do what it takes to win."

"Air Coryell," named for Don Coryell, was the first modern offense with a catchy nickname. In St. Louis with quarterback Jim Hart and in San Diego with Dan Fouts, Coryell coached the league's most explosive and imaginative passing attacks.

He didn't profess to be a genius, though sometimes he acted like one. As Coryell was leaving for work one day, his wife gave him a bag of trash to deposit in the bin at the foot of their driveway. Coryell was barely on the road when he began dreaming up a new play. It took him a very long time to notice the increasing stench in his car.

Levy had boundless respect for George Allen, his boss at Los Angeles and Washington. Yet, Levy couldn't agree with those who called Allen a genius.

"He wasn't," Levy wrote. "He just worked hard and had an indomitable spirit. How come all the geniuses in this world seem to be football coaches? Every time I read the newspaper or turn on my television, a new coaching genius is being discovered. Perhaps the best definition of a genius that I ever heard was offered by former Buccaneers coach, John McKay: 'A genius in football coaching is the guy who won last Sunday.'"

Chapter 5
The Big Splash:
Gatorade Showers

Gatorade couldn't have bought the publicity it began getting for free in the mid-1980s. What more could a sports drink company possibly ask for than to have its product poured over one of the NFL's most famous coaches, in the nation's biggest television market?

GIANTS NOSE TACKLE Jim Burt wasn't thinking about promoting anything or celebrating anything when he first soaked Bill Parcells in the waning moments of a home victory over the Washington Redskins. Burt was thinking about getting even. Parcells had badgered him all week about his matchup against center Jeff Bostic.

"Parcells went to Jim Burt," linebacker Harry Carson recalled, "and said, 'Jeff Bostic is a great player and he kicked a guy's ass last week, and if you're not ready, Bostic's really gonna hand you your lunch.'"

Parcells didn't stop there. Carson added, "He would go to other players' lockers and say, loud enough for Burt to hear, 'You'd better talk to Jimmy because he's gonna get his ass handed to him.' Parcells kept riding him to the point where Burt was getting irritated."

As the clock wound down on a Giants' victory, Burt came over to Carson. "He said, 'That Parcells is a [bleep], we've got to get him with something,'" Carson said. "I said, 'What do you mean, *we?*' He said, 'You're one of Parcells's boys, and if you do something with me, he won't do anything.'"

Carson had become close to Parcells when he coached the Giants' linebackers. "Everybody's jubilant and the game's out of reach," Carson said. "Burt looks around and says, 'Let's get him with the Gatorade.' I said, 'We have to wait until he takes his headset off. We don't want to electrocute him.' When Parcells took his headset off, we got him. I've always owned up to the fact that it was Jim Burt's idea."

Parcells didn't seem like a coach anybody would dare soak. He's well known as a tough, no-nonsense coach, and the Gatorade baths are nothing if not nonsense. But Parcells craves winning as much as any coach and is more superstitious than most. "If you did something one week and won, you did it the next week," Carson said. "That's how it gathered steam."

Burt lost interest in the soakings, but Carson took them to the next level in 1986. Parcells was soaked after each of seventeen victories, the last a 39–20 triumph over the Broncos in the Super Bowl.

"That's when people really noticed; it became a symbol of the season," Carson said. "We lost our first game to the Cowboys on *Monday Night Football*, and then we had to play the Chargers after they scored fifty points and beat the Dolphins. Everybody was so jubilant that we beat them. It was such a difficult task,

I thought, 'Let me get Parcells with the Gatorade.' As the season wore on, everybody knew it was coming; they just didn't know when.

"In the Super Bowl, I got Parcells twice. If you look at the tape, you see me get him one time. But if you look closely, you'll see his shoulder's already wet. That was the second time and it was water. I got him with Gatorade the first time. The second time was to rinse him off."

Parcells seldom saw the baths coming. "It always surprised me," he recalled after taking over the Cowboys in 2003. "I never had enough sense to recognize that potentially this could happen. I was too busy paying attention to what was going on. I avoided several and actually reversed it one time. I got him instead of him getting me."

Parcells, ironically, was nicknamed "The Tuna" because he didn't allow players to put anything over on him. An old TV commercial featured "Charlie Tuna," who desperately wanted to become a StarKist tuna. He was always scheming to get hooked, but always got a rejection message: "Sorry, Charlie, only the best tuna get to be StarKist."

Charlie was easily fooled. Not so Parcells, who was coaching the New England Patriots' linebackers in 1980. "My players were trying to con me on something one time," he recalled, "and I said, 'You must think I'm Charlie the Tuna'—you know, a sucker—and that's how it started."

The Gatorade dunk was quickly copied by winning football teams of all ages. "It was good," Parcells said. "I enjoyed it, and it became popular throughout the country. Now, is it ridiculous? Yeah, but it's fun, too."

Bills coach Marv Levy didn't consider the showers all that much fun. "I told them to knock it off and come up with something new," he said. "How about a couple of boxes of cigars?"

But so far, nobody's come up with a more popular way to celebrate a win. That's fine with Carson, a nine-time Pro Bowl pick, because the Gatorade baths are part of his continuing popularity.

"Women recognize me because I've been on some soap operas," he said, referring to *The Guiding Light, One Life to Live,* and *Loving.* "With kids, it's about the whole Gatorade thing. They think that's neat that I was the one who'd get my coach with Gatorade."

Philadelphia Eagles trainer Rick Burkholder started a controversy by running afoul of the sports drink establishment early in the 2000 season. He gave his players pickle juice to combat cramps during a 41–14 victory on a 109-degree day in Dallas.

Pickle juice is known as "the poor man's Gatorade" because salt retains water and helps avoid dehydration and cramps. But the favorable attention received by Burkholder put him in a bit of a pickle. Because of pickle juice's high salt content, he was criticized in a news release by the Professional Football Athletic Trainers Society.

The release criticized the "escalating media coverage of pickle juice consumption by the victorious Eagles." It added that "the best remedy to prevent cramps associated with dehydration is the scientifically proven combination of fluid and electrolytes— not pickle juice." The release also shilled for Gatorade.

Burkholder was getting a bad rap. He and his staff were testing players daily for dehydration, and for every pound a player lost in practice or in a game, he had to drink twenty ounces of Gatorade and water.

"Rick was loading them up so much that they were constantly walking around feeling like they had to go to the bathroom all week," Eagles coach Andy Reid said.

Burkholder used the pickle juice only after asking Reid if it was okay. Asked how the rotund coach responded, the trainer joked, "He asked if he could have the pickles."

Chapter 6
Cowher Power:
Bill Cowher

As coach of the Pittsburgh Steelers, Bill Cowher
chased a Super Bowl victory for fourteen seasons.
After narrowly grabbing their tenth play-off
spot under Cowher, the 2005 Steelers stormed
through the play-offs and defeated the Seattle
Seahawks 21–10 in the fortieth Super Bowl. No
other active NFL head coach had been with one
team for as long as Cowher, and few rivals could
match his passion and success.

WHEN CHUCK NOLL retired as Steelers head coach after the
1991 season, team chairman Dan Rooney wanted to replace him
with a Pittsburgh guy. Only people who drink Iron City beer and
drive to work through tunnels and over hills and bridges could've
understood Rooney's attitude.

Maybe in college football you hire a favorite son to coach. But
since when did an NFL franchise seek out a local yokel?

But the Steelers are not just any NFL franchise. They take
their steel-city, blue-collar traditions personally. Noll, who hailed
from nearby Cleveland, understood that. So did Cowher, a Pittsburgh native who grew up in the nearby Crafton area.

"He's what that community is looking for," said New England Patriots coach Bill Belichick, whose team won three of the four Super Bowls prior to the Steelers' title. "That [situation] fits his personality and he's what the Steelers want. I think that's the mentality of the ownership and the way the team has been run through the years.

"I love watching him coach. I think he represents the game with his passion for it and his intensity. As a special-teams player, he brings that blue-collar, tough mentality to the game as a coach."

Noll won four Super Bowl rings for Pittsburgh, and Cowher was hired with the hope that he'd bring home "one for the thumb." And he did.

Cowher's intensity stuck out when he played special teams for four years in Cleveland and Philadelphia. When Marty Schottenheimer hired him as Browns special-teams coach in 1985, Cowher, twenty-eight, became the NFL's youngest assistant. He was also the most dangerous. Cowher would sprint down the Browns' sideline, keeping pace with his kick-coverage units, and knock down anybody or anything in his way.

When Cowher became the Steelers' head coach, a TV camera caught him on the verge of jumping off the sideline to tackle a Jacksonville Jaguar headed for the end zone. Cowher barely held himself back.

The 2005 Steelers made the most improbable Super Bowl run ever. They stumbled to a 7-5 record before they won their last four regular-season games to squeeze into the AFC's sixth and last play-off spot. They then became the first team ever to win a Super Bowl after having to win three straight play-off games on the road. Cowher had been preaching that kind of perseverance for years.

"The season is like a roller coaster," he explained. "If you make the decision to be on the team, you strap yourself in at the beginning of the season. And once you strap yourself in, you are going up that first hill and, regardless of what happens, you are going to go up and down a lot more times, and regardless of what happens, you can't get off. If you are part of the team, there is no bailing out, not for sixteen weeks. And if you don't want to make that commitment, if you can't handle the ride, then you better get off right now because *we don't want you*."

Cowher's competitive juices bring out the best and most bizarre in him. While playing golf, he refused to accept a penalty for hitting his ball on top of a storage shed. Cowher climbed on top of the building and hit the ball.

When Cowher was an assistant in Kansas City, he and George Brett, who played for the Royals across the parking lot from Arrowhead Stadium, argued over whether football or baseball required the better athlete. They took the debate outside and Brett pretended to run the ball while Cowher tried to tackle him.

During a pro-am golf tournament, Chi Chi Rodriguez bet Cowher five dollars that he couldn't sink his putt on the eighteenth green. Cowher made the putt and had Chi Chi's bill framed and hung in his office.

When former NFL referee Gordon McCarter died in 2002, most of his obituaries mentioned Cowher. McCarter was in charge when the Steelers were penalized for having twelve men on the field in the first half of a 23–10 loss at Miami on September 18, 1995.

Teams routinely photograph every play from an upstairs booth to help them make adjustments, and the Steelers' print showed they did not have a twelfth man when they were penalized. As he jogged to the locker room at halftime, Cowher stuffed the print into McCarter's shirt pocket. Cowher was fined $7,500.

Sooner or later, just about every NFL official sees Cowher's face contorted with rage. His jaw juts fiercely, his lip curls into a sneer, and sometimes he delivers a "Cowher shower," an involuntary stream of saliva. "Any time you get close to him in a heated moment, you're likely to experience that," referee Ron Winter said.

Cowher had his share of heated moments in 2003, starting in January with a 34–31 play-off loss at Tennessee. After a running-into-the-kicker penalty gave Joe Nedney another chance to beat the Steelers with a field goal, Cowher charged referee Ron Blum, and later termed the penalty "ludicrous." Cowher claimed that he ran after Blum with the faint hope that he might wave off the field goal because the Steelers had belatedly tried calling time-out.

Cowher was fined $10,000 during the 2003 season for criticizing replay official Dale Hamer. Cowher wanted a review of Steelers quarterback Charlie Batch's fumble at the Cincinnati 10-yard line near the end of the first half of a 24–20 Steelers loss. Only the replay official can call for a review during the last two minutes of a half.

When Cowher was told that Hamer, a former on-field official, was in the replay booth, he said, "I guess that's why he's retired."

Cowher surprised onlookers when he chewed out his players for harassing an official during the summer of 2003. Then again, the official was Cowher.

He was refereeing a goal-line drill during training camp when defensive players began griping about his calls. "Get back and shut your yaps," Cowher told them.

Why his change of heart about criticizing officials? "It was all directed at me," Cowher explained. "I don't mind them talking to the offense, but they were all screaming at the official. I took a little offense to that."

NFL officials usually have thick skins, so they don't go home and stick pins in a Cowher doll. A few officials even admit to liking him.

"He's one of the good guys, seriously," Winter said. "He's the kind of guy that will let you know when he disagrees, but when it's over, it's over. He doesn't harbor something that happened in the first quarter and stay on you about it all the way into the fourth quarter.

"For me, anyway, you can deal with that. I have a responsibility to get off that play and get to the next one, so don't badger me about it for the next hour and a half, because now I'm thinking about things that I shouldn't be thinking about. So I appreciate coaches like coach Cowher that will do that—yeah, we disagreed, okay, it's over. There's nothing more that you can ask for."

Despite his background on defense and special teams, Cowher loves trick plays. When Chan Gailey was his offensive coordinator in 1996 and 1997, Cowher constantly urged him to be creative.

"He would come in every week with suggestions and gadget plays," Gailey recalled. "It got to a point where we told him, 'Bill, you can't have more than three gadget plays a week.' We had to tone him down or he'd be doing a bunch of wild things out there."

Why tone the coach down? The Steelers clinched their Super Bowl win over the Seahawks when wide receiver Antwaan Randle El, on a reverse, threw a 43-yard touchdown pass to Hines Ward.

"I'd rather experiment and fail than sit there and try nothing and accept mediocrity," Cowher said. "At some point, if you want to excel, there is risk involved. There are people who live their life based on the averages. That's not me. I have to stay one step ahead of other teams. If I don't stay progressive and remain open to change, then I can't dictate. I never want to be in a position where I am a follower, not a leader."

Chapter 7
Burnout:
Dick Vermeil

Dick Vermeil became a coaching star at UCLA in the mid-1970s, gaining a reputation as a winner and a workaholic. He coached the 1980 Philadelphia Eagles to an NFC title and the 1999 St. Louis Rams to a Super Bowl win. He retired three times, the last time after coaching the Kansas City Chiefs for five years.

VERMEIL'S OLD FRIENDS can chuckle now when they tell stories about how the famous coach burned himself out. Those stories weren't very funny at the time, but now they're central to the lore of how Vermeil came back in 1997 from a fourteen-year coaching sabbatical and took the St. Louis Rams to a Super Bowl title in three seasons.

Vermeil was only the fourth coach to take two franchises to a Super Bowl, the first coach to lead three franchises to 6-0 starts, and the first special-teams coach in NFL history. Yet Vermeil will be best remembered as the poster child for burnout. When Vermeil announced in early 1983 that he was retiring as Eagles coach because his workaholic ways had done him in, burnout and Vermeil became irrevocably linked.

Vermeil was already on the road to physical and emotional exhaustion, and it was only his first summer with the Eagles. He was watching film with his assistant coaches at their Chester, Pennsylvania, training camp the night of July 4, 1976. Their concentration was broken by sizzles, whistles, and booms from outside. Vermeil asked, "What the heck is that?"

He went to the window and saw the sky aglow. Carl Peterson, director of player personnel, told Vermeil he forgot to mention there would be a fireworks display at the Widener College Stadium that night.

"What for?" Vermeil asked.

"For the birthday," Peterson replied.

"Who's having a birthday?" Vermeil demanded.

"You know, the country—it's two hundred years old," Peterson said. "It's the bicentennial."

Vermeil replied, "I don't care whose birthday it is. Tell 'em to shut off the noise."

Vermeil was famous for his tunnel vision. He was diagramming a play for his coaches on a chalkboard in a Veterans Stadium meeting room the night of October 21, 1980. In the stands, Phillies fans were going wild as Tug McGraw, holding a 4–1 lead, was about to strike out Kansas City's last batter in the sixth and final game of the World Series. Police had horses and dogs poised to restrain the crowd.

A club official barged into Vermeil's meeting and announced excitedly, "The Phillies are one out away from winning the World Series."

Vermeil barely acknowledged the remark and went back to his chalkboard.

Vermeil's long days, short nights on his office couch, and tremendous passion helped propel the Eagles to the play-offs in just three seasons. But symptoms of burnout kept surfacing, though Vermeil was the last to spot them.

The Eagles one year wanted a Vermeil family photo for the team's Christmas cards, but the coach was rarely home during the season. Vermeil's wife, Carol, and their children were summoned to the stadium for the photo shoot. A touch of holiday spirit was provided by a Christmas tree borrowed from the lobby.

Carol Vermeil and Eagles general manager Jim Murray convinced the coach to discuss his obsessive work habits with the Eagles' psychiatrist. When his wife asked how the first session went, Vermeil replied, "Criminy, it'll take me a week to straighten that guy out."

Assistant coach Lynn Stiles also worried about the coach's long hours and gave him a copy of a book entitled, *Burnout: The High Cost of High Achievement*. Stiles soon found the book back on his desk, with a note from Vermeil: "This book is not for football coaches."

At times, Vermeil put as much pressure on his players as he put on himself. His players sometimes got so stressed out that they took drastic measures to lighten the mood. Linebacker Bill Bunting, who was out with a knee injury in 1978, drove around Veterans Stadium in a golf cart on a near-freezing day. He was wearing only an athletic supporter, a leather helmet, and sneakers.

"It was Dallas Cowboys week," Bunting recalled. "I knew Dick and the players were on edge. Every once in a while, I would have a wild hair and wouldn't mind what consequences I might face. I would do something to loosen the guys up."

Running back Louie Giammona, who was Vermeil's nephew, once tried to amuse his teammates by picking up a dead bird and biting its head off.

"These guys would ease the feelings of the team," running back Wilbur Montgomery recalled. "We knew we were going to be on the field for four hours. How do we get through this? Someone would do something crazy to make you forget about the four-hour practice so you could relax and have fun. When I played for Dick, I was tired, I was fearful, and I was scared."

Vermeil, trying to mellow a bit, underwent therapy during his career as a TV college football analyst. He turned down repeated offers to return to the NFL, including one from Peterson when he became Kansas City Chiefs general manager in December 1988. Finally, after most people assumed Vermeil was too old or too dis-interested to come back to the NFL, he accepted the Rams' offer in 1997.

Vermeil, sixty, had plenty of passion left. At the news confer-ence introducing him as Rams coach, he spoke for thirty minutes before reporters could get a word in edgewise.

"The single biggest thing that brought me back was, I wasn't proud of what kind of football coach I was when I left," Vermeil said. "I just knew I needed a break. I allowed the game to con-sume me because I loved it so much. I had such a passion for it that it blinded me to my own personal health and everything else going on around me—my wife, my kids. I was a mess.

"I better understand myself from an inner-Dick Vermeil standpoint. I can recognize when it's time to turn the projector off. I think I can recognize when it's time to give the player a break. I think I can recognize when it's time to give the coach a break. I think I can recognize when it's time to chew someone's butt out."

Though Peterson failed to bring Vermeil to Kansas City at first, he succeeded in 2001. Vermeil had retired after the Rams' Super Bowl win to spend more time with his family, but he found that his speaking engagements kept him away from home as much as coaching.

Vermeil took over a losing team, for the third time, and for the third time he reached the play-offs in his third year. The 2003

Chiefs started 9-0, but were knocked out of the play-offs by the Indianapolis Colts.

Peterson's main gripe with Vermeil was that he was too candid with reporters, and even rival coaches. That was certainly the case when the Eagles had the twentieth pick in the 1982 draft and planned to draft wide receiver Perry Tuttle from Clemson.

Before the draft, however, Vermeil told his coaching pal, Chuck Knox of the Buffalo Bills, that he wanted Tuttle. Knox had the twenty-first pick, but on draft day traded up to the nineteenth spot and grabbed Tuttle. Vermeil settled for wide receiver Mike Quick from North Carolina State.

"It proves once again there are no friends in the NFL," Peterson said. "Even though my head coach disagrees with me."

Knox tried to justify pulling a fast one on Vermeil. He said, "I'm sure I know what Carl meant. You can be friends. But business is business."

The Eagles got the last laugh, however. Quick became a four-time Pro Bowl receiver and Tuttle was a bust.

Vermeil was hired by Los Angeles Rams coach George Allen in 1969 as the NFL's first special-teams coach. Even after becoming a head coach, Vermeil tried to stay involved with his kickers.

While the Chiefs' Morten Andersen waited to attempt a 35-yard field goal that could break a 24–24 tie against the Oakland Raiders in 2003, Vermeil promised Andersen a bottle of wine if he made the kick. Vermeil, who hails from California wine country and started his own wine label, offered Andersen a bottle of Bryant Family Vineyards cabernet sauvignon. It was worth at least $500.

Andersen made the kick but never got the wine. The NFL said the reward could be interpreted as a salary-cap violation because it was compensation apart from Andersen's contract. The NFL was a much simpler place in the days when Vermeil was burning himself out.

Chapter 8
Title Town:
Vince Lombardi

Vince Lombardi, a native New Yorker, seemed a
fish out of water when he went to Green Bay in
1959 to revive the Packers. He built the most
famous dynasty in NFL history by winning
six conference titles, five NFL championships,
and two Super Bowls.

LOMBARDI WAS UNDER incredible pressure when he took the
Packers to the inaugural Super Bowl in January 1967. Everything the NFL and Lombardi stood for would go up in flames if
the Packers lost to the AFL's Kansas City Chiefs. NFL owners
kept reminding Lombardi that they were counting on him as the
keeper of the faith.

Lombardi's Super Bowl practices were brutal, even by his
standards. Some players worried they might leave their game on
the practice field. But when the team bus began to leave for the
Los Angeles Coliseum on game day, Lombardi told the driver to
stop. Then he danced a soft shoe in the aisle as players roared

their approval. "They were too tight," Lombardi confided to a friend.

The dance may have loosened up the Packers, but not Lombardi. After his team's historic 35–10 triumph, Lombardi could not loosen his necktie in the locker room. He had tied the knot too tight and the more he yanked it, the tighter it got. Lombardi, almost strangling, got a pair of scissors from an equipment manager and cut the tie loose.

The Packers would be on their way to a second straight Super Bowl, if only they could score on third-and-goal from the 1 with sixteen seconds left in subzero temperatures in Green Bay. The Packers trailed the Dallas Cowboys 17–14 in the 1967 NFL championship game, better known as the Ice Bowl.

The Packers used their last time-out, and quarterback Bart Starr suggested to Lombardi that he sneak between center Ken Bowman and right guard Jerry Kramer. Starr said that despite the icy footing, he could shuffle his feet and lunge into the end zone.

"All he said, which was so typical of the man," Starr recalled, "was, 'Run it! And let's get the hell out of here.' I'm going back to the huddle at this brutally cold time and I'm actually laughing."

Starr got serious long enough to score for a 21–17 win.

Linebacker Dave Robinson learned an early lesson about Lombardi's temper. Robinson had the poor judgment to help the College All-Stars defeat the 1963 Packers, defending NFL champions, in what was then an annual exhibition game in Chicago.

Robinson, a first-round draft choice, and two other Green Bay draftees were invited by a team official to visit the Packers at the Drake Hotel after the game. They were not greeted warmly.

"We walked in and Lombardi wouldn't speak to us, and the rest of the players looked at us like we were lepers," Robinson said. "Marie Lombardi was the only one who came over and talked to us."

Still, Robinson was looking forward to joining the Packers, especially when they reviewed films of the All-Star Game. He expected a compliment as the Packers watched a play on which he beat tight end Ron Kramer and made the tackle.

Instead, Lombardi berated Kramer and added, "That kid probably won't even make the team that drafted him."

Robinson was shocked. Safety Willie Wood leaned over and teased, "Don't buy a house in town, kid." Robinson concluded that Lombardi didn't recognize him on film because he wasn't wearing his usual Penn State number. He also concluded that Lombardi was furious about losing.

"He said that was the most discouraging loss of his career, and he worked the hell out of us," Robinson said. "He was a madman. We had to run extra laps."

The rookie spent the week listening to teammates sarcastically tell him, "Thanks a lot, Robinson!"

When Lombardi went to Green Bay in 1959, he needed a championship quarterback but privately doubted that Starr was forceful enough to fill that role. Lombardi's impression began to change in 1960 after he chewed out Starr for throwing an interception during practice. Starr confronted the coach in his office.

"The ball was tipped, it was not a clean interception," Starr recalled. "I told him not to chew me out in front of the team if he wants me to earn their respect. If he does it in the office I can take the chewing, if I have it coming. But if later he sees he made an error and apologizes in his office, he should apologize out there as well. He never, ever chewed me out in front of the team again."

Quarterback Sonny Jurgensen hoped he would finally lead a team to a Super Bowl title when Lombardi took over the Redskins in 1969. Lombardi had the team pointed in the right direction, but he died of colon cancer before the 1970 season.

"The very first practice, he had me call a pass play and I did it twice," Jurgensen recalled. "He said, 'Look, you're doing it too quickly, give it time to develop.' I said, 'You don't understand; with this offensive line, I've got to get rid of it.' He told me, 'Don't worry about it, we'll get you the protection.'"

Jurgensen stopped by Lombardi's office after a 7-5-2 season and was gratified to be told, "I want to congratulate you, young man, for the way you performed and your attitude this year. You completed 62 percent of your passes and you didn't even know the system. Next year you'll complete over 70 percent." Jurgensen replied, "One question: Look at how many times I got sacked. I thought you told me you were going to get me the best protection I ever had?"

Jurgensen, laughing, recalled Lombardi's comeback: "Yeah, but you knew the personnel better than I did."

Lombardi's trademark play was the power sweep. He made his offense practice it relentlessly. That was fine with middle linebacker Ray Nitschke, who loved pounding the tight end to get to the running back. This was not fine with tight end Gary Knafelc.

"[Nitschke] loved it," wrote Lombardi biographer David Maraniss. "Blood spurting out from his knuckles, smeared on his pants, some of it his, some Knafelc's."

The drill did not end until Knafelc—who feared Nitschke even more than Lombardi—pleaded: "Coach, by this time even Ray knows it's a sweep."

When Lombardi reigned, Green Bay became known as Title Town. Every Packers coach who came after Lombardi was expected to live up to his legacy, but the team went twenty-nine years between Super Bowl wins.

Mike Holmgren finally coached the Packers back to the top in 1996. Yet his players could still sense the ghost of Lombardi and his legendary stars questioning whether the new breed measured up.

"What people don't understand outside Green Bay," defensive end Sean Jones said, "is that we have to exorcise those ghosts: Willie Wood, Willie Davis, Bart Starr, Ray Nitschke. I think Ray Nitschke thinks we stink."

Nitschke insisted he thought otherwise. But nobody could speak for Lombardi.

Chapter 9
The Future Is Now:
George Allen

George Allen was an innovator. He hired the NFL's first special-teams coach, invented the nickel defense, and built the first state-of-the-art practice facility. His methods produced a 118-54-5 coaching record with the Los Angeles Rams and Washington Redskins. So why did owners keep firing him?

ALLEN, AN ICE-CREAM eater and milk drinker, had the diet of a Boy Scout. He also had the mindset of an inventor and a schemer who'd do whatever it took to win. Yet, Allen couldn't win the big one, which frustrated him to no end. When he guided the Redskins to the Super Bowl in January 1973, he wasn't about to let that opportunity slip away if he could help it.

"To win this game, I'd let you stick a knife in me and draw all my blood," he claimed before his team faced the Miami Dolphins in Los Angeles. Allen was fibbing, yet he'd do things to win that nobody else would try—or want to get caught trying.

Before the Super Bowl, Allen hired someone to chart the movement of the sun in the Los Angeles Coliseum in the hours during which the game would be played. This seemed odd, because Allen had coached the Rams in that stadium for five years. His best-laid plans couldn't prevent a 14–7 loss.

"Every time you lose, you die inside," Allen said, "and every time you win, you're reborn."

Allen was quirky and could drive those around him nuts. Three owners fired him. His spending on salaries and his building of Redskin Park led team owner Edward Bennett Williams to say, "George was given an unlimited budget and exceeded it."

Allen also had a fetish for organization and neatness. When he returned to the Rams in 1978, he insisted that linebacker Isiah Robertson pick up a paper cup that he tossed on the practice field. "You have to have discipline," Allen explained. "The field is our living room."

Allen was wary of espionage. In Los Angeles and Washington, he hired a retired Los Angeles police detective, Ed Boynton, to watch for spies. Players nicknamed him "Double-O" and sent him on wild goose chases by yelling, "Spy in the trees," or "Spy on the rooftop."

Though Allen's players joked about his imaginary spies, he was able to convince them that they had enemies nearly everywhere, especially in the news media. "His basic philosophy was, 'Us against them,'" recalled Richie Petitbon, a Rams and Redskins safety. "He was a great motivator and the players loved him."

When future Redskins general manager Charley Casserly applied for a coaching internship in 1977, Allen had him write a paper on three ways he could help the Redskins. Casserly later learned that was a standard Allen technique to challenge a prospective employee and maybe pick up a useful tip.

"People focus on the fact that George was eccentric, and he certainly was that," Casserly said. "He wasn't like anyone you'd ever met in your life. But what sometimes gets overlooked is that he was a great, great football coach. He could coach X's and O's with anyone and was really a defensive genius. His defense would give a team all kinds of different looks. George also knew personnel. He knew good players from bad players."

Allen also knew how to rebuild a losing team. He was hired in 1971 as coach and general manager of the Redskins, who'd been mediocre since the mid-1940s. He declared that, "The future is now," and wheeled and dealed until he had a winning, veteran team. He never kept a first-round pick during his seven seasons in Washington and routinely gutted the upper half of his draft to make deals. Draft choices were, after all, young players, and Allen had little use for them.

In his first six months with the Redskins, Allen acquired fifteen players and four draft choices while trading five players and twenty draft choices. He made nineteen trades before his first season, and eighty-one during his seven years in Washington.

Allen had a nasty habit of trading draft choices he no longer owned. Before the 1971 season, he twice traded his second-, third-, and fourth-round picks for 1973. He used his legitimate second-round pick to compensate the New York Jets for his signing of free agent defensive end Verlon Biggs. He traded that pick again to acquire Petitbon from the Rams. The other two picks initially went to Buffalo for defensive end Ron McDole. Allen used them again to get Chargers cornerback and kick returner Speedy Duncan.

The NFL office didn't monitor trades as carefully as it does today. The Redskins made the play-offs before the league discovered Allen's double-dipping.

"There was no intent to deceive," he claimed. "It was just a matter of a million and one things to do with a team we had just taken over and trying to do them all at the same time. If we finished in last place, this probably wouldn't even have been an issue."

Commissioner Pete Rozelle didn't buy that explanation. He said Allen also traded draft choices twice when he coached the Rams but wasn't penalized because his trading partners would always agree to quick settlements. Rozelle fined the Redskins $5,000, made Allen compensate the Bills and Chargers with legitimate draft picks, and dressed down Allen at an owners' meeting in New York.

Allen generally hated distractions. But he made an exception for the president of the United States. Richard Nixon, who'd been a reserve on the Whittier College football team, was a devoted Redskins fan, and sometimes made low-key visits to their practices. Well, as low-key as he could get with a Secret Service detachment in tow.

Before a 1971 play-off game at San Francisco, Nixon gave the Redskins a pep talk. He suggested they try a flanker reverse with Roy Jefferson, a play Allen had given Nixon in advance. It lost thirteen yards, and the Redskins lost, 24–20.

Allen loved pep talks. His win-at-all-costs reputation seemed to clash with his affinity for high school-like displays of team spirit. When Allen took over the Rams, recalled linebacker Jack Pardee, he suggested the players invent a team cheer. "You could see the players looking around, thinking, 'What's with this turkey?'" Pardee said. "But that's George Allen. His teams take on his personality."

Allen was the Chicago Bears' defensive coordinator in 1963 when they defeated the New York Giants, 14–10, in the NFL championship game. His players awarded him a game ball and on national TV serenaded him with the Bears' song: "Hooray for George, hooray at last. Hooray for George, he's a horse's ass."

Allen took that song with him to the Rams and Redskins. Marv Levy, an Allen assistant, introduced that song to Kansas

City and Buffalo when he became a head coach. It became a popular postgame tune for the Bills as they won four AFC championships from 1990 to 1993. Levy, though, wanted to make sure that Bills owner Ralph Wilson wouldn't find the song offensive.

"The first time we sang it, I explained the reason for it to Ralph," Levy recalled. "I wanted to make sure he understood the impact of it."

Allen's autobiography was entitled, *Merry Christmas—You're Fired!* The title referred to his firing in 1968 by Rams owner Dan Reeves. Although the two did not get along, the firing shocked fans after Allen's teams finished 8-6, 11-1-2, and 10-3-1.

In a rare NFL moment, a city rebelled against a coach's firing instead of celebrating it. About 7,500 signed up for a committee to save Allen's job. He also received the support of virtually his entire roster, and a dozen players stood behind him at a press conference the day after his firing. Six stars, including defensive end Deacon Jones and quarterback Roman Gabriel, said they'd retire unless Allen was rehired.

Reeves relented. But after two more winning seasons and a division title in 1969, Allen's contract was up and Reeves let him go again. This time, it stuck.

Allen kept getting canned even though he never had a losing season. When he left the Redskins in January 1978, he claimed he was fired, but the club claimed he'd been looking for another job. Negotiations for a new contract broke down and Williams said, "I gave George Allen unlimited patience and he exhausted it."

In 1978, Allen returned to the Rams, owned by Carroll Rosenbloom. For the first time, Allen inherited a team ready to win. But for the first time, he found players who wouldn't put up with his quirks. They threatened mutiny when he forbade them to sit on their helmets during practice breaks. Telling Robertson to pick up the cup was considered the snapshot of a fiasco that ended with Allen getting fired in the preseason. The Rams, under Ray Malavasi, reached the Super Bowl a year later.

Allen did not work again in the NFL but still had the urge to coach. He went to the USFL, taking over the Chicago Blitz in 1983 and the Arizona Wranglers in 1984. Then Allen, seventy-two, shocked the football world in 1990 when he took over a Long Beach State University team coming off a 4-8 record. After an 0-3 start, Allen's team rallied to finish 6-5. Allen called that 1990 season the most rewarding of his career.

"There were only two teams in Division I who started 0-3 and wound up with a winning record," he said. "And Alabama has a little more going for it than Long Beach State. Just having enough footballs for practice is a big deal for us."

But Allen's workaholic effort proved a killer. His wife, Etty, found him dead of natural causes on their kitchen floor a month after the season ended. He'd been fighting a cold since his players doused him with ice water after their final victory and he caught the sniffles after standing coatless on the Long Beach State practice field to watch Iowa practice before the Rose Bowl.

"I realized when he went to Long Beach State that I finally understood him," Etty Allen said. "The level of competition is not what matters—it's the competition itself."

Chapter 10
McKay by the Bay:
John McKay

John McKay experienced some of the highest
highs and lowest lows he could have experienced
as a football coach. He won four national
championships at the University of Southern
California, then brought the Tampa Bay
Buccaneers into the NFL with twenty-six straight
losses. Fortunately for McKay, he had a sense
of humor to get him through the Buccaneers'
most hapless days. For every loss, he had half
a dozen one-liners.

"THE MISCONCEPTION ABOUT me is that I'm a funny man,"
John McKay said. "I'm as mean as they come."

It wasn't a total misconception. McKay's one-liners made him
one of the most often-quoted coaches in NFL history. He was
funny, but in a sarcastic kind of way.

McKay had to have a sense of humor to coach the Buccaneers.
Here was a coach accustomed to winning big at USC, yet who in
1976 was leading an expansion franchise bound to lose. It was
not a good omen when, just before the Bucs' regular-season
debut in Houston, they got lost following McKay back to the

locker room after warm-ups. Just minutes before kickoff, the team found a security guard who showed them the way.

Though the Bucs figured to struggle for a while, nobody could have foreseen that they would start 0-26. During this streak, McKay honed his sarcasm to a fine edge. Asked what he thought of the Bucs' execution during their winless first season, McKay replied, "I'm in favor of it."

After a 28–19 loss to the Kansas City Chiefs, he said, "They were absolutely horrible and that's the best thing I can say. Besides that they were bad. These people are not poorly paid, you know."

The 1976 Bucs fell to 0-13 after a 42–0 loss at Pittsburgh. "There were times," McKay said, "I felt like leaving the stadium and hitchhiking home."

A 31–14 home loss to the New England Patriots wrapped up an 0-14 season, and McKay promised, "We will be back. Maybe not this century, but we will be back and we will be a better football team."

The Buccaneers *were* better in 1977. But not by much. They started 0-12 and suffered six shutouts, giving them eleven shutouts in two years. THROW MCKAY IN THE BAY T-shirts became increasingly popular.

After a 10–0 loss to the Los Angeles Rams, McKay said, "We couldn't score against a strong wind."

A 17–0 loss to the Atlanta Falcons moved him to say, "Our offensive line was horrible. I was betting some of our six-foot-six, two-hundred-and-fifty-pound linemen would block somebody. That's what they get paid to do."

The Bucs fell to 0-26 with a 10–0 loss to the Chicago Bears. "I may quarterback the team myself," McKay said, "or go to the damn single wing."

The Bucs' losing streak put a lot of pressure on opponents. Nobody wanted to be remembered as the first team to lose to them. They had to win sometime. Didn't they?

The answer came December 11, 1977, at New Orleans, where the Bucs breezed to a 33–14 victory. McKay was elated and said, "I thought it was the greatest victory in the history of the world."

Now it was the turn of Saints coach Hank Stram to deliver a McKay-like postmortem. "What a nightmare," he said. "It's the worst experience of my coaching career. We're ashamed of our people, our fans, our organization."

But the Bucs weren't through winning. They ended the season with a 17–7 home victory over the St. Louis Cardinals. McKay crowed: "I'm going to go home, take a shower, and tell myself what a great coach I am. Fifteen more and we'll tie the record for most consecutive wins."

McKay was impatient with reporters who kept asking about his transition from college football to the NFL. He did not suffer fools gladly and was touchy if he thought he was being treated like a college coach. Like the time a reporter asked him if the wishbone offense could work in the NFL.

McKay, trying to drive home the point that he belonged in the NFL, declared that he had read the biographies of such great coaches as Don Shula and Vince Lombardi. "I'm as mean as any of 'em," McKay insisted.

Just as McKay finished reeling off the titles of several coaches' biographies, Frank Klein, the cigar-chomping sports editor of *The Tampa Times*, piped up from the back of the room, "And all of them [ghost]written by sportswriters!"

McKay, for once, was speechless.

McKay and John Ralston, former Stanford coach, had been unfriendly college rivals, and McKay usually beat him. But when they met in 1976, Ralston was coaching the Denver Broncos and finally held the stronger hand. He played it for all it was worth.

The Bucs led 13–10 in the third quarter, but the Broncos scored thirty-eight straight points and won, 48–13. Ralston ran across the field to shake McKay's hand but McKay turned away, cursed Ralston, and accused him of running up the score. "I think they wanted to show me I'm really a college coach," McKay said.

He and his players were in so much of a rush to catch their bus to the airport that they left owner Hugh Culverhouse at Mile High Stadium.

McKay showed Tampa Bay in 1979 that he could produce more than one-liners. His team won the NFC Central title, then beat the Philadelphia Eagles, 24–17, in a divisional play-off game. Ricky Bell ran for 142 yards and two touchdowns against the Eagles while carrying thirty-eight times, a play-off record. Asked why Bell had carried the ball so often, McKay replied, "It's not heavy."

The Buccaneers ended their season with a 9–0 home loss to the Los Angeles Rams in the NFC championship game, yet their future looked bright. It wasn't.

McKay guided the Bucs back to the postseason twice but couldn't win another play-off game. They finished 2-14 in 1983, and McKay's frustration grew as he watched kicker Bill Capece misfire in a 12–9 late-season loss in overtime to the Green Bay Packers.

"Capece is kaput," McKay declared. "There will be no more field goals kicked by the Bucs this year, no matter what the score is. I'm tired of being crucified."

Chapter 11
Dutch:
Norm Van Brocklin

Norm Van Brocklin is in the Hall of Fame for his quarterback play, not for his coaching. As a passer, he had the biggest day of all time. As head coach of the Minnesota Vikings and Atlanta Falcons, his big days were few and far between.

BETWEEN HIS FIERY temper, blunt language, and bad teams, it would be hard to imagine Van Brocklin surviving as a head coach in today's NFL. Come to think of it, he was fortunate to survive as long as he did coaching in yesterday's NFL.

Van Brocklin, known as "the Dutchman" or "Dutch," coached for nearly thirteen seasons. Then came his most famous tantrum, after his Falcons lost 42–7 to the Miami Dolphins in 1974. A reporter asked Van Brocklin if he was still a fighter and he replied, "Let's stack the furniture. Anybody who's man enough to fight me, stand up."

That rant, combined with a 2-6 record, got him fired the next day. Van Brocklin, however, got in the last word with sportswriters before he underwent brain surgery. "I want the brain of a sportswriter," he said, "because I want one that hasn't been used."

Van Brocklin wasn't just hard on sportswriters. He was also hard on mistake-prone players, and from 1961 to 1966 in Minnesota, and from 1968 to 1974 in Atlanta, he had more than his fair share of them.

"No one, not even Lombardi, could chew out a player like Dutch and reduce grown men to tears," said former Los Angeles Rams teammate Tom Fears, who went on to coach the New Orleans Saints.

Harmon Wages, a Falcons running back under Van Brocklin, said, "I always envisioned him returning in a chariot, down a road, with a hundred football players crucified on each side, like the final scene in *Spartacus*."

Maybe Van Brocklin would have been a more patient coach if he hadn't been such a great quarterback. With the Rams in 1951, he set an NFL single-game record by passing for 554 yards. In his final game, he and a stubborn defense led the Philadelphia Eagles to a 17–13 victory over the Green Bay Packers in the 1960 NFL title game.

As a player, Van Brocklin could motivate teammates by browbeating them. But that style didn't work for him once he became a coach.

"He was a Jekyll and Hyde," Eagles teammate Sonny Jurgensen recalled. "He could be having fun one minute and the next minute he'd be dead serious. If people were cutting up and having too much fun [on the field] he'd say, 'What the hell is going on?' But he was in control. It was part of his leadership."

For the coach of the Vikings on their maiden voyage, quarterback Fran Tarkenton might have seemed like a godsend. But not to Van Brocklin. Tarkenton had no interest in copying Van Brocklin's classic style, and scrambled his way to the Hall of Fame. His improvisation drove his coach nuts.

"He will win some games for us we shouldn't win, but he will also lose some games we should win," Van Brocklin said.

Former Vikings general manager Bert Rose, recalling the Van Brocklin-Tarkenton era, said: "Fran would scramble, get sacked two straight times, and we'd have a third-and-fifty. Then Fran would scramble again and complete a pass for a first down. It drove Dutch to fits of apoplexy."

Tarkenton didn't throw the prettiest long ball, either. Van Brocklin watched a wobbly deep pass in practice and remarked, "That's right, Francis, give him both ends to catch."

Van Brocklin didn't have much use for the corporate NFL, which commissioner Pete Rozelle was promoting in the 1970s. New Falcons publicist Robert "Hal" Hayes, at the request of NFL Properties, asked the coach to write down his favorite play.

"Gimme that," Van Brocklin snarled as he grabbed the form that Hayes was supposed to return to the league. Hayes beat a hasty retreat from Van Brocklin's office and returned only when the coach called for him. Van Brocklin tossed a crumpled ball of paper at Hayes and said, "There's my selection."

Hayes picked the paper up off the floor, went back to his office, and unfolded it. Van Brocklin had written: "My favorite play: *Our Town* by Thornton Wilder."

Chapter 12
So Jimmy Says to Jerry: Johnson-Jones Feud

You would think that the couple that wins together would stick together. And owner Jerry Jones and coach Jimmy Johnson did stick together for five seasons, in which they restored the Dallas Cowboys to glory. Jones and Johnson led the Cowboys to back-to-back Super Bowl victories in the 1992 and 1993 seasons and might have gotten a few more had they been able to build a wall between their egos.

Dave Wannstedt, a Johnson assistant in Dallas and Miami, said, "God, when you have a great team and you're winning Super Bowls, it's just tough to comprehend that you can't make things work."

JONES AND JOHNSON, also known as "the JJs," were publicly portrayed as being thick as thieves. They were teammates on Arkansas's undefeated team in 1964 and roommates on the road. Many assumed Johnson was in hog heaven, having his old pal as owner and general manager.

"I don't know where those stories started," Johnson said. "I didn't do anything to kill them. I don't know, maybe you don't want to hurt somebody's feelings. We never went out [socially]. We were both offensive guards as sophomores. We did room maybe twenty nights on the road, but that was because of our names [being closest in alphabetical order]. And we were co-captains as seniors—*every* senior was a co-captain.

"I guess our wives got to know each other watching games together when we were on the road. And yes, Jerry and I did stay in touch because I was at Oklahoma State and he did a lot of business in Oklahoma City. But it was never this buddy-buddy thing. Neither one of us ever talked about our futures. Jerry was going to make money and I was going to become an industrial psychologist."

Johnson, instead, became a winning coach at Oklahoma State. He got his big break at the University of Miami, where he won a national championship. Still, many considered Jones naïve when he gave Johnson a ten-year contract and declared, "Jimmy Johnson will be worth five Heisman Trophy winners and five first-round draft choices."

Who could have guessed Jones would be proven right? But that remark was viewed as stomping on legendary Tom Landry's football grave. So was a *Dallas Morning News* photo of Jones and Johnson eating at a Mexican restaurant frequented by Landry. Jones and Johnson had actually asked a hotel clerk to recommend a restaurant where they could enjoy some privacy. Instead, they were directed to a popular spot where they were sure to be noticed.

Criticism kept coming for Jones and Johnson when the Cowboys finished 1-15 in 1989. They knew the team had to be rebuilt, and stockpiled high draft picks, mostly through the controversial 1989 trade of star running back Herschel Walker. Johnson, recalling that first season, said, "It was like going to the dentist twenty times to make sure you wind up with a good set of teeth."

By 1992, Jones and Johnson were headed to their first Super Bowl. Johnson, however, lacked the temperament to tolerate Jones's flamboyance. Jones was involved in personnel decisions, had his own TV show, radio show, and newspaper column, and enjoyed parading his celebrity friends at Texas Stadium.

Jones led an entourage to the field at the end of the third quarter as the Cowboys led the Bears, 27–0, in the last game of the 1992 regular season. Jones's guests included Prince Bandar bin Sultan, the Saudi ambassador to the United States, and six bodyguards.

Then the Cowboys got sloppy, and Johnson was incensed to see Jones and his pals acting as if the game was over. Johnson ordered the first-team offense back on the field before rethinking the logic of risking injury to key players in a meaningless game.

The Cowboys won 27–14 and boosted their record to 13-3, yet Johnson was still fuming. After leaving the locker room, he headed for Jones's suite, with college scouting director Larry Lacewell in hot pursuit.

"When I walked in, their noses were about three inches apart," said Lacewell, one of Johnson's confidants who tried to keep him away from Jones at times like this. "I felt it was pretty heated, so I tried to make some jokes. I mean, Jimmy looked like he was about to blow. Then I said, 'Jimmy, you did win thirteen games. That's pretty damn good. Nobody around here has ever done that.' I think Jerry appreciated I was there. But all Jimmy would do was clench his teeth and say, 'Lace, I'll smile tomorrow.'

"The truth is, Jimmy was probably getting a little tight in the throat about Chicago getting it back to 27–14. It's like he had been hexed by Jerry and the prince."

Johnson never did practice industrial psychology, but still enjoyed getting into others people's heads. He made a career of keeping opponents off balance—on and off the field. Before the Cowboys met the San Francisco 49ers for the NFC title in January 1994, Johnson was driving to dinner while listening to Dallas sports columnist and talk show host Randy Galloway. Johnson grabbed his car phone, called Galloway, and announced,

"You can put it in a three-inch headline: We *will* win the ball game."

San Francisco coach George Seifert had to admit that Johnson had "balls" to go out on a limb like that. He added that the 49ers would find out whether they were made of brass or papier-mâché. The Cowboys won 38–21, then repeated as Super Bowl champions with a 30–13 win over the Buffalo Bills. But that win came without a guarantee.

Johnson often used psychology in coaching. His favorite book was *Flow* by University of Chicago psychology professor Mihaly Csikszentmihalyi. The author explained that true happiness results when people are so involved in an activity that nothing else seems to matter. Johnson used the book to motivate himself and his players.

"*Flow* talks about the difference between pleasure and being truly happy," Johnson said. "Certain things bring you pleasure, but they don't make you happy. A good meal is pleasurable but it doesn't make you happy. So I can experience some pleasurable things, but to be happy, I've got to be challenged, I've got to accomplish things, I've got to have some sense of satisfaction and achievement."

Johnson also motivated players through fear and routinely reminded them that their jobs were on the line. "Everybody needs motivating, from the vice president of IBM to a professional football player to a head coach," he said. "This old b.s. about, 'They're paid a lot to do a job and they've got to be self-motivated'; that doesn't hold water with me."

Johnson could be manipulative. He once told a Super Bowl press gathering that he found the media a convenient messenger to his players. "I don't talk to you," Johnson said smugly. "I talk through you."

The "JJs" broke up at the 1994 NFL meetings in March at Orlando. Jones spotted some Dallas reporters in the lobby of the league hotel and told them they'd be missing "the story of the year" if they went to bed. He said he was thinking about replacing Johnson with former Oklahoma coach Barry Switzer.

"There are five hundred coaches who would love to coach the Dallas Cowboys," Jones said. "I think there are five hundred who could have coached this team to the Super Bowl. I really believe that."

When Johnson heard that, he was livid, especially because he'd disliked Switzer since they were bitter rivals at Oklahoma State and Oklahoma. Johnson told Jones he wanted out and accepted a $2 million settlement. Jones then hired Switzer, who said he felt as if he'd won the lottery.

A late-October game in Miami between the Dolphins, now coached by Johnson, and the Cowboys became the soap opera of the 1996 season. The Cowboys were defending Super Bowl champions, and Johnson again was trying to replace a legend, Don Shula.

Troy Aikman, the first player drafted by Johnson in Dallas, threw for 363 yards and three touchdowns in a 29–10 victory. With two minutes left, the Cowboys were at the Miami 7, and Jones wanted Switzer to rub salt in Johnson's wounds.

"I bet Jimmy would grab the ball and go for it!" Jones yelled. Switzer told his owner that running up the score would be pointless and had Aikman kneel three times and end the game.

"You're too classy for me," Jones replied, laughing.

Chapter 13
So Ditka Says to Buddy:
Ditka-Ryan Feud

Football-wise, this was a match made in heaven. Personality-wise, this match stood no more of a chance than Dennis Rodman and Carmen Electra. Mike Ditka and Buddy Ryan barely coexisted as coaches for four stormy seasons in Chicago that culminated in a championship season for the Bears.

RYAN WAS A feisty, egotistical, and maverick defensive coordinator. Ditka was a Hall of Fame tight end and a tough, blunt, nononsense head coach. They proved that people don't have to like each other to win together.

It's hard to identify the lowest point of their relationship. Maybe it was when Ditka challenged Ryan to a fight during halftime of a loss in Miami in 1985. Or when Ryan kicked Ditka out of a defensive meeting. Or any of their grudge matches when Ryan took over the Philadelphia Eagles and was dying to defeat his old boss.

Ryan had no natural loyalty to Ditka because he was a holdover from Neill Armstrong's staff. Defensive players had lobbied Bears owner George Halas, almost eighty-seven, to let Ryan take over. Halas promised to keep Ryan around but made Ditka the head coach in 1982.

"Buddy Parker is a fine coach, you have nothing to worry about," Halas told Bears defensive players, according to Don Pierson of the *Chicago Tribune*.

Ditka's team finished 3-6 in a strike-torn season, but in his first full season, 1983, the Bears improved to 8-8. Then came five straight NFC Central titles, and in 1985 the Bears went 18-1 and won the Super Bowl.

You might expect that kind of success to encourage coaching camaraderie. Instead, the Ditka-Ryan rift widened. The 1985 Bears boasted one of the best defenses in NFL history and Ryan was in no mood to share the credit. He boasted that he would leave the defensive game plan on Ditka's desk and not even talk to him.

"Have I spoken to him since I left?" Ryan said after leaving the Bears. "Hell, I didn't speak to him when I was there."

The 1985 Bears stood 12-0 and were coming off two straight shutouts before a 38–24 loss at Miami. Dolphins quarterback Dan Marino kept burning the Bears by throwing to his third wide receiver, Nat Moore, and at halftime Ditka told Ryan to cover Moore with a cornerback instead of linebacker Wilber Marshall. When Ryan refused, Ditka challenged him to a fight.

"We can do it any way you want to," Ditka said. "We can go right out back and get it on or you can shape your ass up."

Ryan also knew how to get under his players' skins. But he did that to motivate them.

"We're watching film one week and there's O.J. Anderson [of the New York Giants] running over somebody," defensive end Dan Hampton recalled. "Ryan says to Otis [Wilson], 'Ooh, you better get hurt in practice. I don't want him running over you like that.' That's all he had to say. Otis was ready to go.

"He'd tell [Steve] McMichael, 'I don't care if you go out and get drunk. Just don't take any of the real players with you.' And he'd say it in a way that would have McMichael just fuming."

Hampton claimed Ryan was even able to improve quarterback Jim McMahon's protection. "He'd say to the offensive line, 'You fat-asses can't block anybody in practice; how you going to do it in a game?'" Hampton said. "And [Jimbo] Covert, [Mark] Bortz, and those guys would turn into animals."

The night before the January 1986 Super Bowl in New Orleans, Ryan told his defense that he was leaving to coach the Eagles. The Bears had shut out both play-off opponents, then yielded only seven yards rushing—a Super Bowl record—in a 46–10 victory over the New England Patriots. Ryan's players carried him off the field.

"I'm not happy he's gone, I'm elated," Ditka said. "We'll be better next year."

Ryan acknowledged that he and Ditka were never buddies. "We never went out socially, but then, I'm not much of a socializer," Ryan said. "I should be so lucky to have a Buddy Ryan around. I'd like to have somebody around to take care of me."

With Ryan in Philadelphia, the lid blew off his feud with Ditka. When their teams met in week two of 1986, Ryan announced that the Bears didn't have a chance to repeat as champions. McMichael responded: "The old fat man has been talking a little stuff in Philly, hasn't he?"

The Bears won 13–10 in overtime. They also beat the Eagles 35–3 in 1987 on the first weekend of replacement games during a players' strike. The teams met again in a 1988 divisional play-off game at Soldier Field. Before that game, Ryan alluded to Ditka's two straight play-off losses at home and needled, "I haven't lost a play-off game in Chicago, and I think I'm probably the only guy who can say that."

Ryan claimed his defensive starters, man for man, were better than Ditka's, except for middle linebacker Mike Singletary. Eagles linebacker Todd Bell, one of two Bears who missed out on the Super Bowl season because of salary disputes, ripped the Bears organization and Ditka. He also talked trash during the game, a 20–12 Bears win.

Ryan gave credit to the Bears' defense but not to their coaching. Bears fans showed how fed up they were with Ryan's act when the Eagles visited Soldier Field on a Monday night in 1989. Fans taunted Ryan with chants of *Bud-dy, Bud-dy*, and one sign read RYAN'S NO BUDDY OF OURS.

After a 27–13 victory that made the Bears 4-0, Ditka made it clear that he, too, was fed up with Ryan. "I'm the duck and it's like water off a duck's back," Ditka said. "He's just jealous. You know what they say: 'Empty tin cans make the most noise,' and he's an empty tin can. This is between the Bears and Eagles, not Ditka and Ryan. We all know who would win that one—Ditka, hands down."

Bears safety Shaun Gayle suggested, "Maybe what we could do after the game is all the players circle our cars in the parking lot and we let the two of them go at it."

Singletary, who remained close with Ryan, said, "You feel like a child caught between two parents who don't get along."

Ditka wasn't the only one who sometimes wanted to smack Ryan. When Ryan was Houston coach Jack Pardee's defensive coordinator in 1993, the Oilers took an eleven-game winning streak into a home play-off game against the Kansas City Chiefs. Ryan had arrived in Houston with great fanfare and was billed as the missing link to a championship.

When tight end Keith Cash caught a Joe Montana pass to open the Chiefs' scoring in their 28–20 win, he spiked the ball on an end-zone banner of Ryan's face. It was easy to think of another old tight end who would've loved to do the same.

Chapter 14
Super Bowl Shuffle:
'85 Bears

The 1985 Bears were the reincarnation of Chicago's old Monsters of the Midway. They boasted one of the greatest defenses of all time, former all-time leading rusher Walter Payton, and an incredibly crazy cast of characters. The 1985 Bears won eighteen of their nineteen games, and finished with one of the most dominating Super Bowl victories ever.

IF A CHALKBOARD could talk, it could have warned the New England Patriots what to expect from the 1985 Chicago Bears.

Bears defensive players, always an explosive bunch, had an especially short fuse the night before the January 1986 Super Bowl. They were taking one last look at game films in their New Orleans hotel when end Dan Hampton decided he'd seen enough. So had tackle Steve McMichael, also known as "Mongo" or "Ming the Merciless."

"I'm watching about the sixth play and my heart's beating fast," Hampton recalled. "I can't wait. So I just got up and kicked the projector off the little table it was sitting on.

"Ming, at that moment, leaped up and grabbed a chair and screamed some expletive about the Patriots and swung the chair at the chalkboard that had all these plays diagrammed on it. All four legs stuck in the chalkboard. Nobody said anything. Then I finally just said, 'Let's get the hell out of here.'

"We all walked out of the room, no one saying anything, and went to our rooms and went to sleep. And everybody knows what happened the next day."

In a 46–10 victory, the Bears' defense cemented its reputation as one of the best of all time. The Patriots totaled just 123 yards. "I was ready for Bourbon Street after the third quarter," McMichael said.

Hampton and McMichael were not the only characters among the Bears' defensive cast. Lineman William Perry was nicknamed "The Refrigerator" for an appetite that expanded his girth and shortened his career. Linebacker Otis Wilson was the unit's most reckless player. Middle linebacker Mike Singletary once told Don Pierson of the *Chicago Tribune* that he didn't think Wilson was kidding when he said before a game that he wanted to go out and kill somebody.

"I'm not sure you want to take these characters home," Singletary said. "But you definitely want to take them to war."

Wilson described his teammates like this: "Mike Singletary is the quiet Christian type. I'm the wild one. [Safety Gary] Fencik is the Ivy Leaguer. Dan Hampton is the politician. Steve McMichael is crazy. It makes for a wild bunch."

Singletary was nicknamed "Samurai Mike" and known for his wide-eyed and wild-eyed look which, he said, resulted from trying to see the entire field. His intense, bone-crushing play belied Singletary's stabilizing influence.

"Somebody's got to have some sense, somebody's got to be stable," he explained. "God had given me a great opportunity to balance out a situation. Whatever it was, keep the peace. Keeping the peace is the only way you can progress. Chaos sends you backwards, and it didn't take much to send us into chaos."

Quarterback Jim McMahon often sent the Bears into chaos. Coach Mike Ditka, asked about his relationship with McMahon, replied, "Strange and wonderful. He's strange and I'm wonderful."

Chaos found McMahon during Super Bowl week, and it wasn't entirely his fault. He became embroiled in one of those contrived controversies that will erupt when you have an army of reporters waiting all week for kickoff and desperate for anything that resembles news. All hell broke loose when a local broadcaster falsely accused McMahon of saying that all the men in New Orleans were "stupid" and all the women were "sluts."

This story had legs because the alleged remarks didn't sound out of character for McMahon. He had, after all, mooned a helicopter over the Bears' practice field that week.

"I woke up to two callers who were yelling at me over the telephone," McMahon recalled. "I didn't know what the hell was going on, so I went down to breakfast and the first guy I ran into was [general manager] Jerry Vainisi, who said, 'You really did it this time, didn't you?'

"Next thing I know, we've got women picketing outside our hotel. Men are calling my room and telling me I'm a dead man."

The controversy was blamed for a bomb threat that brought police cars and fire trucks to the Bears' hotel the day before the game. McMahon didn't seem fazed, however. He completed twelve of twenty passes for 256 yards.

When the game started, fans were more interested in McMahon's forehead than his throwing arm. He'd been fined $5,000 by NFL Commissioner Pete Rozelle for wearing an Adidas headband during a play-off game, and was coy over whether he'd adhere to the league's dress code for the Super Bowl. McMahon wore a plain headband, except for the hand lettering, which read ROZELLE.

Next to McMahon, no Bear got more attention during Super Bowl week than Perry. Asked which of the famous New Orleans restaurants was his favorite, the Fridge replied, "I don't know. I don't notice names, I just browse."

Perry enjoyed one of the most celebrated rookie seasons in NFL history. He was the Bears' first-round pick out of Clemson, but when defensive coordinator Buddy Ryan first saw Perry on the practice field, he called him "a wasted pick."

Perry weighed well over 300 pounds, but his quickness and power enabled him to start by midseason. Because of his cameo roles on offense, his enormous size, and likeable nature, he became immensely popular. He received seventeen endorsement deals his rookie year.

Ditka gave Perry a coming-out party when the Bears visited San Francisco in mid-October. Ditka remembered how coach Bill Walsh used guard Guy McIntyre as a blocking back near the goal line in the 49ers' 23–0 win over the Bears in the 1984 NFC championship game. Ditka got even by using Perry in a similar role.

Perry bulled his way into stardom in the Bears' next game, a 23–7 win over Green Bay on Monday night. The Fridge scored on a 1-yard plunge and cleared the way for two Walter Payton touchdown runs. His blocking caused such mayhem that Bears linebacker Jim Morrissey said, "Fridge, you're knocking more guys out of the league than the drug policy."

In a rematch with the Packers, Perry caught a 4-yard touchdown pass in a 16–10 victory. For a crowning touch, Perry scored on a 1-yard plunge in the Super Bowl to give the Bears a 44–3 lead.

But as Perry kept gaining weight, his production waned and the Bears waived him during 1993. He was signed by the Philadelphia Eagles, who kept him through 1994, and he finished his career in the NFL's international developmental league.

Perry returned to world-wide competition in 2003 as a celebrity guest at the Nathan's Famous international hot-dog eating contest in Coney Island, New York. The Fridge, alas, dropped out after eating just four hot dogs in five minutes. The champ, Takeru Kobayashi of Japan, polished off 44½ hot dogs, though he weighed just 144 pounds. Perry could have afforded to lose more weight than that.

The 1985 Bears weren't just one of the most talented teams ever. They were one of the cockiest, too. During the regular season they recorded *Super Bowl Shuffle*, a rap video that would have brought them ridicule had they not gone all the way.

The chorus went like this:

> **"**We are the Bears shufflin' crew,
>   Shufflin' on down, doin' it for you.
>   We're so bad we know we're good,
>   Blowin' your mind like we knew we would.
>   You know we're just struttin' for fun,
>   Struttin' our stuff for everyone.
>   We're not here to start no trouble,
>   We're just here to do the Super Bowl Shuffle.**"**

This song made Joe Namath's Super Bowl guarantee seem modest. Even Singletary, a conservative sort, got in on the act: "Unfortunately," he recalled, laughing. "It was kind of stupid, but it was a great motivator and it brought us together."

Chapter 15
In the Heat of the Moment:
Sideline Spats

Once upon a time, before TV cameras revealed
everything on the field and on the sidelines,
coaches and players could scream, and even
swing, at each other without drawing much
notice. Now, sideline antics have turned into
reality TV.

WHEN THERE'S A spat or a fight, everybody can watch.
Coaches and players like to say these spats are to be expected "in
the heat of the moment," and that nobody takes them personally.
They could have fooled us.

Was that really Herman Edwards, the good-natured New
York Jets coach, nearly coming to blows with running backs
coach Bishop Harris during a 20–17 overtime victory in a play-
off game at San Diego in January 2005?

Edwards began screaming at Harris during the third quarter,
though he wouldn't explain why. It was speculated that Edwards

wanted Harris to get more plays for reserve running back La-
Mont Jordan. Fullback Jerald Sowell had to separate his coaches.

"I look at myself as a peacemaker," Sowell explained. "I don't
like confrontations like that. I knew it wasn't right at the time.
We were trying to win the game."

Edwards apologized to his team, and also to his mother. "The
head coach is supposed to keep his composure," he said. "That's
the one thing I preach to our football team all the time. I let my
guard down and I shouldn't have fallen into the trap."

So who won the argument between the coaches? "The head
coach always wins," Edwards replied.

You would have thought linebacker Kevin Greene had never
been chewed out before, judging by how he reacted on the Carolina sideline in a 28–25 loss to the Redskins in December
1998.

The Panthers had given up touchdowns on three straight
Washington possessions and trailed 21–3 when head coach Dom
Capers and assistant Kevin Steele began lecturing their defense.
When Steele waved an arm near Greene, he leaped from the
bench, grabbed Steele's jacket, yelled, and pushed him back
about ten feet. They were separated by coaches and players.

Greene was allowed to finish the game but was suspended a
game without pay. "I lost my composure in the heat of the moment," Greene, almost in tears, said after the game. "It's an emotional game and I will apologize to the entire team tomorrow."

For Atlanta coach June Jones, it made perfect sense to bench
quarterback Jeff George late in the third quarter of a 33–18 loss
to Philadelphia early in the 1996 season. The Falcons stood 0-3,

they trailed the Eagles 23–10, and George had thrown two interceptions. Jones sent in veteran backup Bobby Hebert.

However, this did not make perfect sense to George. He screamed at Jones and kept screaming while stalking him on the sideline. When Jones had heard enough, he turned around and told George to leave the area.

George was suspended and didn't play again for the Falcons. The top overall pick by the Colts in the 1990 draft, he brought a marvelous arm and a bad attitude wherever he went. After a three-year exile, he finished his career with the Bears in 2004.

"I'm so sorry for what I did," George said after his blowup. "I told Coach Jones I was wrong and I knew I made a mistake. I'm a competitor and it was just a situation where I wanted to compete. But I went about it the wrong way."

Losing coaches don't win many battles with quarterbacks. Jones was fired after a 3-13 season. George signed a five-year, $27.5 million deal with the Raiders.

Raiders owner Al Davis wasn't worried about George's meltdown. "I've seen a lot of other players do a lot worse than he did," Davis said. "That kind of stuff goes on all the time."

Though Buddy Ryan's most famous feud was with Bears boss Mike Ditka, Ryan was on his worst behavior as Houston's defensive coordinator in the 1993 season. He loathed offensive coordinator Kevin Gilbride's "run-and-shoot" offense. He belittled it as the "chuck-and-duck," because it gave quarterbacks little protection.

The Oilers were rolling into the play-offs with an 11-4 record and should have been one big happy family when they faced the Jets. Just before halftime of a 24–0 Houston victory, Oilers quarterback Cody Carlson was sacked and fumbled. Ryan, enraged that the Oilers didn't just run out the clock, punched Gilbride in the jaw.

"It's a difference in coaching philosophy in the heat of the moment," Ryan said.

Gilbride disagreed. "It's a daily, ongoing thing," he said. "The comments, the sarcasm, the denigrating and disparaging remarks toward the offense. We try to just survive it. That's what we're going to do. My best way of handling it is to try to stay far away from the guy and try not to respond to his incessant remarks and just try to stay focused on who I thought the enemy was—the teams we play week to week."

Wade Phillips, who'd been a Ryan assistant in Philadelphia, wasn't surprised by the punch. "He has slugged people on the sideline before," he said. "Assistant coaches who were next to him got it. I was always up in the press box with the headset on, so I didn't."

The curtain began falling on the Ditka era in Chicago when the hot-tempered coach threw the mother of all tantrums at quarterback Jim Harbaugh.

The Bears led 20–0 early in the fourth quarter at Minnesota in October 1992 when Harbaugh called an audible. Harbaugh, reacting to the defensive setup, switched from a fly pattern to a short pass for running back Neal Anderson. Harbaugh, however, had been ordered to avoid audibles because of the Metrodome's extreme noise.

Sure enough, Anderson didn't hear the audible, and safety Todd Scott intercepted Harbaugh's short throw and returned it thirty-five yards for a touchdown. When Harbaugh went to the sidelines, Mount Ditka erupted. The coach screamed at Harbaugh, walked away, then came back to scream at him some more.

That play was the catalyst for a 21–20 Vikings victory. "Audibles are part of the game," Ditka said. "But audibles are to get from a bad play to a better play, not from a good play to a worse play. We went backwards."

So did the Bears. After winning their next two games, they collapsed and finished 5-11, hastening a coaching change. The Harbaugh episode will always be remembered in Chicago as the time when Iron Mike melted down for good.

Chapter 16
So Dan Says to Peyton:
Peyton Manning

Peyton Manning of the Indianapolis Colts won his second straight NFL Most Valuable Player Award after throwing forty-nine touchdown passes in 2004. He became the football world's focus as he led the Colts to a 13-0 start in 2005. Fans pondered the possibility of a perfect season and Super Bowl win, but neither materialized. He hails from a family of quarterbacks that includes father Archie and brothers Cooper and Eli.

DAN MARINO IS Peyton Manning's longtime hero, so it was only fitting that it was Manning who broke Marino's record for most touchdown passes in a season.

"I'm getting all emotional," Manning said after his record-breaking game. "Besides my dad, Dan Marino is my favorite player."

Manning and Marino were hooked up by CBS just after Manning tied and broke the record of forty-eight touchdown passes in the Colts' 34–31 overtime win over the San Diego Chargers the day after Christmas in 2004.

"Congratulations on the record," Marino said. "I know I held that record for twenty years. It's something I'm sure in years to come you'll be very proud of."

Manning replied: "I really appreciate it, man. You know you're my hero."

Yet, Manning would reveal only so much even to his hero. Marino, asked how to design a defense that could stop Manning, replied: "I've actually asked Peyton that. He wouldn't answer it."

Manning made sure that his forty-ninth touchdown pass counted for a lot more than just a record. It came on a 21-yard throw with the Colts trailing 31–23 with a minute left. Edgerrin James's two-point conversion run tied the score, and Manning led the offense down the field in overtime for Mike Vanderjagt's 30-yard field goal.

"To get the record and get the comeback win, this is the sort of game you remember, and it's the sort of game you are remembered for," said Archie Manning, who was present for the historic performance. "That is a double dip."

As Manning got closer to Marino's record, Colts receivers began discussing what they would do after catching the historic ball. None suggested giving it back.

"We've been talking about selling it on eBay," James told *Sports Illustrated*. "I'll tell you this—if he's at forty-eight and I get a little swing pass, I'm going in punt-return mode and taking that thing to the crib."

James didn't catch the record-breaker, though. Wide receiver Brandon Stokley did, after Manning called an audible and told Stokley, "Run a post."

The Colts hadn't run that play in a game and only occasionally in drills. "You think the NFL is real complex," Manning said. "But it turns into street ball real quick."

Said Stokley: "It says a lot about Peyton that here we are, the game on the line, and he calls a play we've never run before. I just didn't want it to hit me in the face."

The ball was stashed in an equipment box and Stokley quickly realized that he wasn't going to get his hands on it again. "The next time I probably see it, it will be in a case somewhere," Stokley said. "But not in my house."

The Colts sent the ball that Manning threw for No. 48 and one of his jerseys to the Pro Football Hall of Fame. They kept the record-breaker for the Colts museum.

Indianapolis fans actually booed when Manning passed up the chance to throw for No. 48 a week earlier. When an interception put the Colts at the Baltimore Ravens 4-yard line with fifty seconds left in a 20–10 home win, Manning took a knee.

"I can't get over the fact they were booing like that," Manning said. "I hope they were Baltimore fans because it's the way you're supposed to do it."

Colts owner Jim Irsay began to imagine Manning in a Colts jersey on the last Sunday of the 1997 season. The Cardinals trailed the Atlanta Falcons by twelve points in the final quarter, and would finish with the NFL's worst record and top draft pick if they lost. The Colts appeared in line to pick next.

"I was thinking, 'Well, it looks like we're going to have the second pick of the draft,'" Irsay recalled. "Then they come back, and with five seconds left Jake Plummer throws a touchdown pass to win it and gives us the first pick, and I just went berserk. The kids came in running, saying, 'What is wrong with Dad?'"

One of Manning's most unusual passes in his record-breaking season didn't produce a touchdown. On the winning drive of a 31–28 victory over the Minnesota Vikings, Manning, under pressure, completed a left-handed shovel pass to James. Manning, who is right-handed, said the throw showed him to be "amphibious."

He explained, "My high school coach used to tell me you have to be amphibious when you're sprinting to your left. I said, 'Don't you mean ambidextrous?' He said, 'No, amphibious.' So I guess I was amphibious on that play."

Once Manning survived a 3-13 rookie season, he led the Colts to the play-offs almost annually. His hardest bump came in 2001, when he topped 4,000 yards passing but threw 23 interceptions as the Colts slumped to 6-10.

Their season began to veer toward a cliff with a 40–21 home loss to the 49ers that dropped them to 4-6. Their defense struggled all year, but that day the Colts also committed five turnovers, including four interceptions thrown by Manning. This produced coach Jim Mora's most famous locker-room eruption. He told his players:

"Let me start out saying this: Do *not* blame that game on the defense, okay? I don't care who you play, whether it's a high school team, a junior college team, a college team, much less an NFL team, when you turn the ball over five times . . . you ain't gonna beat anybody. This was a disgraceful performance . . . we gave it away . . . we gave them the frigging game. In my opinion, that sucked.

"You can't turn it over five times. Holy crap. I don't know who the hell we think we are when we do something like that. We've thrown [five] interceptions returned for touchdowns. That might be a league record. And we've still got six games left, so there's no telling how many we'll have. I mean, it's absolutely pitiful to play like that. Horrible. I mean it's just horrible. Horrible."

Then in his postgame press conference, Mora was asked how the loss affected the Colts' play-off chances. This was like throwing lighter fluid on hot coals.

"Play-offs?" he asked, incredulously. "Don't talk about play-offs. Are you kidding me? Play-offs? I just hope we can win a game, another game."

Manning was stung by Mora's remarks and suggested his coach had gone too far. "I was fully responsible for that loss," Manning said, "but to be called out in front of the whole country, where that press conference is going to be played over and over again . . . that bothers me."

Mora was fired after the season because his defense collapsed. But his explosion after Manning's four interceptions provided the epitaph for the season.

Manning and Mora actually got along fine most of the time. Their association went back to the 1980s, when Mora was head coach in New Orleans and former Saints quarterback Archie Manning was part of the team's radio crew.

Peyton and his younger brother, Eli, who became the New York Giants' starting quarterback in 2004, would go to home games with their father and visit the Saints' locker room. Mora would often throw them out.

"The Saints' equipment guys always put candy bars and gum in everyone's locker," Peyton Manning recalled, "and me and my brother would take all the candy and all the gum."

Manning as a Colts rookie started all sixteen games and threw twenty-six touchdown passes, along with twenty-eight interceptions. He was accustomed to being thrown into the fire after becoming the starter early in his freshman season at Tennessee.

His first time in the Volunteers' huddle, Manning broke into a pep talk about going down the field and scoring. A senior lineman said: "Just call the [bleeping] play, freshman."

Teammates don't talk to Manning like that, anymore.

Chapter 17
Iron Man:
Brett Favre

Green Bay fans were desperate for a return to their glory days, and quarterback Brett Favre took them there. He led the 1996 Packers to their first Super Bowl win since the Vince Lombardi era, and became the first player ever to win three league MVP awards.

ONE OF THE luckiest days in Packer history came in the summer of 1991 when Atlanta Falcons rookie Brett Favre overslept for the shooting of the team picture. The Falcons tired of waiting for Favre to grow up and traded him to the Packers a year later.

He was out having a good time the night before the Falcons' team picture was scheduled and forgot to set his alarm. Favre arrived at team headquarters at 10 a.m., an hour late. As he pulled into the parking lot, he saw coach Jerry Glanville's van pulling out. He stopped to tell the coach he was late because he got stuck behind a wreck.

"You are a wreck," Glanville said after inspecting Favre's bloodshot eyes. "This will cost you fifteen hundred dollars."

Favre recouped some of that cash when Glanville overheard him telling a teammate before a game in Anaheim that he could throw a ball into the upper deck.

"I'll bet you a hundred dollars you can't," Glanville said.

"I reached back and fired a football into the upper deck," Favre recalled. "It was a lot farther than it looked, but the ball cleared the railing. Glanville reached into his pocket and pulled out a hundred bucks. We were never going to be best buddies."

Of the five passes Favre threw in 1991, two were intercepted. The Falcons traded him to Green Bay for a first-round draft choice—a cheap price for one of the top dozen quarterbacks of all time.

Don Majkowski and Wally Pipp have a lot in common. Pipp was the Yankees' first baseman in 1925 who had the bad timing to get a headache and allow Lou Gehrig to replace him for the next 2,130 games. Majkowski was the Green Bay starter who suffered strained ankle ligaments against the Bengals in the third game of the 1992 season.

Favre, whose only NFL completion had been a deflection to himself for a 7-yard loss, replaced Majkowski. Favre made some shaky throws before settling down and leading the Packers to a 24–23, come-from-behind victory. "He drives you crazy sometimes, but he's a talent," coach Mike Holmgren said, and not for the last time.

Favre became the most durable quarterback in NFL history, making 221 straight regular-season starts through 2005. The Eagles' Ron Jaworski, with 116 straight starts from 1977 through 1984, was next among quarterbacks on the iron-man list.

Favre faced a lot of new challenges in Green Bay. Like the quirks of left tackle Ken Ruettgers. He would exasperate Favre by counting down numbers in the huddle.

"This went on for a while," Favre recalled, "and finally, it was driving me nuts, so I turned to Rutt and said, 'What is it?' He looked at me and said, 'The play clock is running.' I'd be like, 'Rutt, would you shut up?'

"Rutt had himself another strange habit. I'd be giving the play in the huddle and he'd be tapping his fingertips along the side of his helmet. Rutt said it helped him remember the play. It aggravated the heck out of me. Now, Rutt's a good guy, an intelligent guy. Probably too intelligent. He was goofy."

Ruettgers also did a fine job protecting Favre's blind side, and that made his quirks easy to forgive.

For Favre, getting his ankles taped became a serious pregame ritual—especially before a 35–21 Super Bowl win over the New England Patriots in January 1997. Favre would allow only assistant trainer Kurt Fielding to tape his ankles. When Fielding was finished, he would predict Favre's performance by writing it on the tape.

"Before the Super Bowl, Kurt wrote down a W for a win," Favre wrote in 1997. "He always predicts a victory. Then he wrote that I'd be twenty-four of thirty-five for two-hundred-seventy-two yards and four touchdowns. Kurt factors in the opposing defense, the weather conditions, and how I practiced all week.

"Sometimes Kurt's predictions are so close to my final statistics it's scary. He used to be a little more erratic because, well, I was a little more erratic. I completed fourteen of twenty-seven passes for two-hundred-forty-six yards and two touchdowns in the Super Bowl, so I didn't make him look too bad."

Favre has had fierce rivalries with some of the NFL's top pass rushers, especially Warren Sapp and John Randle. Nike saw commercial promise in these matchups and in 1998 ran a TV ad that showed the Vikings' Randle chasing a rooster wearing Favre's jersey. The ad ended with Randle standing over a grill and preparing chicken.

This ad angered People for the Ethical Treatment of Animals. It complained that the ad encouraged cruelty to animals and in protest gave the ad first place in its 1998 annual PETA Litterbox Awards.

Packers defensive end Reggie White objected to Nike using Favre's number. "I wish they'd have put another jersey on," he said. "But Randle needs to leave those animals alone."

Anyone who's followed Favre's career knows his life hasn't been all Super Bowl wins and knee-slapping anecdotes. He's endured the arrests of a brother and sister and his addiction to painkillers. His wife, Deanna, was diagnosed with breast cancer in 2004, shortly after her brother was killed in an ATV accident on the Favres' property. A day before the Packers visited Oakland on Monday night, December 22, 2003, Favre's father, Irwin, suffered a fatal heart attack.

Favre was devastated by the death of his father, who was also his high school coach in Kiln, Mississippi. He told his Packers teammates that despite his sorrow, he was obliged to stick with them and would play against the Raiders.

Favre threw for 399 yards and four touchdowns in a 41–7 victory that was pivotal in nailing down a play-off spot for the Packers. He threw for 311 yards and four touchdowns in the first half alone.

"I knew my dad would have wanted me to play," Favre told ABC's Lisa Guerrero in an emotion-packed interview. "I love him so much, and I love this game. It meant a great deal to me, my dad, to my family, and I didn't expect this kind of performance. But I know he was watching tonight."

Chapter 18
Gone Today, Here Tomorrow: Ricky Williams

Ricky Williams spent five seasons as one of the NFL's most productive yet unpredictable running backs. He rushed for 6,354 yards and 41 touchdowns in New Orleans and Miami before abruptly retiring before the 2004 season. Just as abruptly, he returned to the Dolphins after a one-year absence, though he had to accept a backup role.

WE ALWAYS KNEW where Ricky Williams was headed as a runner—between the tackles with tremendous power. Off the field, it was anybody's guess where Williams was headed. He was in Hawaii just before the start of training camp in 2004 when Williams told Miami coach Dave Wannstedt that he was retiring. Then he flew to Tokyo.

Williams, himself, didn't seem sure where he was headed. He was hitting the hole without a playbook or blockers.

"I have no idea what I'm going to do," Williams, twenty-seven, told *The Miami Herald* upon bolting from the Dolphins. "Who knows? I just know it is going to be fun. Going to school again.

Going to travel for the next six months. I'm halfway intelligent. I'll figure something out. I don't feel like I have to explain myself to anyone."

His explanations for retirement kept changing. Initially, Williams indicated he was tired of the NFL grind. In his last two seasons with the Dolphins, he had 383 and 392 carries, respectively, and was a busy receiver besides.

"I just don't want to be in this business anymore," he said. "I was never strong enough to not play football, but I'm strong enough now. I've considered everything about this. Everyone has thrown every possible scenario at me about why I shouldn't do this, but they're in denial. I'm happy with my decision."

But in an installment of CBS's *60 Minutes*, which aired late in the 2004 season, Williams said he retired because two days earlier he had learned that he'd tested positive a third time for marijuana. He said he feared the public's reaction.

"That's the one thing I couldn't deal with at the time—people knowing that I smoke marijuana," Williams said. "That was my biggest fear in my whole entire life. I was so scared to death of that."

Yet, early in 2006, it was announced that Williams had failed a drug test for the fourth time, which brings a one-year suspension under the NFL's substance abuse policy. Since his return to the Dolphins, he'd been required to submit to as many as 10 drug tests a month. While his latest positive test was causing an uproar in the NFL, Williams was studying yoga and holistic medicine in India.

Williams's career was rejuvenated in 2002 when he was traded to Miami and led the NFL in rushing. Between that year and the next, he rushed for 3,225 yards and 25 touchdowns. His career, it seemed, was finally fulfilling its vast promise, which is why Williams's retirement stunned the Dolphins. It was the precursor to a collapse. A rash of injuries, a 1-8 start, and Wannstedt's resignation followed.

The Dolphins took Williams to arbitration for violating his contract and he was ordered to return $8.6 million. He claimed the money meant nothing to him.

"I want to give them every cent back," he claimed. "The money is what made me miserable. I want to be free of that stress. I've been living in a tent for weeks now, paying seven dollars a day. Do you really think money means anything to me? I lost everything, and that's when I realized how much I love to play this game."

If Williams didn't miss the Dolphins, the feeling was mutual. Center Seth McKinney described Williams's departure as stupid and selfish. Williams replied by criticizing McKinney's blocking and claiming that players had no respect for Wannstedt, even making fun of his mustache. Defensive tackle Larry Chester said that Williams was acting like a bitter ex-girlfriend and owed his former teammates an apology.

The possibility of Williams back in a Dolphin uniform then seemed unthinkable. But wherever Williams is concerned, the strangest things continue to happen.

Williams, the Heisman Trophy winner at Texas in 1998, was in the eye of a storm from the start of his NFL career. Before the draft, he signed with No Limit Sports, which was owned by rapper Master P and represented no other major NFL players. After the New Orleans Saints made Williams the fifth player drafted in 1999, Leland Hardy of No Limit Sports boasted he would negotiate Williams's contract on a golf course.

Critics predicted that Williams's choice of agents was a disaster waiting to happen, and they were right. He received more than $10 million in signing bonuses but the rest of his deal included minimum annual salaries laden with virtually unreachable incentives. Williams signed probably the worst contract for a top-ten pick during the free-agency era, and switched to agent Leigh Steinberg in 2002.

Saints coach Mike Ditka announced a week before the 1999 draft that he would swap all six of his draft choices—he was missing a second-rounder—if he could move up in the first round to get Williams. Redskins general manager Charley Casserly, who held the fifth pick, was delighted to grab Ditka's offer. Casserly acquired all the Saints' picks plus their first- and third-round choices in 2000.

Yet, the Indianapolis Colts made Edgerrin James the first back drafted. "It was kind of a shock to be the second running back," said a subdued Williams. "It's flattering to know the Saints made a deal like they did. Now, I hope I can justify that."

"Ricky gives us what Walter Payton gave us in Chicago," Ditka crowed.

That was a high expectation and got only higher once Williams's arrival in New Orleans turned into a circus act. He was advised that he'd reap tremendous publicity by wearing a wedding dress in a mock marriage to Ditka for an *ESPN The Magazine* cover photo.

The photo exposed Williams to ridicule and derision, which was especially troublesome for him because he was diagnosed with social anxiety disorder a year later. This helped explain his extreme shyness and tendency to conduct interviews without removing his helmet. When Williams left the Dolphins in 2003, he claimed that he used marijuana to treat his disorder. He said that Paxil, his prescription drug, didn't fit his diet.

The retirement stunned Ditka, who was fired by the Saints after Williams's rookie season. "Everything he's done has surprised me," Ditka said. "He's not the same person now as he was when I drafted him. I don't really know this guy. I wouldn't take him back. I wouldn't want him on my football team.

"He's not reliable, he's not dependable. He certainly wasn't doing drugs when he came out. He had a little trouble being around people. But we got along pretty well. But he got into a little different environment [in Miami] and met some people, and that probably wasn't the best thing for him. Ricky's not a leader, he's a follower. And that's the problem sometimes—he's too nice a guy. He doesn't know how to say 'No.'"

Williams seemed to be following his own lead when he enrolled at a school for holistic medicine three months after he retired. He began a seventeen-month course at the California College of Ayurveda, named for an ancient Indian medical system.

"I realized a while back that I have an innate ability to be compassionate, and I saw that the strength of compassion is something that healers have and healers use," Williams told the *San Francisco Chronicle*.

"Ayurveda deals with using your environment to put yourself in balance. I've realized, both on a psychological and physical level, that the things we do in football don't bring more harmony to your life. They just bring more disharmony. I loved playing football, but the reasons I loved football were just to feed my ego. And any time you feed your ego, it's a one-way street."

After a year's retirement, Williams decided there was room in his life for football, after all. When Nick Saban took over the Dolphins, he gave Williams another chance, though not before using his first-round draft choice on running back Ronnie Brown. Williams had to sit out the first four regular-season games, the NFL's penalty for his previous drug positive, then successfully moved into a backup role behind Brown.

"I'm having fun," Williams said late in his comeback season. "But I'm to the point where I can have fun doing anything. I sit down and think about life, and it's just really fun to be alive. I've tried to get rid of all the expectations about what's going to come next, and that makes it easy to be happy.

"I wouldn't change anything in my whole entire life. If you change one thing, you're really changing everything. Everything I've been through says who I am, and I'm very happy with who I am right now."

Williams seemed resigned that many, nevertheless, would continue to view him as selfish and unreliable. He said, with a chuckle, "I'm sure my weirdness doesn't help."

Chapter 19
The One and Only Butkus:
Dick Butkus

From 1965 to 1973, Chicago Bears middle linebacker Dick Butkus established himself as the fiercest tackler in NFL history. He was so dominant that not even a career-shortening knee injury nor generally weak Bears teams could diminish his legacy.

DICK BUTKUS, ARGUABLY the best linebacker of all time, always claimed his reputation for meanness was blown way out of proportion.

"I never set out to hurt anybody deliberately unless, it was, you know, important," Butkus said. "Like a league game or something."

What about the time Butkus supposedly bit referee Ralph "Red" Morcroft's finger in a 1969 preseason game in Miami?

"That's all bull," he growled. "It was so hot in August, playing in Miami, and Abe Gibron always made us play the full game. So I told the defensive tackle, 'Let's get in a fight and get out of this.' He started the fight and I got thrown out and they said I bit somebody's finger. Forty years later, now it's probably somebody's arm."

And what about the time Butkus claimed he wanted to knock somebody's head off and watch it roll away? Well, NFL Films recorded that statement.

Butkus insists reporters portrayed him as a brute because he gave few interviews early in his pro career. "I got burned in college by a writer and my first few years I never talked that much," he said. "So they didn't know I ate with a knife and fork."

Detroit rookie running back Altie Taylor quickly learned that Butkus's notorious reputation was well deserved. Lions quarterback Greg Landry recalls that in 1969, after a victory over the Bears, Taylor made the mistake of telling reporters that Butkus was overrated. Teammates told Taylor that he could expect trouble when they visited the Bears at Wrigley Field for the last game of the season. While the Lions got away with another win, Taylor barely got away with his life.

"We called a play to Altie Taylor, an end sweep towards the old third base line, maybe thirty yards from the brick wall," Landry recalled. "Altie ran out of bounds and started slowing down and here comes Fifty-one at him. Next thing he knows, Fifty-one is still coming at him. Next thing, you see a football in the air and Altie Taylor jumping over the wall.

"He came back to the huddle all glassy eyed and said, 'That guy's crazy!' Dick chased him right out of the ballpark. There were things at Wrigley Field that Dick could get away with."

Butkus could rattle people because—well, he could rattle people. Bears defensive end Ed O'Bradovich watched—and heard—Butkus rattle bones for seven seasons. He recalls, "The way Dick would hit people . . . if they had the amount of cameras from all the different angles they have today and the way they make these sound bites, they might have to bar the guy.

"Tackling wasn't good enough. Just to hit people wasn't good enough. He loved to crush people. That takes a sense of timing. You cannot teach that. When he made the tackle, he exploded into 'em. He not only put the fear in the running backs, but in the offensive linemen, too."

Green Bay running back MacArthur Lane once said, "If I had a choice, I'd sooner go one on one with a grizzly bear. I pray that I can get up every time Butkus hits me."

Not even teammates were spared Butkus's wrath. Hall of Fame running back Gale Sayers recalled, "You haven't lived until you've been rammed by him. He didn't hit you low, he hit you in the chest and sort of raked you over. He put his soul into tackling you."

Bears running back Brian Piccolo said, "When Dick is on the other side of the line, glaring at you with those boiling eyes, it makes you wish you could trade places with the equipment boy."

Butkus was such a fierce hitter partly because he was always angry. "When I went out on the field to warm up, I would manufacture things to make me mad," he said. "If someone on the other team was laughing, I'd pretend he was laughing at me or the Bears. I'd find something to get mad about. It always worked for me."

Butkus did not clobber opponents just to intimidate them. He also wanted them to cough up the ball. It's a pity his forced fumbles were never recorded because they surely would have given him the NFL record. His twenty-five fumble recoveries were a league record when he retired, and he also made twenty-two interceptions.

Butkus did not make classic, around-the-waist tackles. He hit upon a more punishing technique while he played fullback at Chicago Vocational High School.

"What bothered me was when somebody hit me high and wrapped their arms around my arms and I had nothing to break my fall," he said. "And when I'm getting hit like that, boy, it really took concentration to hold on to the ball and also brace for hitting the ground.

"I thought, all right, that's what I'm going to start doing. I'm going to put my head in someone's sternum and it won't be picture perfect, but I'll tell you what—they won't come back. I'll put 'em on their backs and somewhere along the line, they'll cough up the ball and that's the whole thing. The idea of hitting somebody hard is not for your ego. It's to make them forget about the ball."

Butkus's tenacity was all the more remarkable because he played his last three seasons in constant pain after suffering a right knee injury in 1970. Surgery was only partly successful and the pain became so severe that he had to leave the field in the fifth game of the 1973 season, the end of his Hall of Fame career.

"They always claim that my threshold of pain was great, but it ran in my family," Butkus said. "One of my brothers, Don, was a welder and he was soldering in his garage in his bare feet and hot solder was dripping on his feet. He didn't even flinch. It smelled like burnt chicken feathers and he didn't interrupt what he was soldering.

"It just makes me want to throw up nowadays when a guy gets hurt, his face is buried in the grass and the trainer is talking to his earhole. The guy gets up and takes his helmet off and runs off the field. I'm not saying how tough we were, but why would I give you the benefit of having you put me out?

"That's what I had to go through my last three years. Guys were taking shots, clipping me, trying to tackle my foot and twist it even more. For what? To make their name that they put me out? I never gave 'em the satisfaction, even if I had to crawl."

Chapter 20
Hollywood:
Thomas Henderson

One of the NFL's most flamboyant characters ever, linebacker Thomas Henderson was drafted by the Dallas Cowboys in 1975. He returned a kickoff for a touchdown his rookie year, played in three Super Bowls, and made a Pro Bowl. He also made a pile of controversy and a mess of his life before he got it together again.

THOMAS "HOLLYWOOD" HENDERSON uttered his best-remembered line when he made fun of Pittsburgh's quarterback before the January 1979 Super Bowl. "Terry Bradshaw couldn't spell 'cat' if you spotted him the 'c' and the 'a,'" crowed Henderson.

Bradshaw got the last laugh by throwing four touchdown passes in the Steelers' 35–31 victory over the Cowboys, yet still alluded to Henderson's taunt ten years later. During his Hall of Fame induction speech, Bradshaw recalled his early friction with Steelers fans and said, "Y'all called me 'Ozark Ike' 'cause I was big and white and dumb actin.' Said I was L'il Abner. Said I couldn't spell 'cat.' Well, y'all didn't, but some fool in Dallas did."

Henderson wouldn't deny he was a fool back then. With his talent, he might have joined Bradshaw in Canton. But he allowed life in the fast lane to ruin his career and, for a while, his life. Fortunately for Henderson, he's had as many lives as a c-a-t.

"Hollywood Henderson had Bobby Bell's skills," recalled former Cowboys player personnel director Gil Brandt, referring to the Hall of Fame linebacker. "He was a great, great player. He was athletic, tremendously fast. He would've been one of the best of all time had he not gone astray. Unfortunately, he went astray."

It didn't take Henderson long to earn his famous nickname. The Cowboys, with two first-round draft choices in 1975, used the second overall pick for Maryland defensive tackle Randy White, and the eighteenth pick for Henderson, from Langston University in Oklahoma. Though White was the Cowboys' marquee choice, Henderson announced, "I haven't had White's publicity because I played at a small college, but you can write this down: I'm just as good a player as he is and maybe better."

Henderson's boasts kept on coming. After becoming the Cowboys' strong-side starting linebacker in 1977, he said, "I have decided I am the best linebacker ever to play pro football. Dick Butkus was just a lineman standing up."

Asked for his opinion on Jack Lambert, the Steelers' great, gap-toothed middle linebacker, Henderson replied, "I don't care for the man. He makes more money than I do, and he don't have no teeth. He's Dracula."

Henderson hung out with celebrities and attended the Grammy Awards with one of the Pointer Sisters. He was a delightful, if sometimes obnoxious, presence, until cocaine addiction brought his world crashing down in the early 1980s.

Henderson's drug use eventually led to his washing out of the NFL. He went to prison, rebounded as an author, entrepreneur, and philanthropist, and struck it rich in the Texas Lottery.

Though he's hardly proud of his off-the-field problems, he doesn't want anybody to forget how splendidly he played linebacker.

"All the people I played with said I was the greatest," Henderson said. "Lawrence Taylor told me he picked number fifty-six because he thought I was the best linebacker in the game. Not only did I talk, but I'd knock your flipping head off. I set the standard for the new linebacker with speed. I don't think there's been a player like that since myself. There are no more Hendersons in the league now."

In some respects, that's just as well. Henderson admitted to inhaling cocaine on the sideline during the January 1979 Super Bowl, and was released by the Cowboys the next November after throwing a tantrum. He drifted to the San Francisco 49ers and Houston Oilers in 1980, and both teams let him go.

Henderson admitted his drug addiction and asked the NFL to place him in rehabilitation. The Miami Dolphins signed Henderson in 1981, but he suffered a broken neck in the last preseason game. His career was over and, worse, he'd relapsed.

Henderson hit bottom in 1983, when he was arrested for having sex with two minors and also was charged with bribery when he tried paying them to drop the charges. He was sentenced to fifty-six months in prison, and served twenty-eight months before he was released.

While in prison, Henderson kicked his drug habit and began co-writing his autobiography, *Out of Control—Confessions of an NFL Casualty*. He returned to Austin, Texas, his hometown, and formed the East Side Youth Services and Street Outreach, which serves his old neighborhood. He also formed Thomas Henderson Films, which educates the prison community about drugs, and he makes speaking tours.

Henderson went on a weeklong hunger strike in 1997 to bring attention to his campaign to add a rubberized track to a football field he'd built on the grounds of his long-closed high school in East Austin. Through his donations and fund-raising, Henderson amassed $250,000 to complete the track in 1999. The facility's long-term maintenance was assured in March 2001 when Henderson won $10.43 million, after taxes, in the Texas Lottery.

"When I won the lottery, I, of all people, wasn't surprised by the gift because there'd been tens of thousands of hours with my hands in the dirt and a shovel in my hand and planting grass and picking up trash," Henderson said.

"When that happened, everybody in my community said, 'You deserved that.' Life is a strange machine."

Chapter 21
Sharpe Tongue:
Shannon Sharpe

Shannon Sharpe retired after the 2003 season as the all-time leading receiver among tight ends with 815 catches, 10,060 yards, and 62 touchdowns. In twelve seasons in Denver and two in Baltimore, his big-play knack helped win three Super Bowl titles. He also was one of the most loquacious players that pro football has ever seen.

SHARPE CLAIMED THAT catching passes was not his best weapon against NFL defenses. "I'm better at getting under their skin," he said.

Sharpe didn't lose many one-on-one matchups, and it's hard to imagine he ever lost a war of words. "I won't talk about somebody's mother," he said. "I won't talk about somebody's girlfriend or wife. But anything else . . . if you have a deformity, I will talk about that."

Before the Broncos' back-to-back Super Bowl victories, Sharpe commanded center stage. Before facing the Packers in January 1998, he told one reporter, "If I touched the ball every time, I'd guarantee the win. If they cover me one-on-one and beat my butt, I'll renounce my citizenship and leave all my assets in a bank account under your name."

The Broncos' offense depended mainly upon its ground game in a 31–24 upset of Green Bay. Sharpe was their leading receiver with five catches for thirty-eight yards.

Before the Broncos met the Falcons in the Super Bowl a year later, cornerback Ray Buchanan unwisely decided to take on Sharpe in a trash-talking contest. Buchanan guaranteed an Atlanta victory, claimed that Sharpe looked like Mr. Ed, and that the Falcons would try to hurt him.

"He called me ugly?" Sharpe asked, incredulously. "His teeth are so big they look like dominoes in his mouth . . . I never called anybody ugly, but do I think he's ugly? Yeah, he's ugly.

"How is Ray gonna hurt somebody? He's not going to tackle somebody; all he'll do is jump on their back and push them out of bounds. When he was in Indy, he never guaranteed anything, except that the other teams would win. He goes to the Pro Bowl for the first time, and all of a sudden, he's great?

"Ray got all that money to sign [as a free agent in 1997], and what he should have done at the end of last year was go in and give half back because he stole last year's salary. He backed up to the window with a mask and a hood on and said, 'Give me my check.' Now to his credit, he earned a little bit of it this year.

"We know if we don't play our best, Atlanta could beat us. We know we'll get their best, they're going to get our best, and then we'll see what happens after that. Then Ray either looks like a genius or he looks like the idiot that he is."

When kickoff arrived, Sharpe didn't exactly bring Buchanan to his knees. He made just two catches for twenty-six yards in a 34–19 Broncos victory.

"Shannon is arrogant," New England Patriots safety Willie Clay said. "But you've got to let it go. Hold a grudge and it messes you up."

Kansas City linebacker Derrick Thomas would have been wise to heed Clay's advice. Instead, he let Sharpe antagonize him into a Monday-night meltdown in November 1998. Sharpe told coach Mike Shanahan that he believed he could rattle Thomas, and Shanahan told him to go for it.

During the fourth quarter of a 30–7 Broncos victory, Sharpe struck. He began taunting Thomas and dived at the legs of linebacker Wayne Simmons. Sharpe drew a personal foul but Simmons was penalized for retaliating. When Sharpe was done taunting, the Chiefs had committed five personal fouls, including three by Thomas, on an 80-yard touchdown drive.

Thomas twice was penalized for violently shaking Sharpe's face mask. There are varying versions of what Sharpe said to enrage Thomas, but all are X-rated. Sharpe was fined $10,000 by the NFL. The Chiefs suspended Thomas without pay for one game and waived Simmons, who'd been playing poorly. Coach Marty Schottenheimer resigned after a 7-9 season.

"Think about what I've done this year," Sharpe reflected. "I got a guy suspended, got a guy cut, one coach resigned . . . I might need to go into politics."

Sharpe also poured salt on the wounds of the Patriots. With the Broncos on their way to a 34–8 victory at New England in 1996, Sharpe picked up a red phone behind the Broncos bench and pretended he was calling the White House.

"President!" screamed Sharpe. "We need the National Guard! We need as many men as you can spare because we are killing the Patriots! So call the dogs off! Call the National Guard, please! They need emergency help! Please! Help!"

"I've always been a talker," Sharpe said. "You don't just wake up one morning and all of a sudden say, 'I think I want to talk a little more.' You either have this gift or you don't."

Sharpe always yakked, even when he had a severe lisp that put him in speech class during elementary school. "The teacher always used to tell us, 'Don't tell the kid the word, let him sound it out,'" Sharpe recalled.

"This guy in our class named Johnny, he got to a word and didn't know how to pronounce it, and I wanted to tell him what the word was. And the teacher said, 'Okay, Johnny, it sounds like . . . it sounds like . . .'"

Sharpe couldn't contain himself. "It sounds like Johnny can't read," he said.

Sharpe also enjoyed agitating the Steelers and their fans. No sooner did the Broncos beat the Steelers 24–21 at Pittsburgh in the 1997 AFC Championship game than he cautioned Steelers fans not to do anything rash.

"Stay away from the Allegheny, the Ohio, and the Mononga-hela!" he said, referring to the rivers that gave old Three Rivers Stadium its name. "I hope they freeze those three rivers tonight because I'd hate to see anybody plunging to the bottom of 'em."

Sharpe was giddy because he was about to get his first taste of a Super Bowl. Yet he knew that critics would not consider the Broncos a great team unless they snapped the NFC's streak of thirteen straight Super Bowl wins.

"No, and they shouldn't," Sharpe said. "You're only great if you win something. I mean, Alexander wasn't Alexander the Mediocre or Alexander the Average. He was Alexander the Great, and there's a reason for it."

Through his fourteen NFL seasons of wisecracks and insults, there was only one remark that Sharpe regretted making. That was after a 38–3 home play-off win over the Dolphins in January 1999 that put the Broncos a win away from the Super Bowl in Miami.

"Tell [Dolphins coach] Jimmy Johnson to have his office ready because we're going to need it to break down film," cracked Sharpe, who knew the AFC Super Bowl team would be using the Dolphins facilities.

But that's not what he regretted saying.

Asked about the Dolphins quarterback, Sharpe said, "I don't want to talk about Dan Marino. I don't talk about losers."

For that, Sharpe was almost apologetic. Almost. "The only thing I've said that I regret is the Dan thing," he said. "People say I called him a loser. I didn't per se call him a loser. I said I didn't want to talk about anybody on the losing side. I said, 'Let's talk about Terrell [Davis], let's talk about John [Elway].' I didn't want to talk about Dan."

Sharpe retired after the 2003 season as a slam-dunk future Hall of Famer. For him, a broadcasting career was a foregone conclusion, and Sharpe joined CBS as a studio analyst. He'd been talking about a broadcast career for a long time.

"I'm going to get me a talk show, a show like Jerry Springer," he said while he was still playing. "Only instead of the guests getting into it, I'm going to get into it with the guests. I'll have Ray Buchanan on and I'll pummel him."

Chapter 22
Bo Knows:
Bo Jackson

Bo Jackson won the 1985 Heisman Trophy at Auburn and was the top overall pick of the 1986 NFL draft. He initially signed a pro baseball contract and became a Raider in 1987. For four years, he was one of the most famous two-sport athletes of all time.

NOT EVEN BO knows how great a running back he might have been had he made pro football his sole occupation instead of his hobby. Jackson had extraordinary speed and power, and in thirty-eight games averaged 5.4 yards per carry for the Los Angeles Raiders. He ran for 2,782 yards and 16 touchdowns.

Jackson, at six-foot-one and 225 pounds, didn't pick up a football each fall until he finished playing left field for the Kansas City Royals. Though he spread himself thin, he relished his celebrated two-sport career. He was the first All-Star ever in two major professional sports. And Nike's "Bo Knows" campaign, featuring Jackson suited up for almost every sport imaginable, helped make him America's best-known athlete.

"Baseball and football are very different games," he said. "In a way, both of them are easy. Football is easy if you're crazy as hell. Baseball is easy if you've got patience. They'd both be easier for me if I were a little more crazy and a little more patient."

Jackson threw himself one of the grandest birthday parties in NFL history. He turned twenty-five on November 30, 1987, the date of a Monday-night game at Seattle. He carried eighteen times for 221 yards and three touchdowns in a 37–14 victory. And Jackson, just a month into his NFL career, personalized each touchdown.

Bo scored on a 14-yard run in the second quarter when safety Kenny Easley, a five-time Pro Bowler, fell down trying to tackle him. Later in the quarter, Jackson cut around left end and ran ninety-one yards into the end zone and down a locker-room tunnel. "He may not stop 'til Tacoma," ABC analyst Dan Dierdorf said, laughing.

Jackson's third score covered only two yards, but he trampled linebacker Brian Bosworth. "If my mother put on a helmet and shoulder pads and a uniform that wasn't the same as the one I was wearing, I'd run her over if she was in my way," Bo said. "And I love my mother."

Jackson prided himself on doing the unexpected. The Tampa Bay Buccaneers learned that the hard way after they made him the top pick of the 1986 draft. Jackson refused to sign, partly because the Buccaneers ruined his senior baseball season by flying him to Tampa for a pre-draft physical. Jackson didn't know the trip violated Southeastern Conference rules and he was declared ineligible after playing just twenty-one games.

"My first love is baseball, and it has always been a dream of mine to be a major league player," he said.

For Buccaneers owner Hugh Culverhouse, Jackson's defection was yet another embarrassment for his hapless franchise. Addressing a press conference on the Jackson fiasco, he said that while driving over he heard the Dionne Warwick song, "That's What Friends Are For." Repeating the lyrics, Culverhouse vowed to "keep smiling, keep shining." Without Bo, of course.

Even after Jackson shunned the Buccaneers, nearly every major league baseball team assumed he'd still play football to maximize his talent and earning power. The Royals, consequently, were able to draft him in the fourth round in June 1986, then shocked the sports world by signing him. But for Jackson, the NFL still beckoned.

While the Royals were playing a key series at Toronto in the summer of 1987, Jackson left the stadium. After the game, his teammates were abuzz over a *Washington Post* story reporting that Raiders owner Al Davis, who drafted Jackson in the seventh round that year, had convinced Jackson to give up baseball.

Jackson had been summoned to the Toronto hotel room of Royals co-owner Avron Fogelman, who had just learned of the Raiders' offer. Fogelman and Jackson met for several hours and agreed Jackson could play for the Raiders after each baseball season.

"Football's my hobby, like hunting and fishing," Bo said. Upon hearing that remark, Royals center fielder Willie Wilson asked sharply, "How can having [Raiders defensive end] Howie Long running into you be a hobby?"

Jackson was a human highlights reel. He had a knack for rising to the occasion, as in his Monday-night football debut. His home runs often were tape-measure jobs. He once cut down speedster Harold Reynolds at home plate with a line-drive throw from the left-field wall of the Seattle Kingdome. Even Bo's strikeouts made *SportsCenter*, especially when he busted the bat over his knee.

Jackson made the American League All-Star team in 1989 and led off with a home run to center field off Rick Reuschel. Jackson added a run-scoring single and stole second and was named the game's MVP. He had 32 home runs and 105 runs batted in that year, a career best, but also led the majors with 172 strikeouts.

Jackson, typically, saved one of his biggest nights for baseball's Broadway stage. At Yankee Stadium on July 17, 1990, he hit three home runs and drove in seven runs.

During a spring-training game in Florida, Jackson hit a home run over the scoreboard, the longest shot ever at the Baseball City stadium. A reporter asked Royals pitching coach Frank Funk, "What did Bo hit?" Funk replied: "A Titleist."

Though Jackson signed with the Chiefs' most bitter rival, Kansas City fans didn't have a problem with divided loyalties. They loved Bo when he was wearing Royals blue and loathed him when he wore silver and black.

Jackson made four trips to Arrowhead Stadium as a Raider. For his first visit, December 13, 1987, fans lustily booed him and displayed dozens of banners poking fun at him. One depicted Bo as a jackass. He suffered an ankle injury after just three carries and sat out the rest of the Chiefs' 16–10 upset victory.

For Chiefs fans, Bo's most memorable moment came at Arrowhead Stadium in 1990. Jackson burst free into the secondary, but safety Deron Cherry knocked the ball loose with his helmet. The Chiefs' fumble recovery set up a field goal in their 9–7 victory.

Jackson was voted to the Pro Bowl in 1990 but never got to play. His career ended the previous month when he was tackled from behind by safety David Fulcher in the Raiders' 21–10 playoff victory over the Cincinnati Bengals. The tackle appeared routine but caused a hip injury that was eventually diagnosed as avascular necrosis. Cartilage and bone around Jackson's left hip joint were deteriorating.

The injury ended Jackson's football career and the Royals released him the next spring. He joined the Chicago White Sox in 1991 but needed a hip replacement, and sat out the 1992 season. He started the 1993 season with a pinch-hit home run off the Yankees' Neal Heaton and finished with sixteen home runs. He was able to play until 1994.

When Jackson first saw the X-ray of his injured hip, he said, "I have dressed deer; I have witnessed the birth of two out of three of my children; and when I saw a black-and-white X-ray of my hip, I just got sick."

Chapter 23
The Boz:
Brian Bosworth

Oklahoma's Brian Bosworth was the nation's top college linebacker in 1985 and 1986, but was suspended from the Orange Bowl and bolted for the NFL. He came into the league with great fanfare but had only a three-year, injury-shortened career. In the end, he offended more people than he tackled.

BOSWORTH SEEMED DETERMINED to become the scratchy fingernail on the chalkboard of pro football. There's never been an NFL player who irritated more people than the linebacker who called himself "The Boz."

He wore a Mohawk haircut and earrings that displayed his jersey number. And he loved to talk trash. If the Seattle Seahawks and their fans expected Bosworth could lead them to the Super Bowl—boy, were they ever disappointed.

Bosworth claimed he had a split personality, which isn't unusual for showbiz types. But he couldn't get many people to warm up to either part of him.

"The Boz is the quotable, outrageous, occasionally obnoxious never-give-a-damn side of me," he wrote in his biography. "The Boz is the guy who's not afraid to be an individual in a world of automatons. Almost everybody has an opinion on The Boz.

"Brian is the quiet, unobtrusive, very professional side of me. Brian likes nothing better than staying home, renting a movie, and putting his feet up. Almost nobody knows Brian. To old farts or people who just think old, The Boz became the symbol of the anti-Christ, the symbol of everything that's wrong with 'damn kids' today—everything that's wrong with everything, period. Every time I get a new design on the side of my head, ten thousand guys in John Deere hats go, 'What'd I tell you, Merle? That there is another sure sign that boy is possessed by a demon.'"

Bosworth was a master of grand entrances and ungracious exits. At Oklahoma, he twice received the Butkus Award as the nation's top college linebacker, but was suspended from the January 1987 Orange Bowl after he tested positive for steroids. He left the Sooners with a year of eligibility left and went to the Seahawks in the supplementary draft. They won a coin toss to get the first pick, and at the time they considered themselves lucky.

Bosworth reported late to the Seahawks because of a contract dispute. He was greeted at the Seattle airport by about two hundred people and several television crews.

"I didn't know it yet, but the people of Seattle were going way overboard already," he wrote. "The radio stations were playing a song about me, sung to the tune of 'La Bamba,' with 'Bosworth' replacing 'Bamba.' And they had gifts waiting, too. They gave me a certificate for a free personalized driveway—complete with my name and uniform number embossed in stone, a pair of three-hundred-and-fifty-dollar Italian shoes . . . for someone who is trying to keep people from knocking on his door all night, what's he going to do with a personalized driveway? The shoes were red, so I don't wear them."

Bosworth signed a ten-year, $11 million contract, which was big money at the time. Then he posed with a Playboy playmate for a poster entitled, "Land of Boz."

The Boz faced his first hurdle in Seattle when he wanted to keep number forty-four, which he wore at Oklahoma. But the NFL required linebackers to wear numbers in the fifties or sixties, and Bosworth wore fifty-five for his opening game. He got his old number back only after taking the league to court.

"I'd played as forty-four since I was a kid," he explained. "I'm extremely superstitious. I couldn't even imagine stepping on the field without wearing forty-four. I had a lot of money tied up in forty-four. My company is called Forty-Four Boz, Inc. And we'd signed a deal to market our own line of clothes and sunglasses called Forty-Four Blues. Now what? I'm supposed to change it to Fifty-Five Blues?"

In his first regular-season game, at Denver, Bosworth showed as much of a knack for marketing as for hitting people. "I can't wait to get my hands on John Elway's boyish face," The Boz boasted. He added that he'd rather get penalized for a late hit than let Elway run out of bounds unscathed.

Bronco fans, predictably, were enraged. About ten thousand of them wore T-shirts featuring Bosworth's face with a slash through it. The shirts read WHAT'S A BOZ WORTH? NOTHING on the front and BAN THE BOZ on the back.

"But if they had looked inside the shirt at the little tag that said 44 BOZ, INC., they would have realized they just paid fifteen dollars for a shirt made by my company," Bosworth wrote. "We gave all the profits to the Children's Hospital. We just wanted to prove how oxygen-deprived Denver fans are."

Bosworth's mother, Kathy, attended the game and watched her son get a special police escort off the field. After watching the commotion caused by her son's pregame hype, the mother of three said, "If he'd been the first, he'd [have] been the only."

Bosworth made a more promising debut in 1987 than did the Seahawks. They lost 40–17, but Broncos center Billy Bryan said of The Boz, "The guy can really play. He hits hard but clean. I can't remember a rookie linebacker [that played] any better."

Bosworth blamed Bryan for a cheap shot from behind. He received more than his fair share of cheap shots, he claimed, and less than his fair share of breaks from officials.

"I guess it's no wonder I never get a holding call from the refs," Bosworth wrote. "I came to the sideline against Houston and I said to [linebacker] Keith Butler, my guru on the Seahawks, 'Man, I never get the damn call.' And he said, 'Of course, you don't, you moron, and you never will.'"

"Why not?"

"Because it's *you*, you dumb [bleep]."

The Seahawks stood 7-3 in 1987 before their season came unglued with a 37–14 Monday-night loss to the Los Angeles Raiders. That's also when, according to Bosworth, the world got on the "Ban the Boz" bandwagon. On a 2-yard touchdown burst, rookie sensation Bo Jackson ran him over and fans around the nation were delighted.

"It was my own fault," Bosworth recalled. "He came up inside and I didn't know if he was going to cut it back and try to run it inside or go outside. So I hesitated for a second and that's all it took. I wasn't set and he knocked my [butt] over. I'm sure they ran that one back a few times in the ABC booth.

"That wasn't bad, but losing to Pittsburgh and the planet's worst quarterback, Mark Malone, the next week was worse."

Bosworth ultimately bit off more controversy than he could chew. He sounded miserable as his rookie season, disrupted by a players' strike, drew near a close.

"The three months that I've been here, they've been the most uncomfortable three months of my whole entire life," he said. "So far, I've probably had zero amount of fun playing the game that

I'm supposed to have the most fun in my life playing. I have asked myself why and I've asked dear and close friends why. And there's really no answer. After contemplating the question over several weeks, I know it's not my fault.

"This is the one thing I love to do more than anything in the world, and the people around me are making me hate it."

Bosworth's unhappiness did not elicit much sympathy, especially not as his injuries piled up and his performance slid. He failed the Seahawks' physical in July 1990 because of a shoulder injury and ended his NFL career after playing just twenty-four games.

Bosworth turned to acting. His first film, *Stone Cold*, bombed in 1991, but he found a niche in action movies. He played a linebacker for the prison guards facing off against the convicts in *The Longest Yard*, a 2005 remake of a Burt Reynolds film.

Bosworth also remained visible as an XFL television commentator in 2001. As unpopular as The Boz may have been, he stayed a lot more famous than Brian ever did.

Chapter 24
The Tooz:
John Matuszak

John Matuszak was the top pick of the 1973 NFL
draft, but his wild behavior kept his career
sputtering. Finally, he became another renegade
who found a last resort and success in Oakland.
In 1976, he became a starting defensive end for
the Raiders and finished the season by winning
a Super Bowl.

JOHN MATUSZAK WARNED anybody reckless enough to go
barhopping with him: "You can get bruised when you cruise with
'The Tooz.'" He was a six-foot-eight, 280-pounder who lived hard,
died young, and personified the Raiders' old outlaw image. Matuszak would walk into a bar, rip his shirt open, and growl like a
lion. He could be a beast on the field, too. But his wild lifestyle
often got in the way of his ability.

Quarterback Ken Stabler recalled that Matuszak's revelry in
Denver on New Year's Eve of 1978 came back to haunt the Raiders
in the AFC championship game. Matuszak got back to his room
the morning of the game and yanked down the drapes, prompting

a hotel employee to tip off the Broncos that Matuszak wasn't in great shape. Sure enough, he was too worn out to stop the Broncos from running over him as they killed the last three minutes of a 20–17 win over the defending Super Bowl champions.

Raiders coach Tom Flores knew Matuszak could help his defense if only he could be kept under control. Before the 1979 season, Flores asked Stabler to take Matuszak into his condo, explaining, "We'd like him to move out of the trunk of his car."

Stabler agreed. He didn't have to buy a lot of groceries for Matuszak, who lived on bagels, Cheez Whiz, and Crown Royal. Stabler could usually calm down Matuszak when he'd start insulting strangers. But Stabler couldn't stop him from buying a .357 magnum pistol.

While Stabler was home watching the Monday-night game, he got a call from Matuszak's lawyer, who asked Stabler to accompany him to jail. Matuszak was arrested for shooting at road signs and driving while intoxicated. Stabler took him home.

Oakland was the end of the line for the NFL's misfits and malcontents. They knew if they couldn't play for owner Al Davis, they couldn't play for anybody. Matuszak's aberrant behavior had kept him on the move since his college days.

He went to the University of Missouri as a tight end but was suspended from the team after he severely beat an Air Force cadet who Matuszak said was making improper advances toward his girlfriend. Matuszak transferred to the University of Tampa in 1971 and became the nation's top defensive player. The Houston Oilers made him the first overall pick of the 1973 draft.

Matuszak soured on the Oilers, he said, when they cut seven teammates at the end of a players' strike in 1974. He jumped to the Houston Texans of the World Football League, and as Matuszak stood on the sidelines at the Astrodome, he was served with an injunction filed by the Oilers to prevent him from playing. Matuszak waved to the crowd as he left the building. The

Oilers traded Matuszak to Kansas City before the 1974 season for nose tackle Curley Culp and a first-round draft choice.

If Chiefs coach Hank Stram thought he could tame Matuszak, he was mistaken. During one training camp, Matuszak quarreled with his wife, Yvette, and she tried to run him down with a car. Matuszak ran into a nearby cemetery, stood behind some gravestones, and laughed while his wife swore at him.

After the 1974 season, the sometimes-happy couple stripped down to relax in the sauna off the Chiefs' deserted locker room. They were discovered by mild-mannered trainer Wayne Rudy. Shocked, Rudy went looking for coach Paul Wiggin, who replaced Stram in 1975, and sputtered, "The Tooz! The Tooz!"

Wiggin expelled the sweaty couple from the sauna. He also would expel Matuszak from Kansas City, but not before saving the wild man's life.

Matuszak wrote in his biography that during the 1976 training camp, he mixed beer and sleeping pills while he waited for his wife at a bar. She found him collapsed outside and summoned Wiggin, who rode with Matuszak to a hospital in an ambulance. On the way, Matuszak's heart stopped and Wiggin beat on his chest and revived him.

Matuszak was placed in intensive care. He recovered but had worn out his welcome with Wiggin and was traded to Washington for an eighth-round pick. He didn't stick with the Redskins, but his career finally was about to turn around.

The Raiders signed Matuszak during the 1976 preseason because they were worried about whether left end Charles Philyaw would ever get up to speed. When coach John Madden asked linebacker Ted Hendricks what he thought of adding Matuszak to a roster of eccentrics, Hendricks replied, "Look around you, John. What's one more going to hurt?"

Matuszak began the season as a backup but led a goal-line stand in a 14–13 victory at Houston in week three. Philyaw was injured a week later and Matuszak became a starter as the Raiders marched to their first Super Bowl title.

Matuszak also played in the January 1981 Super Bowl, a 27–10 victory over the Eagles in New Orleans. Letting the Raiders on Bourbon Street was like leaving a bunch of rowdy teenagers home alone with a full liquor cabinet. Matuszak tried to play the elder statesman and told reporters, "I'm going to see that there's no funny business. I've had enough parties for twenty people's lifetimes. I'll keep our young fellows out of trouble."

Matuszak was spotted a night later on Bourbon Street at 3 a.m., four hours after curfew, and he overslept for a press conference the next morning. Rival coach Dick Vermeil, asked about Matuszak's behavior, replied, "If he were on the Eagles, he'd be back on a plane to Philadelphia right now."

Matuszak always seemed like a character right out of the movies, and that's exactly what he became. He'd already started acting when his NFL career ended after the 1982 season. He appeared in *North Dallas Forty*, *Caveman*, *The Goonies*, and *One Crazy Summer*.

In *The Goonies*, Matuszak played Sloth, a huge, deformed creature who was a child of the villainous Fratelli family and was kept chained in a basement. He was befriended by the Goonies, a bunch of kids who saw in Sloth a kindred spirit.

Matuszak was only thirty-eight when he died in 1989 from an accidental painkiller overdose. In his biography, he wrote: "The truth is, I did have a dark side, a self-destructive side, which I never clearly understood myself. All through my career, I seemed to place obstacles in my path. Just when it appeared my life was going smoothly, I would go and screw things up again. It was a side of me I didn't like, and it never surfaced when I was clean. Almost every heartache I've ever had, every time I've lost my self-control, every time I've hurt someone I cared for, it was related to foreign substances. I mean alcohol and drugs."

Chapter 25
Hacksaw:
Jack Reynolds

Linebacker Jack "Hacksaw" Reynolds seldom lost his edge during fifteen years with the Los Angeles Rams and San Francisco 49ers. After starring at the University of Tennessee, he was the Rams' first-round pick in 1970 and went on to play in three Super Bowl games.

MOST FOOTBALL NICKNAMES aren't meant to be taken literally. This one was.

Linebacker Jack Reynolds was called "Hacksaw"—not because he was tough, relentless, or would quickly cut down blockers and ball carriers, though he had all those qualities. And Reynolds didn't take the nickname to call attention to himself. In fact, he became weary of the publicity it brought him, especially when he met the media before his Super Bowl games with the Rams in January 1980 and the 49ers two years later.

Reynolds would tell the "Hacksaw" story for three straight days of pregame interviews. He would retell the story every fifteen minutes when a fresh wave of reporters arrived. So Reynolds greeted reporters covering the January 1985 Super Bowl between the 49ers and Miami Dolphins with sheets explaining how "Hacksaw" got his nickname during his college days.

The details were excruciating, especially for an old car abandoned on a bluff overlooking the Tennessee campus. That car was on the receiving end of Reynolds's anger and frustration after a 38–0 loss to Mississippi in his senior season.

"When I got back to school, I decided to cut that old Chevy in half to make a trailer for a new Jeep I had purchased," Reynolds wrote.

"It was a good outlet for my frustrations. I went to Kmart and bought the cheapest hacksaw they had, along with thirteen replacement blades. I cut through the entire frame and drive shaft, all the way through the car. I started on Sunday and finished Monday afternoon. It took me eight total hours. I broke thirteen blades.

"When I finished, I got one guy from the dorm, Ray Nettles, to witness it. The next day we took the rest of our friends from the dorm up the hill to see it. When we got there, both halves of the car were gone, with just the thirteen blades lying on the ground. To this day, I don't know what happened to that car!"

Because Super Bowl interviews are so crowded and chaotic, reporters often get close enough to a player only to hear snippets of conversation. And reporters routinely swap quotes, which often get mangled, then circulate like viruses.

Reynolds, after handing out the "Hacksaw" diary, mentioned he was living in San Salvador, an island in the Bahamas. One reporter thought Reynolds said he lived in San Salvador, capital of El Salvador, and asked how he was surviving in the midst of a civil war. Reynolds replied, sarcastically, "I have a machine gun and a machete."

Everybody got the joke. Or so it seemed. One reporter heard this story secondhand and went around excitedly telling colleagues:

"Did you hear? Hacksaw lives in El Salvador and he's got a machine gun and a machete!"

"Hacksaw" wasn't Reynolds's first nickname. It was just the one that stuck. While growing up in Cincinnati, he was also called "Horse," "Animal," "Crazy Jack," and "The R.C. Kid," because he drank so much Royal Crown Cola. He was already hacking at large objects.

"Four or five of us would climb up in a tree and then another guy would cut it down and we'd crash," he recalled. "We used to do some really weird things. We'd roll tires down a grass hill and the kid at the bottom had to catch 'em or spear 'em with a stick. Half the time those tires would knock you down. The ones that really hurt were the ones that had the rims."

Reynolds was knocked down again after the 1980 season. Though he made his second Pro Bowl, the Rams no longer considered him one of the NFL's top run-stopping linebackers and released him. Bill Walsh, the 49ers coach, was happy to sign Reynolds.

Though the 49ers' 1981 season is best remembered for quarterback Joe Montana's stardom and Dwight Clark's catch that put them in the Super Bowl, the 49ers couldn't have won a championship without rebuilding their defense. Walsh drafted three defensive backs, most notably Ronnie Lott, and all started. Walsh obtained veteran talent and leadership in pass rusher Fred Dean and Reynolds.

Walsh was asked before the 1981 NFC championship game whether a veteran like Reynolds could still be fresh after playing four games in the preseason, sixteen in the regular season, and one in the play-offs.

"If we were playing fifty games, it would make Jack that much happier," Walsh said. "He is consumed with football, even more than any addicted coach."

Defensive tackle Warren Sapp, left, has thrived on confrontations. Here he's challenged by Green Bay coach Mike Sherman, who's furious because Sapp injured Packers tackle Chad Clifton during an interception return in the Buccaneers' 21–7 victory over the Packers in 2002. Neither the officiating crew nor the league office penalized Sapp. *Chris O'Meara/AP Photo.*

New Orleans Saints wide receiver Joe Horn got on the horn to make the most notorious phone call in NFL history. He'd just made his second of four touchdown catches in a 45–7 win over the New York Giants late in the 2003 season when Horn called his mother from a cell phone that was stashed under the goalpost padding. He may have had unlimited minutes, but the NFL billed him $30,000. *Andrew Cohoon/ AP Photo.*

Any photo showing Terrell Owens happy as an Eagle must be a collector's item. He flashes the No. 1 sign after catching eight passes for 101 yards in a 15–10 home victory over the Baltimore Ravens in 2004. Owens bounced back from a late-season ankle injury to catch nine passes for 122 yards in a 24–21 Super Bowl loss to the New England Patriots. During the next season, however, Owens constantly clashed with coaches and teammates and was finally sent home. *Rusty Kennedy/AP Photo.*

Mike Ditka, coaching the Saints, shows his famous temper to back judge Bill Lovett during a 20–3 loss to the Atlanta Falcons in 1997. Though it was his first season in New Orleans, the loss left Ditka feeling so low that he said after the game that he might quit if his team didn't improve. They didn't, but he stayed another two years. *Alan Mohner/AP Photo.*

Philadelphia cornerback Herman Edwards is about to pounce on the fumble of Giants quarterback Joe Pisarcik and return it to the end zone for a 19–17 win. Pisarcik, who made an errant handoff to Larry Csonka, can only watch in horror as the Miracle of the Meadowlands begins to unfold in November 1978. The Eagles' unlikely victory propelled them into the play-offs for the first time in 18 years. *Burnett/AP Photo.*

You'd think Peyton Manning would wear out his arms by raising them after every touchdown pass. The Indianapolis Colts quarterback celebrates another score, against the New England Patriots in 2003. A year later he threw 49 touchdown passes, breaking Dan Marino's all-time record. *Darron Cummings/AP Photo.*

Brett Favre reached the pinnacle of his career when he led the Green Bay Packers to a 35–21 Super Bowl win over the New England Patriots in January 1997. He threw two touchdown passes and reacts happily to a two-point conversion pass to tight end Mark Chmura that put the finishing touches on a championship. *Ed Reinke / AP Photo.*

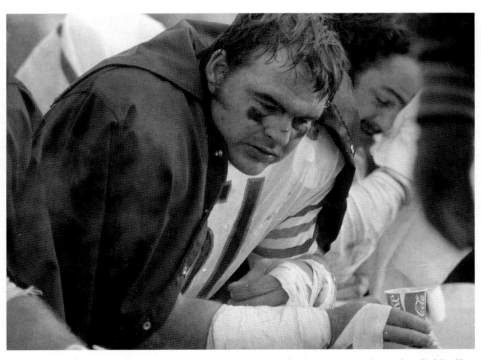

Relentless Chicago linebacker Dick Butkus might have stayed on the field all day if you let him. But he took a well-deserved rest as the Bears' offense operates in a 20–19 loss to the Packers at Green Bay in 1970. Butkus seldom got a chance to rest for long and was one of few bright spots during mostly dark days for the Bears. *AP photo.*

Media Day at the Super Bowl must have been invented with Denver tight end Shannon Sharpe in mind. Given his own podium and microphone, Sharpe kept hundreds of reporters entertained before the Broncos' 34–19 victory over the Falcons in January 1999. He spoke non-stop about how he acquired his gift of gab and how he would make Atlanta cornerback Ray Buchanan pay for his pre-game taunts. *Ron Heflin/AP Photo.*

John Riggins sported many looks during his Hall of Fame career. He had an afro hairstyle for the New York Jets' training camp in 1972, only to shave it in favor of a Mohawk when he ended a contract holdout in 1973. Riggins became a lot better known for his running than for his hair. *AP Photo.*

Deion Sanders has been one of the showiest, as well as the best, cornerbacks of all time. He points jubilantly to the Dallas crowd as he helps the Cowboys sew up a Super Bowl trip with a 38–27 victory over the Packers in the NFC Championship game in January 1996. *Ron Heflin / AP Photo.*

Joe Namath could win with his arm and disarm with his charm. This Jets quarterback was one of the most famous and charismatic stars ever in New York, and that's saying a lot. "Broadway Joe" nailed down a permanent place in the lore of his sport and city when he guaranteed the biggest upset in NFL history, then delivered with a 16–7 Super Bowl victory over the Baltimore Colts in January 1969. *AP Photo.*

Pittsburgh running back Franco Harris has just grabbed the Immaculate Reception and heads for the end zone to finish the most famous play in NFL history. Defensive back Jimmy Warren can't catch Harris after he grabbed a deflected pass and gave the Steelers a stunning last-minute play-off victory in 1972. *Harry Cabluck/AP Photo.*

Pittsburgh quarterback Terry Bradshaw usually could find the humor in any situation, but not this one. He presses a towel to a thumb that was injured by Los Angeles pass rusher Cedrick "Nasty" Hardman during the Steelers' 45–34 loss to the Super Bowl-bound Raiders in a Monday-night game in 1980. *AP Photo.*

Have you ever wondered why Pittsburgh
coach Bill Cowher is nicknamed "The Face,"
or "The Chin?" Few coaches have ever
displayed a game face as intense as Cowher's,
though you'd never guess that he's watching
a 40–21 play-off victory over the Buffalo Bills
in January 1996. The Steelers then went on
to win their first AFC championship under
Cowher. Ten years later they won a Super
Bowl for him with a 21–10 victory over the
Seattle Seahawks. *Gene Puskar/AP Photo.*

Chapter 26
Riggo:
John Riggins

A country boy from Centralia, Kansas, John Riggins broke a lot of tackles, records, and stereotypes. His roots suggested he might be overwhelmed by the bright lights of New York and Washington. Actually, there wasn't a city too big or too bright for Riggins.

He was an unpredictable eccentric, whether he was in a football uniform or mingling in the most exclusive circles of government. He was the first-round draft choice of the New York Jets in 1971, and totaled 11,352 yards rushing and 116 touchdowns over fourteen seasons with the Jets and Redskins.

RIGGINS GAINED NOTORIETY as a rebel in 1973, when he held out for most of the Jets' training camp because of a contract dispute. When he returned, he sported a Mohawk haircut, which coach Weeb Ewbank described as the "damnedest sight." The coach saw an even stranger sight when Riggins sat at Ewbank's desk to sign his contract.

"He had that Mohawk haircut and he was stripped to the waist, and he was wearing leather pants and a derby hat with a feather in it," Ewbank recalled. "It must have been what the sale of Manhattan looked like."

Holdouts became a Riggins trademark. He rode his motorcycle out of the Redskins' training camp in July 1980 because the club wouldn't renegotiate his contract. After sitting out the next six weeks, Riggins announced his retirement. The Redskins suspended him and he sat out the entire season.

Joe Gibbs was named Redskins coach early in 1981 and traveled to Riggins's farm in Lawrence, Kansas, to see if he'd return. Riggins came back that summer with a brief explanation: "I'm bored. I'm broke. I'm back."

Riggins didn't reward Gibbs for his visit until late in the 1982 season. Then, he let his coaches and teammates know he wanted the ball. "He said it many a time: Just hitch the wagon up and he'll carry the load," guard Russ Grimm recalled. "Come Sunday, you didn't want anybody else back there."

Riggins became a tank, not a wagon, during the 1982 playoffs. He rushed for 185 yards on thirty-seven carries against the Minnesota Vikings and was motivated to have another big day against the Miami Dolphins in the Super Bowl.

"He came to the offensive line the night before," tackle Joe Jacoby said. "He told us he'd been in trouble with the coaches and could we open some holes for him? Not big holes, he added. Just ones that would let him get four or five yards. He didn't want anything where—fifteen or so yards down the field—he might run out of gas."

Riggins bolted 43 yards for the game-breaking touchdown in the Redskins' 27–17 victory over the Dolphins. He was named MVP after rushing for 166 yards, a Super Bowl record.

"Ronnie [Reagan] may be president," Riggins cracked, "but I'm king for the day." As it turned out, his reign lasted much longer than a day.

"Not many athletes have a big game in the biggest game there is and it changed my life in a number of ways," Riggins said. "One of them was that it made Washington kind of a small town for me, Centralia all over again. I'd walk down the street and people would be calling, 'Riggo.'

"You have to remember, Washington has only two things that most of the people there care about: government and the Redskins. And a lot of the time they don't care for the government."

Riggins behaved like a fullback charging into the end zone when he attended an annual black-tie affair for Congress at the National Press Club in 1985. He was seated across from Supreme Court Justice Sandra Day O'Connor and her husband, John. Riggins had been drinking and said, "C'mon, Sandy, baby. Loosen up. You're too tight."

Riggins got up to chat with John O'Connor but collapsed under a chair. Wearing a tuxedo and cowboy boots, Riggins slept on the floor, snoring, for about an hour. He snoozed through a speech by Vice President George Bush before he was awakened and escorted out by security guards.

"I must have been like an eighteen-wheeler lying there," recalled Riggins, who sent Justice O'Connor a dozen roses as an apology. "In those days, I thought people in Washington didn't allow themselves to enjoy a party. They were stiff. That wasn't my idea of a real hoedown good time. I liked to have people swinging from the chandeliers. I'd like to think I've grown up a little since then."

Riggins had a lot of growing up to do during his playing days. He didn't see much value in pregame preparation.

"I'm not much for meetings and X's and O's," he said. "All that stuff really can't prepare you for a defense. You have to adjust to what they do from play to play. That's why I like to carry the ball a lot. It lets me get a feel for what the defense is doing."

Nor did Riggins believe in a monastic existence the night before a game. "For me, football was easy," he said. "A little too easy, actually. I was constantly creating little diversions. I needed pressure to perform. I put self-induced pressure on myself over the years and it's helped me."

Riggins, who set an NFL record with twenty-four touchdowns in a season, was inducted into the Hall of Fame in 1992. Not surprisingly, he put an unusual spin on the moment.

"Kind of like giving your own eulogy at your funeral," he said. "Enshrining, entombing the football spirit. It's the end of a football act, you might say."

Riggins's choice of a Hall of Fame presenter seemed unusual, too. He picked NFL Commissioner Paul Tagliabue—staid, conservative, and not even a close friend.

"You go to a wedding, you get a priest," Riggins explained. "You get to the Hall of Fame, you get the commissioner. Makes pretty good sense to me."

Chapter 27
Rosso:
Tim Rossovich

If not for a major knee injury in 1972, Tim Rossovich would be remembered as one of the best linebackers of his era instead of as the kookiest. A linebacker from the University of Southern California, Rossovich was the fourteenth overall pick of the 1968 NFL draft. He was voted to one Pro Bowl and enjoyed a colorful but all-too-brief career.

ROSSOVICH WAS THE NFL's first flower child. One of the last, too. Who else could balance peace, love, and happiness with playing middle linebacker?

Wired for sound during a 13–13 tie against the Atlanta Falcons in 1970, Rossovich yelled across the line: "I love you, man, but I gotta wipe you out."

Oh, there were other counterculture types in the NFL, but none like Rossovich. Dave Meggyesy looked the part and expressed the anger and protest of the '60s. He wrote a book that blasted football as brutal and dehumanizing. Rossovich agreed with the brutal part, but he relished that. He didn't burn flags or his draft card. Just his hair.

"He spent a lot of time tie-dying T-shirts," recalled Steve Sabol, president of NFL Films. "He had that big afro and wore bell-bottom pants. He was the first to embrace that Haight-Ashbury style. The football establishment never took him seriously, but his teammates did because he was tough and never quit.

"He was totally fearless, one of the most intense players I ever saw. He had to get himself into that restrained insanity in order for him to play. Linemen who challenged him outweighed him by seventy or eighty pounds. I don't want to say he was out of condition, but he never ate right."

Sabol, a former college football player, vicariously lived Rossovich's NFL career. During his early days with NFL Films, Sabol roomed with Rossovich in Philadelphia and featured him in *The New Breed*, a nationally televised show that captured Rossovich's eccentricity and talent.

One night when Sabol was having a party, he answered the door and found Rossovich standing there in flames. Sabol and a guest knocked down Rossovich and put out the fire with blankets. Rossovich got up and said, "Sorry, I must have the wrong apartment," and left.

Rossovich was as familiar with flames as an arsonist. For a 1971 *Sports Illustrated* cover photo, he applied lighter fluid to his afro and set it on fire. That set the tone for John Underwood's story, "He's Burning to be a Success."

Readers were treated to dozens of outrageous tales painstakingly compiled and verified by Underwood. Few could believe the stories then. Fewer would believe them now.

Rossovich was hell on wheels. He drove a motorbike off a pier. He drove some friends to a bar and stopped the car by slamming it into the bar's outside wall. Once in a bar, Rossovich would use his teeth to open bottles and chew glass.

He had a contest with Eagles teammate Mike Ditka to see who could open the most beer bottles with his teeth. Rossovich was ahead, one hundred bottles to three, when he started drinking the beer from a glass, then eating the glass. Ditka, a legendary tough guy, withdrew.

Rossovich also munched on insects, cigarettes, and playbook pages. Bored at a birthday party, he went to the bathroom, returned naked, and dove into the cake. He opened his mouth to give a speech and a sparrow flew out. He took a compass on the road to make sure he slept with his head facing north because, Sabol explained, Rossovich wanted to let magnetic waves run through him and revitalize him.

Rossovich's antics were legendary at USC. Recalling that he once punctured his leg jumping from the second story of his future wife's sorority house, Rossovich said, "It was a bad week for me. I fell off two roofs and set fire to myself jumping over a car [that he and friends set ablaze]."

When Rossovich was a freshman, he and some friends were swinging on a rope over a river and made a bet on who had the nerve to land nearest a rock cliff. Rossovich won by deliberately crashing into the rocks and, luckily, escaped with only cut elbows. But the cuts became badly infected when Rossovich jumped into a contaminated fish pond at a fraternity party. He went into a coma and was hospitalized. In the hospital, he threw chairs and smashed a television set. Worse, he was told he couldn't play for eight weeks.

But when Rossovich left the hospital, he insisted to assistant coach Marv Goux that he was ready to play. He tried to prove his point by banging his head into a locker and repeated this daily, hoping the coaches would relent. They did not.

Rossovich, six feet and 245 pounds, normally did not waste his ferocity on lockers. Eagles Hall of Famer Chuck Bednarik, who'll never be confused with a flower child, said, "You've got to be like an animal to play that position and Rossovich is that way."

The Eagles, declining to meet Rossovich's salary demands in 1972, traded him to San Diego for a first-round draft pick. He suffered torn knee ligaments in his first preseason with the Chargers and lasted only through 1973. This was a cruel twist of fate because it was Rossovich's hair, not his career, that was supposed to go up in flames.

Chapter 28
Butch and Sundance:
Larry Csonka

Hall of Famer Larry Csonka was the Miami
Dolphins' bluntest weapon in their perfect
1972 season. He, close friend Jim Kiick, and
Mercury Morris gave the Dolphins the
unstoppable running game that helped make
them a three-time Super Bowl team.

CSONKA WAS THE Bronko Nagurski of the Super Bowl era. He
was a burly fullback with an oft-busted nose who never met a
collision he didn't like. Defensive players dreaded running into
Csonka the way offensive players dreaded running into Chicago
Bears linebacker Dick Butkus.

"Csonka's like a Caterpillar with 9.5 speed," said Hall of Fame
safety Larry Wilson of the St. Louis Cardinals. "Not one of those
fuzzy little things, but one of those big yellow jobs. He's brutal."

Csonka, six-foot-three and 235 pounds, was quicker than
most people realized. Still, he would rather run over a defender
than around him.

"I wasn't fast enough to run away from people," he said. "So I figured the shortest line was the best line. When they weigh two-hundred-fifty-five to two-hundred-seventy, it's a good idea to hit them as hard as you can, as quick as you can."

Csonka was a throwback. The heat and humidity of Miami and the hardness of the artificial turf in the Orange Bowl were not his cup of tea. He preferred playing on the road in chilly weather and on real grass or in mud. "I like to be able to shake a little dirt out of my helmet," he said.

Csonka was right in his element on a chilly, windy day in Buffalo in September 1971 as the Dolphins beat the Bills, 29–14. Csonka, despite a broken nose he suffered early in the fourth quarter, rushed for 103 yards. Teammate Jim Kiick, despite a gashed forehead, rushed for 108.

"I got in the huddle and there was a steady stream of blood coming from my nose, running on the ground," Csonka said. "[Tight end] Marv Fleming's eyes got a little big, he felt a little woozy. It was running on his shoe at one point and he drew it back real quick. If Jim had bled a little more from that cut in his forehead, he'd have gotten the game ball. I sacrificed a pint of blood to get a game ball."

Csonka and Kiick saw kindred spirits in the movie, *Butch Cassidy and the Sundance Kid*. Yet the running backs never decided which of them was Butch and which was Sundance.

"They've been asking that for over thirty years and I still don't know who is who," Csonka said in 2003. "We managed to get in a lot of trouble all the time with everyone, so that's probably why we got that title."

While most Dolphins were afraid of Don Shula, the Dolphins' demanding, no-nonsense coach, Kiick and Csonka delighted in seeing how far they could push him. At training camp one year, they staged a joint contract holdout, a la Sandy Koufax and Don Drysdale. They once showed their lack of enthusiasm for training-camp life by posing behind bars for a summer issue of *Dolphin Digest*.

Csonka claimed to have dropped a baby alligator in Shula's shower and forced him to dash out, in the buff, in front of a receptionist's desk. Csonka also said he threw a black rubber strip, which he claimed was a snake, at Shula and watched the coach yell with alarm and take off.

When Kiick was backing up halfback Mercury Morris, he got some hometown pals from Lincoln Park, New Jersey, to help him lobby for more playing time. During a game against the Jets at Shea Stadium, the pals held up a sign that read RUN KIICK OR TRADE SHULA. Kiick said the coach was steamed for three days.

Csonka was seldom caught speechless. When he was named Super Bowl MVP of the Dolphins' 24–7 victory over the Minnesota Vikings in January 1974, he said, "I won a car; only a Hungarian could win a car in the year of the gas shortage."

During that game, Vikings linebacker Wally Hilgenberg tried to intimidate Csonka as he rushed for 145 yards and two touchdowns. "He told me if I ran his way one more time he'd bite my head off," Csonka recalled. "And I told him if he did that, he'd have more brains in his stomach than he's got in his head."

Csonka was the seventh overall pick of the 1968 draft and reported to the Dolphins' camp two weeks late because he played in the College All-Star Game, in which he was named MVP. Ray Jacobs, a huge defensive tackle, welcomed the highly publicized rookie to the NFL by spitting tobacco juice on his suit.

"I grabbed Ray's lamb-chop sideburns and gave him a big smooch," Csonka recalled. "They left me alone after that."

The next summer, Csonka got his first look at Butkus in an exhibition game in Miami. He took a handoff from quarterback Bob Griese, then saw two Dolphin linemen collide and give Butkus a clear path to the ball. Csonka tossed it back to Griese.

"I'll never forget the look on his face when I gave it back to him," Csonka said. "I said I was a slow farm boy, not a dumb one."

The Dolphin dynasty, which included back-to-back Super Bowl wins, ended after the 1974 season. Kiick, Csonka, and wide receiver Paul Warfield joined the Memphis Southmen of the World Football League for that league's final season.

Csonka, when asked what he'd learned from his WFL experience, replied: "That you can make a lot of money in sports. I would've preferred to stay in Miami, as would've Jim and Paul Warfield. But we had an opportunity to make nearly twentyfold or more of what we were making in a relatively short term, and did."

Csonka returned to the NFL in 1976 as a Giant. His main legacy in New York was his role in quarterback Joe Pisarcik's 1978 fumble—the most infamous play in franchise history. Csonka, who never had a chance to cleanly take the handoff, can't understand why such a big deal is made about that play.

"It would've been a lot bigger game if the Eagles had gone on to do something in the play-offs, or we could've got into the play-offs," he said. "But as it turned out, it was kind of like, 'What difference does it make?'"

Csonka proved he could go home again and still knock defenders over. He rejoined the Dolphins in 1979 and in his final season rushed for 837 yards and 12 touchdowns. Shula bore no hard feelings from Csonka's 1975 exit. Referring to their shared Hungarian ancestry, the coach said, happily, "I've got my hunky back."

Chapter 29
Looney:
Joe Don Looney

Maybe he felt obliged to live up to his last
name. Maybe he was a nomad trapped in a football player's body. Or maybe he was just ahead
of his time as a boorish, spoiled athlete who
squandered enormous talent. It's hard to say,
because nobody has fully explained the eccentric
and seemingly pointless behavior of Joe Don
Looney.

Teams kept taking chances on Looney because
they kept thinking they might get him to grow
up and fulfill his vast potential. Of course, he
never did.

LOONEY ALREADY HAD a checkered past when the New York
Giants made him their top draft pick in 1964. He made college
stops at Texas, TCU, a junior college, and Oklahoma. He was
through at Oklahoma after he hit a student assistant.

Giants owner Wellington Mara was asked if he'd considered
Looney's bad attitude before drafting him. "I have considered
those shoulders, those legs, and those two-hundred-and-twenty-
four pounds," Mara replied.

Looney could run 100 yards in 9.8 seconds, shoulder-press
290 pounds, and squat 450. But he never made much use of those
assets. Looney didn't feel the need to practice, attend meetings,

or adhere to team rules. Nor even to run through his assigned holes. "Anyone can run where the holes are," he said. "A good football player makes his own holes."

Looney preferred playing catch with a nine-year-old fan on the sidelines to running patterns for quarterback Y.A. Tittle. One day he told coach Allie Sherman he wasn't going to practice anymore.

"I know the plays," Looney explained. "It doesn't make any sense for me to go out there and run around doing stuff I've already learned. Let me know when you're going to get into something new."

Sherman put up with Looney for twenty-eight days before trading him to the Baltimore Colts on August 25, 1964. Just before he left the Giants, Looney vented his frustration by attacking a tackling dummy. It recoiled and knocked him down.

If Colts coach Don Shula, a noted disciplinarian, couldn't rein in Looney, nobody could. One night, Shula sent running back Alex Hawkins to Looney's apartment to keep an eye on him.

"I watched him pace up and down the apartment," Hawkins said. "I listened to him rant and rave. I heard of his grand scheme to buy an island near New Guinea, buy a boat, get some girls and some Texas buddies and go down there and breed a new race. Joe eventually went to sleep. I didn't dare close my eyes."

Looney was a talented punter and after booting a 60-yarder in practice, he looked up and said, "How'd you like that one, God?"

Looney averaged 42.4 yards per punt in 1964 and ran 58 yards for a touchdown against the Chicago Bears. That gave the Colts reason to hope he was coming around. But in November, Looney broke down the door of an apartment and punched a man inside. Looney was arrested and claimed at his trial that he and a friend were looking for the apartment of some nurses. He added that he was still upset because Barry Goldwater had lost the presidential election.

A week after the trial, Looney jumped into the ring during a tag-team wrestling match in Baltimore involving Red Berry and Bruno Sammartino. He seemed to think he was protecting the wrestlers from hostile fans. Shula traded him to the Lions in January.

Detroit's Harry Gilmer was the next coach who believed he could discover what made Looney tick. He claimed that Looney would become the hub of his running attack. But Looney's nasty habit of skipping practice resurfaced. Assistant coach Joe Schmidt, a Lions legend, found Looney in his dormitory room and explained that he was risking a fine. Looney asked Schmidt how long he'd been going to practice every day.

"Fourteen years," Schmidt replied.

"Joe," Looney said, "you ought to take a day off once in a while."

Looney soon got into a parking lot fight over who should pay a $3.28 check at a local pancake house. The last straw for Gilmer came in a September game when he told Looney to give a message to quarterback Milt Plum. "If you want a messenger, call Western Union," Looney replied.

Looney got a message that he was traded to Washington.

Once again, there were signs that Looney might be growing up. He scored a touchdown in his first game for the Redskins in 1966 and explained to reporters, "It was a twin-two-sweep-trap . . . that means as much to me as it does to you."

Looney actually remained a Redskin in 1967, but he was unhappy with his contract and said he'd play out of his option. Instead of finding a new NFL team, Looney spent the 1968 season in the army.

Looney resurfaced with the New Orleans Saints, his fifth and final NFL team, in 1969. He owned a mastiff hound, which he loaded down with barbells, supposedly to build up its leg muscles. But the dog was accused of raiding a henhouse.

"I might have known," Saints defensive end Doug Atkins said. "The minute the kid straightens out, the dog goes bad."

Looney's old teammate, Hawkins, caught up with him in 1983 and wrote about Looney's life after football. He said he'd found inner peace through Indian yoga and meditation.

"[He wore] long hair, beard, sandals, beads, the whole nine yards," Hawkins reported. "He met a guru, Swami Muktananda, Baba to his friends, followed him to India, trimmed his weight to 150 pounds, and worked as a common laborer and keeper of the swami's elephant. He shoveled elephant droppings. When Baba died in November 1982, Joe Don came back to Texas and joined Baba's successors, a brother-sister team. I might add, the sister is not short on looks."

But after Looney's death in 1988, he was accused of having harassed and intimidated young women who alleged they were sexually exploited by Muktananda. While there was a light side to Looney, there was a dark side, too.

Hawkins concluded: "He has found the answers, he says. I hope he has, because if he hasn't, you ain't heard the last of Joe Don Looney yet."

Chapter 30
Good-Time Max:
Max McGee

Wide receiver Max McGee played for five NFL
champions during his twelve years in Green Bay.
He led the Packers in receptions four times
and also punted. Yet this free spirit is best
remembered for starring in a game in which
he never expected to play.

MCGEE ONCE RETURNED from a night on the town to tell his
Green Bay teammates he'd met a woman named Will Rogers.
"She said she never met a man she didn't like," McGee explained.

McGee never met a curfew he did like. Not even before a
Super Bowl. The night before the first NFL-AFL championship
game, against Kansas City in January 1967, McGee was eager to
get better acquainted with Los Angeles. He met a few flight at-
tendants at the bar of the team's hotel and agreed to meet them
later. Roommate Paul Hornung declined to join McGee, though
neither expected to play the next day.

The next Packer to see McGee was quarterback Bart Starr. He was in the lobby early the next morning when McGee came in. Starr couldn't say he was surprised.

"He was extremely talented—'clutch' is what he was," Starr recalled. "He and Hornung didn't like curfews, but nobody worked harder in practice."

McGee had an unorthodox attitude about performing in the clutch. "When it's third and ten, you can take the milk drinkers and I'll take the whiskey drinkers every time," he said.

If that remark set back clean living a few years, McGee's Super Bowl performance set back clean living for decades. When the game started, McGee and Hornung, who was sidelined by a shoulder injury, were on the bench, discussing plans for Hornung's impending bachelor party and wedding. They were interrupted by coach Vince Lombardi, who was screaming for McGee. At first, the receiver worried that Lombardi had just found out about McGee's night on the town. Instead, he was sending McGee into the game.

Starter Boyd Dowler found he couldn't play because of pain from a shoulder injury suffered in the NFL title game. McGee was so startled that the only helmet he could find belonged to a lineman.

Fortunately for McGee, he had studied film of the Chiefs' pass defense. He'd even napped an hour when he got back to the hotel. And the Chiefs weren't covering him on the opening series, which he pointed out to Starr.

On the next series, McGee broke free over the middle, reached back to make a difficult catch, and went thirty-seven yards for the first touchdown in Super Bowl history. He caught seven passes for 138 yards and two touchdowns in a 35–10 victory.

"I'd like to see every one of them stay out all night and do what he did," Hornung said thirty years later.

McGee had plenty of practice working on short sleep. Lombardi's hapless predecessor, Ray "Scooter" McLean, was a players' coach who ran a loose ship. McGee, not surprisingly, took a lot of unauthorized shore leave.

In McLean's lone season, 1958, the Packers finished 1-10-1. After a 24–10 loss to the Bears, McGee and Hornung persuaded McLean to let them stay overnight in Chicago rather than go home with the team. McLean reluctantly agreed, only after telling them he didn't want to read about their exploits in the Chicago papers.

"So Hornung and I go down and see Don Rickles at the Playboy Club and he sees us and takes a shot at us in front of everybody, and then we go to Chez Paree and end up with a couple of those dancing girls, and we got back to Green Bay just in time for Tuesday morning practice," McGee recalled.

"And there's Scooter sitting at his desk. 'Get in here, guys— look here!' and he points at 'Kup's Corner,' where [gossip columnist] Irv Kupcinet writes about how Hornung and McGee, after losing to the Bears, were seen dancing with Chez Paree adorables at two in the morning. And he tried to put his foot down. Never again! When he said he was fining us it pained him more than it pained us. It was hard for Scooter to get tough."

It was not hard at all for Lombardi to get tough, and it seemed just a matter of time before he'd clash with McGee. Yet, McGee survived the entire Lombardi era. The legendary coach took nothing for granted and began his 1961 training camp by holding up a pigskin and announcing, "Gentlemen, this is a football."

McGee, from the back of the room, said, "Uh, coach, could you slow down a little? You're going too fast for us."

Lombardi laughed. But he found plenty of occasions to chew out McGee and Hornung. Once when they knew they were going to get chewed out, they hid a tape recorder just outside Lombardi's office. When they replayed his tirade, they doctored the tape with their own expletive-filled comebacks. When they listened to the altered version, they laughed uproariously. Privately, of course.

McGee wasn't always able to pull one over on Lombardi, who was wise to his late-night socializing. Lombardi once caught McGee and fined him twice within a few days for breaking team rules. Lombardi soon caught him a third time and screamed during a team meeting, "Max! That will cost you five hundred dollars." That was a lot of money then.

Lombardi added, "Max, if I catch you again, the fine will be one thousand dollars." Then, the coach, not known for delivering punch lines, added, "Max, if you find anything worth a thousand for sneaking out, call me and I'll go with you."

The Packers won their first NFL title under Lombardi in 1961 and their second a year later. Their only loss in 1962 came at Detroit on Thanksgiving Day, when the Lions sacked Starr eleven times while beating up the entire Packers offense. Starr asked his receivers late in the game if any thought he could get open, and McGee replied, "Bart, why don't you throw an incomplete pass and nobody'll get hurt?"

Chapter 31
Motor Mouth:
John Randle

Hardly anybody had heard of John Randle when
the Minnesota Vikings gave him a tryout in 1990.
Once he got his opportunity, every opponent
heard Randle, whether they wanted to or not.
The chatty defensive end made seven Pro Bowls
before he retired after the 2003 season with 137½
sacks. That tied for fifth on the all-time list.

RANDLE WAS ONE of the best pass rushers of all time. And one
of the craziest. He went after opponents with small talk, insults,
and a fury seldom matched on the field.

"See, you are this guy who is six-one, and you see a guy who
is six-seven, and someone tells you to go out there and beat his
ass and get around him," said Randle, who weighed 290. "That's
not normal. So you got to have a little insanity to do what we do.
You got to be crazy."

Randle's craziest moment came during the Vikings' 34–16 play-
off victory over the New Orleans Saints in January 2001. After

sacking quarterback Aaron Brooks, Randle dropped to all fours and lifted a back leg, imitating a dog marking a fire hydrant.

The Metrodome crowd went wild with laughter, but the NFL fined Randle $7,500 for excessive—not to mention tasteless—celebration. The Vikings were punished worse a week later when they lost 41–0 to the Giants in the NFC championship game.

Randle got his ammunition for trash-talking by studying the opposing team's media guide. By kickoff, he knew his opponent's hobbies, businesses, favorite charities, hometown, and the names of his wife and children. When Randle asked Lions guard Mike Compton how his family was doing, Compton returned to the huddle and asked, "How does he know my kids' first names?"

Once, Randle was trying to distract Chicago Bears guard Todd Burger by talking about his wife, "Jennifer." But he couldn't get a rise out of his normally talkative rival.

"John," another Viking informed Randle. "Burger's wife is Denise. Jennifer is [tackle] Andy Heck's wife."

The Bears claimed that was the only time they found Randle at a loss for words.

When John Teerlinck was the Vikings' defensive-line coach, he told his linemen to think of themselves as sacred cows of India. Randle interpreted this to mean that no one should touch him or else he'd lose his power.

"Don't touch me, don't touch me," he would yell on the field before a game. If anybody touched him, Randle would rub his hands on teammates supposedly to drain some of their power and replenish his.

Randle liked being a sacred cow. "It is like taking a vacation," he said. "You've got to get by the red lights and get into the open road and take off."

The Sporting News decided to find out just what kind of trash Randle was talking. With help from NFL Films, the magazine put a microphone on Randle for the Vikings' 24–3 victory over the Bengals in 1998.

After pregame introductions, Randle stared at Bengals left tackle Kevin Sargent, who'd be his primary opponent, and yelled at Vikings linebacker Ed McDaniel: "Hey, [Sargent] is scared. He turned his back. They all turned away. They don't want this war. They aren't worth anything."

On his fourth defensive series, Randle tried getting into Sargent's head. "Can I be your friend?" Randle asked.

Ignored by Sargent, Randle looked at quarterback Neil O'Donnell. "Hey, Neil, I see you, brother," Randle screamed. "Hey, Neil, why don't you run it yourself? I want you to run it yourself."

O'Donnell kept throwing, and once got rid of the ball just in time to deny Randle a sack. Randle was livid. "You know what?" he yelled to the Bengals while pointing at an imaginary wristwatch. "It's time for me to get after your asses."

Back on the bench, Randle was seething. "I missed that sack," he said, slamming his helmet to the ground. "I am not closing the gap. I am not doing my part. Damn it! Damn it!"

Even as the Vikings had the game wrapped up and Randle had one sack, he was frustrated, especially with guard Anthony Brown. "I want to kill that guard," he yelled to teammate Derrick Alexander. "I will kill his butt! Are you with me? Are you with me?"

Randle still couldn't get another sack, though, and was fuming when line coach Andre Patterson came over to congratulate him. "I'm just telling you," Randle replied, "if I don't come in tomorrow, you know what happened. I committed suicide."

Randle loved action movies. He was inspired by the main character in *Predator* to smear his face with war paint, but had to ditch that special effect in 1998 when the NFL cited the paint as a uniform code violation and fined him $15,000.

"You look into the stands at the Metrodome and see kids with their faces painted like me, and what is wrong with that?" Randle asked. "I have to find some other way to get psyched up for the game. No one will deny me the power."

Randle had an unusual energy reserve, even for a pro athlete. His arms, legs, and, of course, his mouth rarely stopped moving. Before a game, he'd dance around like a fighter and throw punches in the air. He'd also swat the goalposts and sing.

Randle would arrive at the Metrodome three hours before kickoff, an hour earlier than required. Instead of relaxing, he would go out on the field alone for a hard workout that would have left most players too tired to play decently.

Randle was even in constant motion while buying groceries. Early in Randle's career, assistant coach Paul Wiggin spotted him moving around a supermarket as if he were on the practice field. Randle sprinted from one aisle to the next and juked around displays as if they were offensive linemen.

"Here's Johnny, doing a swim move against a pile of potato chips," Wiggin said. "I couldn't believe what I was seeing. Johnny was playing football in the grocery store. I knew we had something special then."

Chapter 32
The No-Fun League:
Rules Breakers

A lot of great players have revolutionized
pro football, though not in the way you might
imagine. Sure, there are players who revolutionized their positions—Lawrence Taylor
at outside linebacker and Kellen Winslow at
tight end, for instance. But let's also give
credit to those stars who changed pro football
by changing the rules—because they were so
clever at gaming the old ones.

WHEN "EXCESSIVE CELEBRATION" became unsportsmanlike conduct, it was clearer than ever that the NFL really was the
No-Fun League. Fines had failed to discourage showy touchdown
celebrations, so stiffer measures were enacted. In both 2004 and
2006, the NFL imposed 15-yard penalties for specific types of
flamboyant touchdown displays.

New Orleans Saints wide receiver Joe Horn's cell-phone call
from the end zone in 2003 was among the last straws. He apparently hadn't gotten the memo that went out a year earlier, after
San Francisco 49ers wide receiver Terrell Owens scored and
pulled a Sharpie out of his sock to autograph a football. That

memo warned players they would be disciplined for bringing any foreign object on the field.

But more than memos were needed to keep phones, markers, and who knows what else off the field. So starting in 2004, possession of foreign or extraneous objects and multiplayer demonstrations would result in unsportsmanlike-conduct penalties.

Now, about those multiplayer demonstrations . . .

The Bob 'n' Weave was a touchdown dance started by the St. Louis Rams during their 1999 Super Bowl run. Players would form a circle where they would crouch and bob and weave like boxers. When eight Rams bobbed and weaved in a 2000 game against the Minnesota Vikings, they were fined $90,000. Five were repeat offenders, including wide receivers Isaac Bruce and Torry Holt. Each was fined $20,000, and Holt, who invented the routine, exclaimed, "I tripped out at the number they threw at us."

The bottom line was this: In the No-Fun League, spikes, dunks, Lambeau Leaps, spins, dances, and simple celebrations were okay. Any prolonged, made-for-TV demonstrations were not.

Dallas Cowboys running back Emmitt Smith scored so often that his end-zone celebration was thoroughly polished. He would spike the ball and rip off his helmet with a flourish. Many players wanted viewers to see their faces because helmets were hurting their endorsement opportunities. To discourage players from showing their faces, the NFL in 1997 made it unsportsmanlike conduct to remove a helmet on the field.

New York Jets defensive end Mark Gastineau was the NFL's premier sack artist of the early 1980s, and the sack dance became his trademark. The NFL wearied of his routine, however, and starting in 1984 assessed a 15-yard penalty for such dances. That didn't cramp Gastineau's style. That year, he totaled twenty-two sacks, then an NFL record.

Los Angeles linebacker Ted Hendricks boasted at the January 1984 Super Bowl that no other team had forced as many rules changes as the Raiders. Rules makers, indeed, struggled to keep up with the Raiders' penchant for winning by hook or by crook.

Oakland Raiders cornerback Lester Hayes in 1980 led the NFL with thirteen interceptions, with an assist from stickum. That was the goo he smeared on his hands, in the best tradition of Hall of Fame receiver Fred Biletnikoff. The league wasn't worried about Hayes getting an unfair advantage, but he was making a mess of game balls. Stickum was outlawed in 1981, and Hayes had only three interceptions.

They didn't call Raiders quarterback Kenny Stabler "the Snake" for nothing. The Raiders trailed 20–14 at San Diego in 1978 and were at the Chargers 14 with time running out. Stabler was getting sacked when he deliberately fumbled toward running back Pete Banaszak, who clumsily kicked the ball toward the goal line. Tight end Dave Casper then kicked the ball into the end zone and fell on it for a touchdown and a 21–20 victory.

"The play is in our playbook," guard Gene Upshaw said. "It's called, 'Win At Any Cost.'"

The play would have been illegal had the officials determined that the fumble was deliberate, as Stabler later admitted. The next year it became illegal to advance a fumble in the last two minutes of a half, except by the player who fumbled.

The Raiders also get major credit for the 1976 rule prohibiting a defender from "running or diving into, or throwing his body against or on a ball carrier who falls or slips to the ground untouched and makes no attempt to advance, before or after the ball is dead." Ben Davidson's blatant spearing of Kansas City Chiefs quarterback Len Dawson in 1970 helped inspire that rules change.

Dawson and "Big Ben" filmed a TV commercial in 1989, in which Davidson cracked, "It's always fun to drop in on you, Len."

Kickers, as a rule, don't showboat or take cheap shots. So why have they been targets of so many rules changes? For one thing, their increasingly powerful legs were making the game too easy for them. So the goalposts were moved from the goal line to the back of the end zone and kickoffs were moved gradually from the 40- to the 30-yard line. The original rules makers never dreamed how many games would be decided by field goals.

But a rule directed at Tom Dempsey seemed unusually harsh. Long before Casey Martin, who was denied a golf cart on the PGA Tour despite his severely painful and atrophied leg, the NFL made an example of Dempsey, a kicker with a disability.

Dempsey was an inspirational athlete born with no right hand and no toes on his right foot. Yet he kicked for five NFL teams from 1969 to 1979. He set a league record in 1970 by kicking a 63-yard, game-winning field goal for the Saints.

Because he had no toes, Dempsey wore a plate on the front of his right shoe that gave him an extra-large kicking surface. Dallas Cowboys general Tex Schramm complained that Dempsey had an unfair advantage and pushed for the 1977 rule that said "a shoe on an artificial limb must have a kicking surface that conforms to that of a normal kicking shoe." The rule applied to Dempsey, even though his right foot wasn't artificial.

Green Bay kicker Don Chandler's 27-yard field goal against the Colts in a 1965 play-off for the Western Conference title is perhaps the most controversial place kick of all time. "Wide by three feet," claimed Baltimore tackle Lou Michaels. That kick tied the score, 10–10, and Chandler's 25-yarder in overtime put the Packers in the NFL title game.

Kicks were harder for officials to judge then because the up-rights were so short. They were raised to twenty feet above the crossbar in 1966.

Lou (The Toe) Groza, a Hall of Fame tackle and kicker, had his place kicks down to a science. He would keep a roll of tape in his helmet and mark off the exact distance for his approach. Groza scored 1,608 points and his technique was widely copied but ultimately outlawed. In 1956, his twentieth season, a new rule allowed "no artificial medium to assist in the execution of a kick."

Nobody familiar with the NFL's uniform inspectors, who police each game for wardrobe malfunctions, would be surprised by how many rules have been changed in the name of fashion. Wearing logos of non-NFL sponsors is prohibited. So are non-league do-rags. The list goes on and on.

Tear-away jerseys, which left many a would-be tackler clutching a piece of cloth instead of a running back, once were popular. Gregg Pruitt of the Cleveland Browns, one of the league's top rushers and kick returners of the late 1970s, wore jerseys that tore almost as easily as tissue paper. The tear-away jersey was outlawed in 1979.

Ben Hawkins of the Philadelphia Eagles, who led the league in receiving yardage in 1967, considered it unfashionable to buckle his chinstrap. He let it hang loose, which prompted the rule that a chinstrap must be buckled at both ends.

Hall of Fame end Bill Hewitt, who played for the Chicago Bears and Philadelphia Eagles during the 1930s, didn't worry about chinstraps. He didn't even wear a helmet. But when he was among the many retired players who rejoined the NFL during World War II, Hewitt found himself in a new world. While he was gone, the NFL passed a rule requiring all players to wear helmets.

All these dress rules make you wonder—how'd the NFL ever get caught napping by Janet Jackson's exposed breast during halftime of the Super Bowl in January 2004?

Chapter 33
Babygate:
David Williams

Football coaches didn't have to worry about
missing a player because of his child's birth
until Houston Oilers tackle David Williams came
along. Or, more accurately, until Scot Cooper
Williams—all nine pounds and fifteen ounces of
him—came along.

A TRADITIONAL FOOTBALL wife was expected to have her
babies during the off-season if she wanted to be sure Dad would
be there for the delivery. Old-school coaches and players can tell
plenty of war stories about missing the births of their children.

Howard Schnellenberger, who coached the Baltimore Colts and
won a national championship at the University of Miami, was an
Alabama assistant in the 1960s out recruiting a hot prospect when
his wife, Beverlee, was giving birth. Schnellenberger returned to
see their newborn, kiss his wife, and tell her she'd done a good job.
Such devotion to football was not uncommon.

Ultimately, football's military mentality of the 1940s clashed with male sensitivity of the 1990s. Sensitivity lost the opening round. In an episode known as "Babygate," Williams was fined for attending a childbirth instead of a kickoff.

Debi Williams was giving birth on October 16, 1993, a night before the Oilers played at New England. David Williams was committed to staying with Debi until their child was born, especially because she had suffered a miscarriage a year earlier. The baby arrived at 6:25 p.m., making it tricky for Williams to fulfill his obligations to both mother and team.

He missed the Oilers' afternoon charter flight and the last evening flight from Houston to Boston, too. Williams said he checked into chartering a flight to Boston, but that Logan Airport was fogged in. He claimed he had no way to make kickoff, but the Oilers suggested he should have found a way. General manager Mike Holovak fined him a game check.

"He doesn't make $125,000 a week to stay home and watch television," offensive line coach Bob Young said. "They ought to suspend him for a week, maybe two.

"Everybody wants to be with his wife, but that's like if World War II was going on and you said, 'I can't go fly. My wife's having a baby.' You have to go to work—especially when you get paid like that."

Offensive coordinator Kevin Gilbride also criticized Williams. "I don't think I can put into words how disappointed I am," he said. "I understand the support of your family—that always has to come number one—but there's a judgment, too. He fulfilled his commitment to his family. His place had to be with us with our backs up to the wall."

Williams did not second-guess himself. "I don't regret what I've done," he said. "I wanted to be there for my child to be born and I was going to stay there until he was. We lost one last year. I didn't want anything to happen. That's the way I felt about it. I'm sorry they can't accept that. I'm sorry they don't understand it."

The Oilers snapped a three-game losing streak with a 28–14 victory at New England, and Williams brought a box of cigars to the next practice. Though Young claimed that Williams had let his teammates down, none of them agreed.

Kevin Donnalley, who replaced Williams at right tackle, said, "His wife was probably saying, 'Dave, I need you here.' He made a lifelong commitment to her, but football's his job. I didn't envy his situation."

For the Oilers, fining Williams was a public-relations fiasco. His lawyer, Leigh Steinberg, said Williams did "what any 1990s father would do." He added, "Football players are not magically removed from the responsibilities of fatherhood."

Anna Quindlen agreed in a scathing column on the editorial page of *The New York Times*. Quindlen pointed to the prevalence of boorish and criminal behavior among many pro athletes and was incredulous that the Oilers would punish Williams. She also noted that Jimmy Johnson in his zeal to rebuild the Dallas Cowboys in 1989 had dumped his wife of twenty-five years so she wouldn't be a distraction from coaching.

"And along comes David Williams standing for the principle that the goal of life is something more than the end zone," Quindlen wrote. "The Oilers should put him on commercials, send him to high schools, make him a poster boy for the revolutionary concept that professional athletes—and professional men—can learn to put their work in its proper place."

The Oilers didn't take Quindlen's advice. Since then, however, pro football players routinely have been permitted to miss games for the birth of a child, a funeral, or a family crisis.

Maybe NFL clubs had a change of heart about family obligations. Or maybe they just noticed that the Oilers, minus Williams, started an eleven-game winning streak.

Chapter 34
Prime Time:
Deion Sanders

Cornerback Deion Sanders would've been an attention-getter if only for his two-sport career, highlighted by his game-breaking plays in the NFL. But his flamboyance was what turned him into "Prime Time." He made eight Pro Bowls and played for two Super Bowl champions. In 641 major league baseball games, he hit .263 with 186 stolen bases.

SANDERS CHOSE TO wear number thirty-seven when he came out of a three-year retirement to join the Baltimore Ravens in 2004. He said he wanted opposing receivers to remember his age.

After a slow, injury-interrupted start to his comeback, Sanders made two interceptions in a 20–6 victory over the Buffalo Bills in late October. He returned one 48 yards, scoring his twenty-third career touchdown, and high-stepped the last thirty yards before performing an end-zone dance.

"At breakfast this morning," Sanders said, "I told the guys, 'When I get into the end zone, stand back and let me dance first. Then you can congratulate me.'

"They talked about me before I came: 'He's too old. He shouldn't be doing this.' I'm a thirty-seven-year-old kid out there."

He was a thirty-eight-year-old kid for the Ravens in 2005, and warned receivers they should still be wary of him. "I'm not as good as I once was, but I'm good once as I've ever been," he claimed. "And you never know when that once is. They don't know, if you try me, that might be that once. I can cover in my sleep."

Sanders was nicknamed "Prime Time" by a Florida high school pal after Sanders scored thirty points in a basketball game for North Fort Myers High School. He also went by "Neon Deion." In the NFL, he lived up to those nicknames by making big plays in big games, dancing in the end zone, and sporting expensive jewelry and clothes. Under his football pants, he wore good-luck boxer shorts, decorated with gold dollar signs.

When Sanders returned in 2004, however, he said he no longer felt compelled to live up to his old reputation. Did that mean "Prime Time" was gone?

"When did I stop being Prime Time?" he asked, grinning. "I didn't get that memo."

Asked if he was worried about staining his Hall of Fame resume, Sanders replied: "That's already written. I've got twelve years' worth of great film that they cannot erase."

Sanders briefly disavowed "Prime Time" after an amazing Monday-night road performance for the Dallas Cowboys against the Giants early in 1998.

He scored on a 59-yard punt return and a 71-yard interception. He set up another touchdown with a 55-yard catch and finished the 31–7 victory over New York with 226 yards in returns and receptions.

"Prime Time? I'm trying to bury that," said Sanders, who professed to have become a devout Christian in 1997. "Prime time is God's time now."

A year before his comeback, Sanders tried to return to the Falcons, but not as a player. He declared himself the best candidate to succeed coach Dan Reeves, who was a sure bet to be fired after the 2003 season. Sanders was an NFL studio analyst for CBS and seemed unfazed by his lack of coaching experience.

"I can make them a better team, and I know that, because I know the things that really need to be done there," he said. "I put so much time into preparing every week for my Sunday job, watching tape and talking to players and coaches, that I still live football. It's still a big part of me. I talk to head coaches and assistants, guys with whom I'm close, every week. I know what the job involves, believe me, and I know I can do it."

Falcons owner Arthur Blank didn't call Sanders. He hired Jim Mora instead.

Sanders was the first athlete to hit a home run in the big leagues and score a touchdown in the NFL in the same week, the first to play in a World Series and a Super Bowl, and the first to suit up for major league baseball and NFL games on the same day.

Sanders attempted his daily double October 11, 1992. Playing in Pittsburgh for the Atlanta Braves in the National League play-offs, Sanders flew to Miami after a Saturday-night game and played for the Falcons the next afternoon. Then he hopped a charter flight back to Pittsburgh on Sunday night and hoped to come off the bench.

Critics questioned whether Sanders's loyalty lay mainly with the Braves, the Falcons, or Nike, the athletic apparel giant with which he had an endorsement deal.

Sanders made two tackles, returned three kicks, and caught a pass in the Falcons' 17–7 loss to the Dolphins. Braves manager Bobby Cox said he didn't know if Sanders would be back for the game. Sanders arrived at Three Rivers Stadium just seventeen minutes before game time and never got off the bench.

Broadcaster Tim McCarver, a former big league catcher, criticized Sanders's two-sport stunt as selfish. Sanders hit .533 against the Toronto Blue Jays in the World Series, and while the Braves were celebrating their clinching win, he snuck up on McCarver from behind and dumped ice water on him.

"You're a real man, Deion," McCarver said, sarcastically.

Sanders never did seem to get along with catchers. When he played for the New York Yankees in 1990, he didn't run out a pop fly against the White Sox. Chicago catcher Carlton Fisk pointed out to Sanders that big leaguers run out fly balls.

On Sanders's next at bat, he drew dollar signs with his bat in the dirt, as he often did. Then he told Fisk, "The days of slavery are over."

A shouting match ensued with Fisk saying, "There's a right way and a wrong way to play this game, and if you don't play it right, I'm going to kick your ass right here in Yankee Stadium."

When Sanders in 1996 participated in 50 percent of the Cowboys' offensive plays as a wide receiver and 80 percent of their defensive plays, he became the NFL's first two-way player since Philadelphia's Chuck Bednarik in 1962. Comparisons of Sanders and Bednarik were inevitable, though the old Eagle didn't appreciate them.

Bednarik, a center and linebacker, played more than fifty minutes three times during one season. "The positions I played, I made contact one hundred percent on every play," he said. "I snapped on extra points and punts. Some of these guys who think they're playing both ways don't have to touch anybody. Deion Sanders? Talk about somebody claiming to be a two-way player? He never made a tackle and just came up and did a little dance.

"I'm a Czech and we'd call what he does a polka step. That's nightclub entertainment, not sport. Nobody likes that kind of stuff. Besides, he does a bad polka step."

A dangerous one, too. While dancing after a 93-yard interception return for the 49ers against the Falcons in 1994, Sanders suffered a pulled groin muscle.

Sanders signed a one-year contract with the 49ers upon becoming a free agent in 1994. A baseball strike enabled him to play nearly the entire season and he made the most of it. He returned three interceptions for touchdowns and was named NFL defensive player of the year. He had four tackles and an interception in a 49–26 Super Bowl victory over the San Diego Chargers.

The next year, Sanders signed a seven-year, $35 million deal with the Cowboys and helped them beat the Pittsburgh Steelers 27–17 in the Super Bowl.

Green Bay Packers general manager Ron Wolf, who was no fan of free agency, said, "The only free agents who ever worked out were Reggie White and Deion Sanders."

Sanders didn't enjoy success as a free agent when he went to Washington in 2000. He came in for lots of criticism after an ordinary season, which he climaxed by walking away and keeping most of his $8 million signing bonus. But it was nothing new for Sanders to rub a lot of people the wrong way.

"Some people will come out to see me do well," he said. "Some people will come out to see me get run over. But love me or hate me, they're going to come out."

Chapter 35
He Hate Me:
Rod Smart

Rod Smart's unique nickname helped make him the poster child of the XFL, founded by wrestling promoter Vince McMahon. Smart parlayed his success in that short-lived league into an NFL career highlighted by a Super Bowl appearance.

SMART DIDN'T JUST have a chip on his shoulder. He wore one on his uniform.

Smart is best known as "He Hate Me," the nickname on his Las Vegas Outlaws jersey in 2001. For many XFL fans, he was known only as "He Hate Me."

Smart was an instant hit in the XFL, which promoted pro football like pro wrestling. The Outlaws began their first and only season in a home game against the New York/New Jersey Hitmen that was televised by NBC. For Smart, this was the perfect opportunity to showcase himself and his nickname.

"Who hates you?" he was asked in a pregame interview. He was still hearing that question three years later when he completed the unlikely transition from XFL running back to a special-teams demon who helped the Carolina Panthers reach the Super Bowl in February 2004.

The "He" in his nickname, Smart explained, was, "Anybody against me—guys on defense, guys on special teams, and anyone I'm going against."

Smart's nickname was a spontaneous, fun idea. No promotional wizard could have contrived a nickname so original, right down to its grammatical flaw.

"When they were doing the jerseys, they asked what I was putting on the back of my jersey," Smart recalled. "I was like, 'I guess my name.' [Then I said], 'You can put whatever?' And they said, 'Yup.' Me and the other running backs went in and brainstormed for a minute. I had 'He Hate Me.' Chrys Chukwuma had 'Chuckwagon,' and Ben Snell had 'Thoro.'

"That's how it went. That league was fun and helped some of us get in the NFL. The main thing was, I was able to play good and that went with the name. If I hadn't, it would've been just a name. I had to show 'em I could ball."

Smart rushed for 555 yards, second most in the XFL, which played a ten-week season before it folded. He stuck with the Philadelphia Eagles in 2001, but was waived before the 2002 season and was claimed by the Panthers.

Rejections were old hat for Smart. No NFL team drafted him in 2000 even after he rushed for 1,249 yards in his senior season at Western Kentucky. The San Diego Chargers signed him as a free agent but cut him within a month. He went to the Edmonton Eskimos of the Canadian Football League and was cut after a week.

"To go to Canada, to come from the country that has the best football and get cut?" Smart asked. "That was the low point for me. After that, I said, 'I'm not leaving the country again to get cut.'"

Smart found his niche on Panthers' special teams. He scored his first NFL touchdown on a 100-yard kickoff return in 2003 in a 19–13 win over the New Orleans Saints. That year against the Jacksonville Jaguars, he blocked a punt that produced a safety in a 24–23 victory. He led the Panthers with twenty-four special-teams tackles in 2002.

Smart needed no introduction in an NFL locker room. Guard Kevin Donnalley was among the Panthers who remembered "He Hate Me."

"That was weird," Donnalley said. "They could put anything they want on the back of their jerseys and some guys had some crazy stuff. It made you think, 'Who hates him?' But that stuck. It has lasting power, and it stays with him now."

Carolina fans began hanging banners that read I LOVE ME and I DON'T HATE ME. It became a guy thing to wear Panther jerseys with SHE HATE ME on the back, a reference to wives and girl-friends left home on game days. Panthers quarterback Jake Del-homme named a Thoroughbred filly She Hate Me in honor of Smart.

"I love the way Rod goes about his business," Delhomme said. "Great work ethic, always hustling. Loves the game. I asked him if he'd mind if I did this, and he got a big smile on his face. He loved it. Hopefully, she'll have some of Rod's speed."

No doubt the Thoroughbred was more highly strung than Smart. Despite all the attention from his nickname, he remained pretty mellow.

"I'm the same person with two names," Smart said. "It's not like a Dr. Jekyll-Mr. Hyde-type thing. There is no make-believe here. I'm a cool, calm, and laid-back guy. I love to make people laugh. I grew up around fights and arguments, and that is something I don't like. When I see everybody happy, it makes me happy."

Smart escaped a dangerous neighborhood in Lakeland, Florida. He has a brother, Jad, whose name starts with a "J" because their mother was in jail when he was born. Rod eventually moved in with his high school principal. "I feel fortunate," he said. "I had some people who really helped me get through it."

That wasn't the last time Smart proved he could make something of himself if only given a chance. Who would have guessed an XFL refugee would wind up returning kickoffs in a 32–29 Super Bowl loss to the New England Patriots?

"You get a lot of people in the same situation I was in, going unnoticed and then have a team go all the way to the big show," Smart said. "It can happen anywhere.

"I've been to the Super Bowl but haven't won one, so there's always an extra step I have to go to get where I want. I've come a long way as an individual to be where I'm at, and my goal is to go farther."

Chapter 36
The Bachelor:
Jesse Palmer

Jesse Palmer was an unlikely celebrity. Yes, he was a quarterback in New York, but he wasn't going to play much once the Giants acquired Eli Manning in 2004. Yet most single males would've much preferred playing the role of Palmer than Manning.

REALITY TELEVISION IN the NFL once meant NFL Films capturing the grunts, groans, and hits on the field. Fast forward to the new millennium, when reality TV gets inside the most personal aspects of people's lives.

It was only a matter of time before an NFL player showed up on a reality show. So it was hard to understand why Palmer ruffled so many feathers by starring on ABC's *The Bachelor* in the spring of 2004. Palmer had his choice of twenty-five women to pick out Ms. Right. This, naturally, invited a lot of puns about Palmer's ability to make a pass.

"Anybody who knows Jesse knows he is a real good guy for that kind of thing," said Giants center Wayne Lucier. "He's good-looking. He's bright. He's easy to talk to. They definitely picked the right guy."

Yet, fuddy-duddies suggested that Palmer was jeopardizing his football career. It's more acceptable for a quarterback to make the cover of *Sports Illustrated* than *People*. Which is odd, because who ever heard of a *People* cover jinx?

Many assumed that Palmer's TV work meant he couldn't be working hard in the off-season or that his success as a ladies' man wouldn't sit well with new coach Tom Coughlin, famed for being stern and humorless. Palmer seemed behind the eight ball, anyway, because the Giants were cleaning house at quarterback.

They obtained Manning, the nation's top college quarterback, through a draft-day trade. They signed free agent Kurt Warner, a former NFL and Super Bowl MVP, to start until Manning was ready. Palmer hadn't been impressive while auditioning as the starter in the last three games, all losses, in 2003.

Still, criticism—or was it just jealousy?—of Palmer's spring fling seemed unreasonable. NFL players routinely keep busy in the off-season by appearing at awards banquets, golf tournaments, charity benefits, and card shows. Some players even appear on TV shows. So why the big deal over Palmer's stint as *The Bachelor*?

Palmer defused *The Bachelor* controversy by working hard in off-season sessions and training camp. Coughlin, who would cut Palmer before the 2005 season, described him as "tough" and "courageous."

Running back Tiki Barber wasn't surprised that Palmer returned to the Giants with strong resolve. "It's funny because everyone sees him as this reality TV star," Barber said. "He's just a player to us, same guy he's always been. A little bit of a ham, but a good guy to have around."

Palmer became an irresistible target for teammates' teasing. Especially when star-struck young women lined up to get Palmer's autograph at the Giants' training camp in Albany, New York.

And during the show's early episodes, teammates gleefully noticed, Palmer was clumsy sometimes. "Of course he has said some things [to some women] that probably were a little embarrassing, but those things happen" Lucier said. "And we've had some fun with him. But he's handled it pretty well. He seemed to really like the experience."

TV viewers were more interested in who survived Palmer's final cut than whether Palmer survived Coughlin's final cut. Palmer's choice was Jessica Bowlin, a twenty-two-year-old California law student.

Palmer told Bowlin on the final episode in May that his "gut instinct" was that they were meant to spend their lives together. But he added, "I am not ready to propose to you tonight. I think that we need more time to grow and learn about each other."

If it sounded like Palmer was getting cold feet, he was. The next month, he and Bowlin said they'd agreed to end their relationship. BACHELOR SACKS TV GIRLFRIEND, one headline announced.

"Jessica and I shared an incredible romantic journey on the show that began with a friendship that remains strong today," Palmer said. "We simply realized that, individually, our next steps take us in different directions."

Said Bowlin: "With too much distance and too little time, these were not ideal circumstances in which to start a relationship. Jesse is a great guy and has a wonderful family. Who knows what the future holds?"

The couple never could've guessed that Palmer in 2005 would wind up in San Francisco, briefly playing for the 49ers before he was cut. He always knew that being a star on reality TV wouldn't make him a star in the NFL.

"It won't make me throw more completions," he said. "I wish it would."

Chapter 37
Foot in Mouth:
Controversial Kickers

Being a kicker is like being left-handed. From an early age, people around you make you feel different. "I was a drummer in a band and people said I wasn't a real musician," recalled Nick Lowery, one of the NFL's best kickers from 1979 through 1996. "Then I became a kicker and people said I wasn't a real football player. That's the story of my life."

Players who wake up Monday morning feeling like a bucket of bruises all wish they were kickers. But when a tough field goal needs to be made in the closing minute, only kickers wish they were kickers.

FRICTION BETWEEN KICKERS and teammates usually remains private. Yet, here was Indianapolis Colts quarterback Peyton Manning saying of teammate Mike Vanderjagt: "He's a good kicker. But he's an idiot."

Manning said this during the 2003 Pro Bowl, normally the least controversial game of any NFL season. Vanderjagt, a Canadian, had told a Toronto-based cable sports network that Manning and coach Tony Dungy needed to be more fiery.

"We need somebody who is going to get in people's faces and yell and scream," said Vanderjagt. "I've gone over there to the offense and said, 'Come on.' They're just like, 'Mike, go sit down.

You're the kicker.' I have more emotion probably than anybody. I can't tolerate watching eleven guys just walk off the field after you get stuffed and really show that you don't care. That is frustrating to me.'"

Dungy's first year with the Colts, 2002, saw a turnaround from a 6-10 finish to a play-off spot. Yet, Vanderjagt questioned Dungy's leadership.

"I think you need a motivator," he said. "I think you need a guy that is going to get in somebody's face when they're not performing well enough. Peyton and Tony are basically the same guy. They work hard, they mark their X's and O's, and go out and execute. If that doesn't happen, there's nothing we can do about it."

Even though Vanderjagt publicly apologized three days before the Pro Bowl, Manning was still steamed. During a sideline interview in Hawaii, he said: "I'm out at my third Pro Bowl, I'm about to go in and throw a touchdown to Jerry Rice, and we're talking about our idiot kicker who got liquored up and ran his mouth off."

Both players patched things up by phone. "I was concerned they would cut me and no one else would want me," Vanderjagt said. "We both said things we shouldn't have said, and certainly in the forum we shouldn't have said them in."

Vanderjagt popped off again two years later during the play-offs, but this time he was offending the opponent. Before the Colts met the Patriots, the defending Super Bowl champs, in January 2005, Vanderjagt said, "I think they're ripe for the picking."

This drew a sharp rebuke from Patriots safety Rodney Harrison, who said, "He should focus on making the field goals, not [worrying] about what we're doing over here, okay? I mean, he has to be a jerk, Vanderjerk, if he sits there and criticizes Peyton Manning and Tony Dungy. And then for him to put his foot in his mouth again just shows what type of character he has."

Vanderjagt, actually, just showed how poor a prognosticator he was. The Patriots won, 20–3. The Colts were knocked out of the play-offs a year later when Vanderjagt, despite being the NFL's all-time leader in field goal accuracy, badly missed a 46-yard kick near the end of a 21–18 loss to the Pittsburgh Steelers. That was his last kick for the Colts before he moved on to Dallas.

It's no secret that a kicker who gets brushed by an opposing rusher is expected to fling himself to the ground as if he's been shot. He just might draw a penalty. But when Tennessee kicker Joe Nedney jokingly said he took a dive in a January 2003 play-off game, you'd have thought he'd admitted to robbing a bank.

Nedney got a second chance—actually, a third chance—to kick a game-winning field goal in overtime because Pittsburgh tight end Enron Kinney ran into Nedney's left leg and knocked him to the ground. The kick missed, but Kinney was penalized and Nedney made a 26-yarder for a 34–31 victory that put the Titans in the AFC championship game.

Nedney joked that he might take up acting. That didn't go over too well in Steeler country. In fact, it inflamed a nationwide controversy.

"I know there's a lot of people in Pittsburgh right now who are flaming mad and people around the nation that are flaming mad, and I'm sure the comment I made afterward left a really bad taste in everybody's mouth," Nedney said the next day.

"I sincerely apologize for doing that, but it was only meant as a joke. I didn't mean to come off sounding cocky or put it in anybody's face."

The game's ending was controversial even before the penalty. It appeared that Nedney sealed the win with a 31-yard field goal, but officials ruled the Steelers called time-out before the snap. Then came Nedney's miss and game winner.

Steeler fans, naturally, wondered how you knock down a six-foot-five, 225-pound kicker. "I pride myself on not being a small, frail, unathletic kicker," Nedney said. "He got me down and I got another chance. That's it."

When a lineman misses a block, hardly anybody notices. When a kicker misses the ball, everybody notices. You could ask Sean Landeta. Although he's one of the most venerable punters in league history, he made one of the most embarrassing punts ever.

Landeta and the New York Giants got off on the wrong foot in a play-off game against the Chicago Bears in January 1986. Backed up to his goal line and under a heavy rush, Landeta barely grazed the ball. It was scooped up by Shaun Gayle for a touchdown in a 21–0 victory.

"I couldn't believe it," said Landeta, who was credited with a 7-yard punt. "It's something that never happened to me before. I mean, you don't even miss a ball just fooling around."

It was a Monday night fit for neither man nor beast . . . nor kicker. A blizzard blew into Denver for an October 1984 game against Green Bay that became known as "The Snow Bowl." The Packers' first two plays resulted in fumbles returned for touchdowns and a 14–0 Broncos lead. Yet they still needed a field goal from Rich Karlis.

He was a highly reliable, barefooted kicker, but teammates feared Karlis's foot would get frostbitten. He made the kick, anyway. Coolly, of course, in a 17–14 win.

Though the Mile High Stadium field was clear for a 1985 game against San Francisco, the stands were filled with snow from the previous day's storm. Bronco fans, naturally, pelted the 49ers with snowballs. The Broncos led, 17–16, when, on the final play, the 49ers' Ray Wersching lined up to try a short field goal. But as he was about to kick, a snowball splattered near the ball and he missed.

Fans don't want to hear legitimate excuses from place kickers when they miss. So you can imagine their reaction to dubious alibis offered by the Dallas Cowboys' Rafael Septien.

When he missed four of five field-goal attempts against the Houston Oilers in 1985, Septien said, "I was too busy reading my stats on the scoreboard." When he missed a field goal on the artificial turf of Texas Stadium, he explained, "The grass was too tall."

He blamed one miss on being distracted by the play clock. After another miss, he said, "My helmet was too tight and it was squeezing my brain. I couldn't think."

Buffalo Bills kicker Booth Lusteg did not make excuses. After missing a 23-yard field goal that could have snapped a 17–17 tie against the San Diego Chargers in 1966, he was confronted by four angry fans outside the stadium. They jumped out of a car and asked him if he was Booth Lusteg.

Lusteg said yes and was punched in the nose. When Bills official Jack Horrigan asked Lusteg why he didn't call the police, he replied, "Because I had it coming." Insult was added to injury when the Bills released Lusteg.

Chapter 38
Super Laughs:
Championship Comedy

It's not surprising that the biggest game of the NFL season has produced some of the biggest plays in league history. What is surprising is that the Super Bowl has also showcased so many boneheaded plays.

Credit AFL founder and Kansas City Chiefs owner Lamar Hunt for naming the Super Bowl. He named it after the high-bouncing "Super Ball" that amused his three children. For its first two years, the event was known simply as the AFL-NFL Championship game, and Hunt couldn't have imagined what an extravaganza the game would become. Nor that it would produce so many laughs.

DALLAS COWBOYS DEFENSIVE tackle Leon Lett became the poster child for premature celebrations during a 52–17 victory over the Buffalo Bills in January 1993.

The lumbering Lett recovered a fumble at the Dallas 36 late in the game and had clear sailing. But he slowed down to showboat before crossing the goal line and was oblivious to Bills wide receiver Don Beebe frantically giving chase. Beebe arrived just in time to knock the ball loose and through the end zone for a touchback.

"I learned," Lett said, "not to celebrate too soon."

First, Buffalo running back Thurman Thomas lost his head. Then he lost his helmet, and then the Bills lost the game.

Thomas wasn't happy when the Bills arrived in Minneapolis to face the Washington Redskins in January 1992. He still hadn't forgotten that New York running back Ottis Anderson, and not Thomas, was voted MVP of the previous Super Bowl, a 20–19 Giants victory over the Bills.

A few days before facing the Redskins, Thomas was upset to read that offensive coordinator Ted Marchibroda had called quarterback Jim Kelly the Michael Jordan of the Bills' offense. When Thomas read that quote, he stormed out of the Bills' breakfast and refused to attend that day's press conference.

"I think *I* am the Michael Jordan of this team," Thomas said. "Guess I will have to go out and win the MVP."

Bills tackle Will Wolford explained: "You have to understand Thurman. If you don't know him, you'd think he was an idiot. We've known him for two or three years and now we know he's an idiot."

Thomas did little to prove that Wolford was joking. He missed the Bills' first possession because he couldn't find his helmet and the Redskins rolled, 37–24. Bills coach Marv Levy, however, insists that Thomas got a bad rap for the helmet episode.

"When they played the national anthem, all the players took off their helmets and put them next to themselves," Levy explained. "The player standing next to Thurman grabbed the wrong helmet. He was a defensive player and went down to the other end of the bench and just held it in his lap. The helmet Thurman tried to put on was too small or something. To this day, Thurman has not disclosed the name of the culprit. Talk about being a good teammate!"

Butch John of *The Clarion-Ledger* in Mississippi became the most unfairly maligned sportswriter in history for a question he asked Redskins quarterback Doug Williams before a 42–10 win over the Denver Broncos in January 1988. John is generally known as the bozo who asked, "How long have you been a black quarterback?" What he actually asked was, "Doug, it's obvious you've always been a black quarterback all your life. When did it start to matter?"

Pittsburgh linebacker Jack Lambert, nicknamed "Dracula" for the gap in his teeth, was not somebody you wanted to rile. But Dallas Cowboys safety Cliff Harris did just that in the Steelers' 21–17 victory in January 1976.

When Steelers kicker Roy Gerela missed a field-goal attempt, Harris tapped him on the helmet and taunted him. Lambert threw Harris to the ground and wasn't penalized.

"It wasn't something I thought about—it was a split-second thing, but I couldn't permit anyone to intimidate our team," Lambert said. "Luckily, I didn't throw any punches or I probably would have been thrown out of the game."

The Miami Dolphins were on the verge of ending pro football's first perfect season with an exclamation point. They led the Redskins 14–0 in the closing minutes of the January 1973 Super Bowl when Garo Yepremian lined up for a field goal. The snap was low and the kick was blocked, right back to Yepremian. He picked it up and tried to pass but the ball slipped and he batted it into the air. It was grabbed by cornerback Mike Bass, who sprinted forty-nine yards for a touchdown.

"I thought I was doing something good, something to help the team," Yepremian said. "Instead, it was almost a tragedy."

Coach Don Shula discussed the play with Yepremian on the flight back to Miami. "You know that pass you threw yesterday?" Shula asked. "If you ever try it again, I'll kill you."

There were, however, some bad Super Bowl plays that Shula couldn't very well complain about. Like the one from President Richard Nixon.

Shula was home watching game tapes when his phone rang at 1:30 a.m. on January 3, 1972. "Must be some nut calling at this hour," Shula thought. He was informed that the President of the United States was on the line.

Nixon wanted to talk about the Dolphins' upcoming game against the Cowboys. Though Nixon was a diehard Washington Redskins fan, he told Shula he also rooted for the Dolphins because of his winter residence on nearby Key Biscayne.

"Mr. Nixon alerted me that the Cowboys are a real strong team," Shula said. "But he told me, 'I still think you can hit [Paul] Warfield on that down-and-in pattern.'"

Cowboys coach Tom Landry didn't sound worried. "Actually," he said, "the president gave them a play they run every week."

The first time the Dolphins ran the presidential play, it was deflected by cornerback Mel Renfro. Harris, who was also in the area, cracked, "Nixon's a great strategist, isn't he?"

The Dolphins lost, 24–3. A year later, after defeating Nixon's beloved Redskins, Shula said, "I also want to thank the president for offering *not* to send in any more plays."

Linebacker-turned-sportscaster Tommy Brookshier had the dubious distinction of conducting the worst post–Super Bowl interview ever. His interviewee was Cowboys running back Duane Thomas, who ran for ninety-five yards and a touchdown against the Dolphins in January 1972. Unhappy with his contract, Thomas stopped dealing with the media.

When any reporter approached him, Thomas would ask, "What time is it? A little late for socializing, isn't it?" He was asked at the Super Bowl how he could seem so blasé before the "ultimate game." Thomas replied: "If it's the ultimate, how come they're playing it again next year?"

Thomas gave Brookshier an exclusive postgame interview— sort of. Thomas was accompanied by Hall of Fame running back Jim Brown, who fixed a stone-faced, intimidating stare on Brookshier. Thomas seemed determined to embarrass Brookshier by giving one-word answers that left the old linebacker scrambling to come up with the next question. Brookshier became flustered and his questions became desperate.

He asked: "Are you that fast, are you that quick, would you say?"

Thomas hung him out to dry again. "Evidently," he replied, dryly.

Brookshier later admitted that interview gave him nightmares for years.

One of NFL Films' best moves ever was to put a microphone on Kansas City coach Hank Stram during the Chiefs' 23–7 victory over the Minnesota Vikings in January 1970. Stram loved the limelight and strutted like a rooster. He held a rolled-up sheet of paper in one hand and waved it like a bandleader's baton while he excitedly observed the history unfolding before him.

"Come on, Lenny, pump it in there," he yelled to quarterback Len Dawson. "Just keep matriculating the ball down the field, boys."

When he saw Vikings safety Karl Kassulke appear confused, Stram said, chortling, "Look at 'em, boys. They're running around like it's a Chinese fire drill."

Stram's ultimate moment of glory came when he called the play that resulted in a 5-yard touchdown run by Mike Garrett for a 16–0 lead. "Sixty-five toss power trap," Stram crowed. "This thing just might pop wide open . . . Was it there, boys? . . . I told you that baby was there. Yes sir, boys."

Most viewers considered the tape a classic. But not Vikings coach Bud Grant. He made his players watch the tape before they met the Chiefs in their 1970 opener at Minneapolis. Enraged, the Vikings won, 27–10.

First, the New York Jets did the impossible in January 1969. They backed up quarterback Joe Namath's brash prediction of victory with a 16–7 win over the Baltimore Colts, who were seventeen-and-a-half-point favorites. Then the Jets did the unthinkable. They forgot to take the sterling silver championship trophy on their flight home the day after the game.

"That wasn't exactly our finest hour, especially coming right after our finest game," Jets public relations director Frank Ramos recalled. "After all the celebrating that went on, I don't think anybody was in any condition to think about things like who had the trophy. Some of the guys had enough trouble just finding the airport.

"When we got home, a big crowd was waiting. It sure was embarrassing when all those fans asked to see the trophy we'd won and we didn't have anything to show them."

The trophy turned up, along with some forgotten equipment, at the Jets' hotel in Fort Lauderdale.

Chiefs cornerback Fred "The Hammer" Williamson was the pioneer of Super Bowl hype. Before the inaugural game against Green Bay, he vowed to use his personalized clubbing technique to knock out the Packers' receivers.

"Two hammers to [Boyd] Dowler, one to [Carroll] Dale should be enough," Williamson boasted.

Williamson, to the great amusement of the Packers, was knocked out of Green Bay's 35–10 victory after he tried to tackle running back Donnie Anderson.

Chapter 39
Just Win, Baby:
Al Davis

As a coach, general manager, and owner, Al Davis turned the Raiders from a doormat in the early 1960s into a five-time Super Bowl team. He also turned them into the black sheep of pro football. Davis moved the Raiders from Oakland to Los Angeles and back to Oakland, while filing lawsuits everywhere he went.

NFL COMMISSIONER PETE Rozelle was asked if his opinion of Al Davis had changed since the maverick owner successfully sued the league to move the Oakland Raiders to Los Angeles in 1982. Rozelle replied that he once considered Davis a "charming rogue" but had come to see him as an "outlaw."

Detractors have described Davis as selfish, ruthless, unscrupulous, and sue-happy. His boosters paint him as a brilliant football mind with a big heart for old players, friends, and loved ones. Davis once moved into the hospital room of his wife, Carol, to see her through recovery from a heart attack. He's also been a pioneer in diversity hiring in the NFL. And Davis's all-consuming devotion to the Raiders paid off with their fifth Super Bowl, a 48–21 loss to Tampa Bay in January 2003.

"It's a tunnel vision, a tunnel life," he said. "I'm not really a part of society."

Davis's exhortation, "Just win, baby," is among the most popular mottos in sports. The Raiders' silver-and-black logo is among the best known. It features two swords crossed behind a helmeted man wearing an eye patch.

"We all believe in the patch," Davis said, almost reverently. "Just like Disney says, 'Mickey Mouse [is the symbol] of the entertainment world,' I believe this is the patch of the sports world. I believe the Raiders are global."

Davis's wardrobe is almost entirely black and white. He typically wears warm-up suits, slicks back his hair in a 1950s pompadour, and wears dark glasses—an appearance that reinforces his image as the NFL's godfather.

San Diego Chargers quarterback Dan Fouts was asked before the 1980 AFC championship game against the Raiders if he regarded Davis as sinister. "I think that his tailor is sinister," Fouts replied.

Davis was immortalized as a dirty trickster when Harland Svare, coaching the Chargers in the early 1970s, suspected his locker room in Oakland was bugged. Svare looked up at a light fixture and said, "I know you're up there, Al Davis."

Davis, flattered that he inspired such paranoia, later said, "I'll tell you this: The thing wasn't in the light fixture."

When Weeb Ewbank coached the New York Jets from 1963 to 1973, he became especially guarded the week before a Raiders' visit. If a helicopter flew overhead during practice, Ewbank would say, "Al Davis has someone watching." He'd stop practice until the helicopter flew away.

When it comes to the art of the deal, Donald Trump never had anything on Davis. A typical Davis deal is entirely one-sided.

Ewbank's distrust of Davis can be traced partly to a deal during Ewbank's first Jets training camp. He sent offensive lineman Bob Mischak to the Raiders for guard Dan Ficca. Davis neglected to mention that Ficca was still in the military and wouldn't be available for another six weeks.

When New York Giants coach Bill Parcells, one of Davis's closest coaching pals, was low on healthy cornerbacks in 1985, Davis offered to help. Davis sent him Ted Watts, a former first-round pick, for a draft choice. Watts had a bum knee and couldn't help the Giants, yet Davis kept the draft choice.

These deals were pretty fair compared with the 1987 deal between Davis and the small city of Irwindale, twenty miles east of Los Angeles. Irwindale offered to turn a gravel pit into a 65,000-seat, $115 million stadium for the Raiders. For signing a stadium agreement with the city, Davis received $10 million, nonrefundable.

The project seemed like a fantasy from the start, and soon collapsed. But the money kept by Davis was real. "We didn't get the team and Al Davis still took all that money," city councilman Patricio Miranda recalled in January 2003. "It hurt because we only have one thousand people living here. I was the only councilman to vote against giving him the ten million dollars, nonrefundable, just to talk. I guess I have to blame my people more than I blame Al Davis."

Eight Raiders asked Davis, a 1992 Hall of Fame inductee, to present them at their inductions. Running back Marcus Allen was never going to become the ninth. Not after he and Davis had the most famous feud in Raider history.

Allen was MVP of the Raiders' 38–9 Super Bowl victory over the Washington Redskins in January 1984, and for the rest of the decade was the NFL's most complete back. Then he inexplicably was reduced to a backup role in 1991 and 1992.

While there was widespread suspicion that Davis ordered Allen's benching, Allen remained quiet until an interview that was aired during the halftime of a Monday-night game in December 1992. Allen, asked if he was being punished by Davis, replied: "Absolutely, no question about it. He told me he was going to get me . . . I don't know for what reasons, but he told me he was going to get me, and he's done that.

"He's tried to ruin the latter part of my career, tried to devalue me. I think he's trying to stop me from going to the Hall of Fame. It's just been an outright joke to sit on the sidelines and not get the opportunity to play. The last two years have been the most frustrating, painful, and humiliating thing I've ever gone through."

Davis offered no explanation except to say, "He was a cancer on the team."

Allen took advantage of the advent of free agency and went to Kansas City. He scored twelve touchdowns for the Chiefs in 1993 and helped them reach the play-offs in four of his last five seasons.

Davis is the only pro-football figure to have worked as a head coach, general manager, owner, and league commissioner. He reluctantly agreed to step down as Raiders coach and succeed Joe Foss as American Football League commissioner in April 1966. Davis might have been even more reluctant had he known that Kansas City Chiefs owner Lamar Hunt and Dallas Cowboys general manager Tex Schramm had been secretly negotiating an AFL-NFL merger for six weeks.

If there was to be a merger, Davis wanted one on his terms, with the NFL becoming part of the AFL. But the AFL merged into the NFL, as was announced June 8, and Davis returned to the Raiders in July as managing general partner.

"Al Davis taking over as commissioner was the strongest thing the AFL ever did," longtime San Diego sportswriter Jerry Magee said. "He thought the peace was a detriment to the AFL. It was a disappointment to him that they merged."

Former NFL executive Don Weiss, however, suggests that Davis's role in achieving the merger has been exaggerated. "In my opinion, he was not the catalyst he has long claimed to be, but one of several," Weiss wrote.

"Undeniably, he stirred up lots of anger and accelerated discussions. The trouble Davis triggered was a mere episode in an entire drama written and directed by Tex Schramm, Lamar Hunt, and certainly, Pete Rozelle. The last thing Al Davis wanted was a merger. He wanted capitulation."

Chapter 40
Kick 'Em in the Head Ted: '70s Raiders

The Raiders of the 1970s and 1980s collected three Super Bowl trophies and dozens of eccentric characters. Owner Al Davis specialized in finding talented players who'd been misfits elsewhere but were perfect for the Raiders.

Defensive end Pat Toomay, a free spirit, had played for the Cowboys, Bills, and Buccaneers before he joined the Raiders in 1977. "I knew," he said, "that somewhere in the league there must be a club like this."

WHEN JOHN MADDEN coached the Oakland Raiders, he said of linebacker Ted Hendricks: "Ted's elevator doesn't go all the way to the top."

When Hendricks joined the Raiders in 1975, he rode a horse on to the practice field at Santa Rosa, California. He was wearing his Raiders uniform and a spike-topped German World War I helmet painted silver and black. He held a traffic cone as a lance. Hendricks doesn't recall any of his new teammates acting as if his entrance was unusual.

"I guess Madden had seen everything with our group, and everybody else had seen everything," he said.

That didn't mean the Raiders didn't appreciate Hendricks's antics. Quarterback Ken Stabler wrote in his autobiography, "Most Raiders loved to party, but Ted Hendricks was a party all by himself."

One Halloween, Stabler recalled, Hendricks came to practice with a pumpkin squashed on his head as a helmet. During a Monday-night game, he was wearing a fake nose when an ABC camera caught him on the bench.

Hendricks's strength belied his lanky, six-foot-seven frame. He didn't like to lift weights and sabotaged the efforts of assistant coach Myrel Moore to bulk up his linebackers. Hendricks ignored Moore's weight program and instead lifted a bar with two empty cans, each marked 500 POUNDS. When Moore made the linebackers push a heavy medicine ball to help them fend off low blocks, Hendricks stole the ball and left it at a local bar.

Hendricks didn't need help dodging blocks. He often leaped over blockers and sometimes his feet caught a lineman or running back in the head. Hendricks accidentally knocked fullback Marv Hubbard cold in practice, and quickly became known as "Kick 'Em in the Head Ted."

Lester "the Molester" Hayes fancied himself as a defensive back in the nastiest Raider tradition of Jack Tatum and George Atkinson. Hayes, though, was a lot messier. He smeared his hands and jersey with stickum to improve his chances for interceptions.

And Hayes talked incessantly, despite a severe stutter that might get him stuck on a sound for fifteen or twenty seconds. Listeners would cringe sympathetically but Hayes wasn't fazed. He'd just wait for his tongue to get unstuck and keep rolling. He ended nearly every statement with, "So be it."

Hayes's favorite movie was *The Empire Strikes Back*, which he claimed to have watched three hundred times. He loved to discuss that movie and once declared, "I am the only true Jedi in the National Football League."

When Hayes retired after the 1986 season, he was tied with Willie Brown for the team's most career interceptions—thirty-nine. He claimed some in the Raiders organization didn't want to see him break Brown's record.

"There are some individuals in silver-and-blackdom who would rather run through a gauntlet of pit bulls wearing pork-chop underwear than see me break the record for interceptions by a Raider," Hayes said.

He helped the Raiders win two Super Bowls, which he said were more important than his salary. "There comes a time when you have enough deceased presidents and you play for the ring," he said.

Hayes moved with the Raiders to Los Angeles in 1982 and blamed a Hollywood mentality for the team's decline in the late 1980s. "We had the opposing team so psyched that they hated going to Oakland," he recalled. "Without that intangible mystique, we're a normal team. It distresses me. It causes mental malfunction. It bothers me to watch the mentality of the new Los Angeles Raiders. It's important to get the mentality back to our heritage, which is going out and biting, scratching, and dusting eyebrows."

The Raiders were infamous for biting, scratching, and dusting eyebrows. Linebacker Matt Millen, the first player to earn a Super Bowl ring for three different teams, claimed he was branded as a dirty player simply for donning silver and black.

"At Penn State, I was one of [Joe] Paterno's boys, a good kid," said Millen, who was named president and CEO of the Detroit Lions in 2001. "Then I get drafted by the Raiders. What am I? A dirty player. Once I got to San Francisco, I got in a fight, they'd say, 'Look how competitive he is.' With the Raiders, I was just a dirty player."

Millen didn't improve the Raiders' reputation when Washington Redskins tackle Joe Jacoby claimed that he'd run over his own mother to beat the Raiders in the January 1984 Super Bowl. "To win," Millen said, "I'd run over Joe's mom, too."

Because of the Raiders' high profile, some players who would've been anonymous elsewhere became household names. Like defensive tackle Otis Sistrunk.

The Raiders, known as "The Kings of *Monday Night Football*," played the Monday-night opener in 1974 at Buffalo. Sistrunk did not attend college and when a camera zeroed in on his menacing expression and shaved head, ABC announcer Alex Karras cracked, "That's Otis Sistrunk. He's from the University of Mars."

That one-liner helped Sistrunk gain his first and only Pro Bowl berth.

George Buehler was just another 285-pound guard before his fondness for remote-controlled toys became big news as the 1976 Raiders reached the Super Bowl.

Buehler once brought a $700 model airplane to camp and worked painstakingly to get the plane airworthy. Buehler's teammates went to a field to watch its maiden flight.

"The plane was terrific and so was George," Stabler wrote. "He had it doing loops, diving, climbing, banking, all kinds of maneuvers. We let out cheers and he was rightly proud. Then as he brought the plane down low for some lazy circles and figure eights, [tight end] Dave Casper came walking by.

"The plane dived once right over Casper, and he sort of waved it away, like King Kong swatting at the bothersome planes that dove at him in the movie. When Buehler's plane made a second pass, Casper was ready. He grabbed a handful of lava rocks from the path and threw them at the plane—hitting the engine. The plane pitched straight down and crashed, pieces flying in every direction."

The next year, Buehler had a remote-controlled tank. Stabler and running back Pete Banaszak taped firecrackers to the tank and lit a long fuse calculated to set off an explosion as it rolled into the coaches' offices. Madden ran out screaming and looking for the culprit.

"And while John stood there hollering and turning pink and pulling at his hair as he tended to do whenever he got excited," Stabler wrote, "we ran that little tank between his spread legs and brought it on home."

Chapter 41
Heidi:
The Author Remembers

Author Jonathan Rand offers his remembrance of
one of the most famous sports telecasts of all
time. He had no idea what he was missing. And
he wasn't alone.

HEIDI CAUGHT ME totally unaware. One minute I was watching football in Oakland and the next minute I was watching a little girl in the Alps.

I was sitting in a college bar in Columbia, Missouri, watching my hometown New York Jets play the Oakland Raiders on November 17, 1968. It was a lazy afternoon and I kept getting distracted as I chatted with friends, none of whom showed much interest in this important game.

But it was better to be in a bar watching a game with people who didn't care than ornery drunks who hated the Jets. I ran into a lot of them as an undergraduate in Buffalo, where fans didn't appreciate anybody hostile to the Bills. Especially not Jets fans.

I'd followed the Jets as they came into the world in 1960 as the New York Titans, a charter member of the American Football League. I was thirteen when I attended one of their first-year training camp practices at Bear Mountain, New York, and had no idea what a motley crew I was watching.

I was part of an intimate gathering at the Polo Grounds in 1962 while watching the Titans lose, 52–31, to the Dallas Texans. I probably had no clue that the Titans had run out of money and been taken over by the league three days earlier.

Those ragamuffin Titans became the Jets in 1963, and by 1968 were a force to be reckoned with. Jets fans hated the Raiders even worse than the Giants, and every Jets-Raiders game was filled with ill will and cheap shots. The Jets and Raiders totaled nineteen penalties for 238 yards.

But the penalties couldn't mar a riveting game between 7-2 teams. Joe Namath threw for 381 yards and a touchdown for the Jets and Daryle Lamonica threw for 311 yards and four touchdowns. This was a classic AFL game—hard-hitting, mean-spirited, pass-happy, and high-scoring.

I figured the Jets had sewn up a hard-fought victory when Jim Turner kicked a field goal for a 32–29 lead with 1:05 to play. When NBC went to a commercial, I turned back to my friends and almost forgot about the Jets. When I turned back to the TV, the game had given way to a pig-tailed Swiss girl who herded goats. She was Heidi, heroine of a children's book made into a TV movie.

I assumed the game had ended while I was blabbing and I couldn't believe I had been so absentminded. Little did I realize that NBC had pulled the plug on the game to show the movie at 7 p.m., Eastern time. I was dumbfounded to learn later that the Raiders came back and won, 43–32.

All I missed in sixty-five seconds was a 43-yard touchdown pass from Lamonica to Charlie Smith and a fumbled kickoff that allowed Preston Ridlehuber to score the clinching touchdown. I must say I took this all pretty well. A lot better than most fans.

Angry viewers made so many calls to NBC headquarters in Manhattan that the switchboard broke down. Network president Julian Goodman apologized the next day for interrupting the game.

The game had started at 4 p.m. and back then, before so many ads were sold, three hours were usually enough for a pro-football telecast. But all the penalties and passes caused the game to run late. Dick Cline, NBC supervisor of broadcast operation control, adhered to network policy and broke away from the game to start the movie on time.

That policy was soon junked and ever since, networks have stayed with football games until their conclusions, no matter what's on next. Because Cline couldn't make or receive calls once the switchboard went down, NBC installed for him a phone line with its own exchange. This became known as the "Heidi Phone."

The ramifications of *Heidi* went far beyond NBC policies. The public outcry demonstrated the nation's devotion to pro football, which in another two years would be regularly televised on Monday nights. And that game put a spotlight on Namath and the Jets, which would get even brighter as the season neared its climax.

It became much easier for Jets fans to laugh about *Heidi* when their team, in the "Revenge of Heidi" game, beat the Raiders 27–23 in New York for the AFL championship. Then the Jets defeated the Baltimore Colts 16–7 in the Super Bowl.

Considering the Jets were seventeen-and-a-half-point underdogs, who could've guessed you'd be able to turn off the Super Bowl with sixty-five seconds left and know the Jets' lead was safe?

Chapter 42
Broadway Joe:
Joe Namath

Joe Namath became the toast of New York when, in January 1969, he led the Jets to the AFL's first Super Bowl victory. Though knee surgeries diminished Namath's enormous talents, he played thirteen years. He had plenty of good days, and plenty of good nights.

THERE'VE BEEN BETTER quarterbacks than Joe Namath, but none more charismatic or more beloved by a city. He was "Broadway Joe," celebrated almost as much for his Friday and Saturday nights as for his Sunday afternoons.

Opponents would've rather sneaked a peek at Namath's little black book than his playbook. He looked formidable in a Jets' jersey but made his fashion statements with white football shoes, fur coats, and panty hose. Namath was pro football's Muhammad Ali—brash and mouthy and winner of a championship, despite many rooting for him to get knocked on his rear.

Plenty of athletes became larger than life playing in New York. But no jock ever cut a finer figure on the city's stage than Namath. Boston Patriots owner Billy Sullivan called him "the biggest thing in New York since Babe Ruth."

Every Namath retrospective starts with The Guarantee.

The Jets were seventeen-and-a-half-point underdogs to the Baltimore Colts in the January 1969 Super Bowl in Miami. The Green Bay Packers had smashed AFL opponents in the first two Super Bowls, and Namath was fed up with hearing about the supposed superiority of the Colts and NFL. He was accepting an award at the Miami Touchdown Club three nights before Super Sunday when a heckler said, "Hey, Namath, we're gonna kick your ass on Sunday."

Namath replied, "Wait a minute, pal, I've got news for you. We're going to win on Sunday. I guarantee it."

Jets coach Weeb Ewbank hit the roof when he saw Namath's guarantee in a front-page headline. "I could have shot him," he said.

Ewbank advised Namath that Colts coach Don Shula would use his prediction to fire up the Colts. Namath wasn't chastened. "Joe shrugged," Ewbank recalled, "and said, 'Coach, if they need press clippings to get ready, they're in trouble.'"

Jaws dropped all over America as the Jets won, 16–7, the most famous upset in pro-football history. Though Namath relied more on his defense and running game than his powerful arm, he was voted the game's MVP. Had he never played another down, his legacy in pro football would've been guaranteed, too.

"One game does make a difference in a lot of people's lives," Namath said. "That game made me a buddy with every underdog in the world. That game was not just for the Jets and the AFL. It was for every underdog out there."

Namath had the Colts riled even before the guarantee. He claimed the AFL had six quarterbacks, including himself, more talented than Colts starter Earl Morrall. When Namath and Jets safety Jim Hudson stopped in a restaurant on their first night in South Florida, they were confronted at their table by Colts defensive end Lou Michaels and offensive lineman Dan Sullivan. The conversation went something like this:

MICHAELS: "Namath . . . you're doing a lot of talking."

NAMATH: "There's a lot to talk about. We're going to beat the hell out of you."

MICHAELS: "Haven't you ever heard of humility?"

NAMATH (AFTER A TENSE SILENCE): "You still here?"

MICHAELS: "Damn right, I'm still here. I wanna hear everything you gotta say."

NAMATH: "I'm gonna pick you apart."

MICHAELS: "You're gonna find it tough throwing out of a well."

NAMATH: "My blockers will give me time."

MICHAELS: "I never heard Johnny Unitas or Bobby Layne talk like that."

NAMATH: "I believe that."

MICHAELS: "Even if we do get in trouble, we'll send in Unitas, the master."

NAMATH: "I hope you do, because that'll mean the game is too far gone."

MICHAELS: "Suppose we kick the hell out of you, what will you do?"

NAMATH: "I'll sit right down in the middle of the field and cry."

Namath paid the check with a $100 bill and offered the two Colts a ride back to their hotel. When Michaels refused, Namath said, "Don't be silly; we'll drop you off."

Back at their hotel, Michaels told Sullivan: "He's not such a bad kid after all."

Jets owner Sonny Werblin showed the AFL was here to stay when he signed Namath to a $427,000 contract on January 2, 1965. That proved a major step toward the AFL-NFL merger in 1966.

Yet, Namath wouldn't have been a Jet had Werblin grabbed the quarterback he originally wanted. Werblin was a high-powered show-business agent and envisioned Jerry Rhome of

Tulsa as the quarterback who would make New Yorkers respect the Jets. The Jets took Rhome in the 1964 draft as a future pick, then brought him to New York before the 1965 draft to offer him a contract.

"What happened next was a faux pas that may have changed the course of professional football," wrote former Jets offensive line coach Chuck Knox in his autobiography. Knox had coached against Namath's junior high school basketball team in western Pennsylvania and lobbied Ewbank to draft him after his senior year at Alabama.

Knox recalled that Werblin soured on Rhome when he jumped into the backseat of a limousine ahead of Werblin's wife. "I don't believe this!" Werblin sputtered. "This . . . this is not star quality."

The Jets traded their rights to Rhome to the Houston Oilers for a 1965 first-round pick, which was used to pick Namath. Werblin's star search was over. He soon had one of the most talented and flamboyant quarterbacks who ever lived.

"Flamboyant?" Namath asked in 1991. "It was probably my white football shoes, when all other players wore black. I stood out, but that was the idea. Sonny Werblin had a lot to do with molding my style. He was a show-business exec, and he became the first owner of a sports team to promote a star system. Maybe he and I were both a little ahead of our time."

Namath took full advantage of Manhattan's Upper East Side singles-bar scene. "I don't like to date so much as I just like to kind of, you know, run into something," he said. Asked to elaborate on his preferences, Namath replied, "I like my Johnnie Walker Red and my women blonde."

Jets running back Ed Marinaro was hanging out in a bar with Namath one night until Namath picked up a companion and left. Marinaro told Namath that he couldn't believe he was leaving with a woman who didn't rate even close to a "10."

Namath replied, "Eddie, it's three in the morning and Miss America just ain't coming in."

Sometimes, it was three in the morning and Namath just wasn't coming in. One night in Denver, Ewbank came to Knox, who was Namath's confidant, and frantically told him that Namath had missed the 11 p.m. curfew. Knox sent equipment manager Bill Hampton to search the bars. When Namath was found, Knox asked him by phone to come back to the hotel.

"Now, wait a minute, Chuck," Namath said. "If I come in now, it's gonna cost me a five-hundred-dollar fine. If I come in two hours from now, it's still gonna be five hundred. So what's the use? I might as well get my money's worth."

Knox could not find a hole in this argument and told Hampton to just make sure Namath got back in one piece. "In a couple of hours, Joe comes home and he's fine," Knox wrote. "So fine, in fact, he is carrying a very messed-up Bill Hampton."

Though he settled down after retiring in 1977, Namath's roguish reputation surfaced in 2003 as he slurred his words during an interview with ESPN's Suzy Kolber.

She asked, "Joe, it's been a difficult season for Jets fans. What does it mean to you now that the team is struggling?"

Namath replied, "I wanna kiss you," and leaned toward Kolber. "I couldn't care less about the team struggling. What we know now is we can improve. Chad Pennington, our quarterback, missed the first part of the season and we struggled. We're looking to next season, we're looking to make a noise now and . . . I wanna kiss you."

ESPN quickly cut short the interview. Namath apologized to Kolber and a month later entered alcohol counseling.

Five knee operations kept Namath in constant pain and shortened his prime. But they provided him at least one endorsement opportunity—a popular panty-hose commercial. And to think Namath had outraged people by wearing a fur coat!

The ad began by panning up a pair of attractive, shaved legs. A female voice said, "This commercial is going to prove to the women of America that Beautymist Panty Hose can make anybody's legs look like a million dollars."

The camera then revealed green shorts, a Jets jersey, and Namath. He grinned and said, "If Beautymist can make my legs look this good, think what they can do for yours."

For every fan who considered Namath arrogant and spoiled, many more found him fun and likeable. "Namath was in a different class," Oakland Raiders coach John Madden said. "It didn't matter if he won or lost. He was still a star.

"One time I was leaving the house for a Jets game and my wife [Virginia] said, 'You have to stop Namath today.' I said, 'Yeah, I know. That's all we talked about all week.'"

The Raiders won, 38–29, in a 1967 game best remembered for Ben Davidson knocking off Namath's helmet a few plays after Ike Lassiter broke his cheekbone.

"Hell of a game," Madden recalled. "I came out of the locker room afterward and my wife was standing there, really mad. First thing she said was, 'You didn't have to hurt him.' She didn't care that we won the game. She was mad that we whacked Joe. I said, 'But that's part of stopping him.'"

Chapter 43
Brain Lock:
Infamous Blunders

Great plays make us ooh and ah, and remind those of us on the couch that we could never compete with the great athletes on the field. But when a professional athlete commits a boneheaded mistake, it makes us think, if only fleetingly, that maybe they're not always as superior to us as we thought.

No, we could never make those great plays. But, yes, we could make those dumb plays. And at our own level, most of us have.

CLEVELAND LINEBACKER DWAYNE Rudd thought the Browns' 2002 opener was over and won. And it would've been if he'd just left his helmet on his head.

The Browns led Kansas City 39–37 with four seconds left before Rudd, thinking he'd sacked Chiefs quarterback Trent Green, tossed his helmet to celebrate. Rudd didn't see Green flip the ball to tackle John Tait, who ran to the Cleveland 25 as time ran out. Rudd was penalized for removing his helmet on the field and the ball was moved half the distance to the goal line. Morten Andersen then kicked a 30-yard field goal.

"I'm sick," Browns coach Butch Davis said after the 40–39 loss. "To have something like that happen at the end is inexcusable."

The Browns were leaving the field when referee Ron Blum called them back for the field-goal attempt. Rudd was mortified.

"I thought he was down," he said. "When I tackled him, he rolled over on my face mask. I looked up and saw triple zeros on the clock and thought the game was over."

Rudd remained a target of ridicule until the sixteenth game, when his goal-line stop of Atlanta Falcons running back Warrick Dunn helped preserve a 24–16 victory that enabled the Browns to finish 9-7 and slip into the play-offs. "I will get a chance to get a little more sleep at night now," Rudd said. "You've got to have short memories in this league."

Pittsburgh rookie wide receiver Plaxico Burress was enjoying himself as he grabbed a 19-yard pass from Kordell Stewart during the Steelers' 24–13 victory over the Jacksonville Jaguars early in 2000. Burress fell after the catch, then jumped up and spiked the ball.

Maybe he was overly excited about the catch. Or maybe Burress thought he was back at Michigan State, where he'd be ruled down as soon as his knee touched the ground. In the NFL, a player isn't ruled down until an opponent touches him, and nobody touched Burress. Jaguars linebacker Danny Clark alertly grabbed the ball and returned the fumble forty-four yards.

Teammates didn't soon let Burress forget his blunder. "We call him the Prop Forty-Eight of wideouts," joked running back Jerome Bettis, referring to a college eligibility rule for partial academic qualifiers.

During practice the next week, teammates would wait for Burress to make a catch, then yell, "Spike! Spike! Spike!" By then, the rookie knew better.

You wouldn't expect the smartest players on the field to make some of the dumbest mistakes. Then again, quarterbacks have a lot on their minds. In addition to calling signals and reading defenses, they're staring into the eyes of people who want to dismember them. Throw in a few shots to the head, and it's understandable if even some of the best quarterbacks forget where they are and where they're supposed to be.

Bob Griese was the thinking man's quarterback and led the Miami Dolphins to back-to-back Super Bowl wins. But no Super Bowl unnerved him as much as his introduction to Chicago Bears linebacker Dick Butkus in a 1969 preseason game.

Butkus was famed for bone-crunching tackles, and he also liked to distract quarterbacks by jumping up to the line and growling at them. Griese, entering his third NFL season, took one look at Butkus and lined up behind the right guard.

"Larry Little must have jumped about six feet in the air when I put my hands underneath him," Griese recalled.

Denver quarterback John Elway wasn't always the poised veteran who ended his career with back-to-back Super Bowl wins. The first player drafted in 1983, he was under tremendous scrutiny and pressure as a rookie, and started the opener against the Pittsburgh Steelers. Though the Broncos won, 14–10, Elway completed just one of eight passes and was replaced by Steve DeBerg. The rookie wasn't sorry to get away from the gap-toothed Steeler linebacker who was nicknamed "Dracula."

"I wanted to click my heels together and say, 'Auntie Em, bring me home; you can have my signing bonus back; I don't want to see Jack Lambert spitting and drooling at me, anymore,'" Elway said upon his Hall of Fame election in 2004. "So for me to be standing here today, thinking about that game, it's a miracle."

Elway also pulled a Griese late that season. Near the end of a 31–7 loss at San Diego, he tried to lead a two-minute drill. Having been sacked four times, he probably was rattled because he lined up behind left guard Tom Glassic.

"He had his hands under me and I was trying to kick his foot with mine to tell him he was in the wrong place," Glassic said. "I was already in a set position so I couldn't move. But I bobbed my head and wiggled my behind and shouted, 'Hey, John, wrong guy! I don't have the ball.'"

Center Billy Bryan yelled to Elway, "Over here! Over here!"

Glassic could understand Elway's confusion. "All of us linemen have big rear ends, so it was easy to mistake one for another," he said. "Looking back on it, it was a disastrous day. But if you don't laugh, you cry."

Phil Simms already had been a Super Bowl MVP when he lined up behind a guard during a 23–16 win over the Atlanta Falcons in 1988. Simms was in the shotgun formation on third-and-eight and stuck deep in his own territory.

"I was looking to see what kind of coverage they had," he said. "I was really intense because we needed to score. Then I noticed what I thought was our guard waving his hand behind his back at me. I couldn't understand what he was doing. I mean, he was frantic.

"Then it dawned on me that I had lined up over the right guard. I quickly moved over. But I was so flustered that I couldn't even remember what play I had called in the huddle. So when I got the snap, I just threw it to the first guy I saw open and by some miracle he caught it for a first down."

Center Bart Oates recalled: "In the huddle after the play, I smiled at Phil and all he said was, 'Shut up.' Then he broke into a smile, too."

At least Griese, Elway, and Simms knew their mistakes weren't unique. Minnesota Vikings defensive end Jim Marshall had no such consolation. He stands alone as the pro version of Roy "Wrong Way" Riegels, who ran almost seventy yards the wrong way to set up a safety in California's 8–7 loss to Georgia Tech in the 1929 Rose Bowl.

Marshall's 62-yard, wrong-way run at San Francisco in 1964 didn't cost the Vikings a win. But it made the game a lot more interesting, not to mention unforgettable. "You can imagine how it was for me," he said. "I have never been so humiliated."

Marshall helped give the Vikings a 27–17 lead. He forced a fumble by 49ers quarterback George Mira that was returned by end Carl Eller forty-five yards for a touchdown. Marshall was closing in on Mira again early in the fourth quarter when Mira threw a swing pass to halfback Billy Kilmer, who was hit hard and fumbled. Marshall turned around, scooped up the ball, and started running—to pay dirt, he thought.

But he'd lost his bearings. Teammates screamed for Marshall to stop and turn around, but he sprinted to the end zone. "I thought they were cheering for me," he said. "About the 5-yard line, I looked around and things just didn't seem right."

When he crossed the goal line, Marshall saw quarterback Fran Tarkenton, yelling from the sideline and pointing the other way. Marshall, flustered, threw Tarkenton the ball. By tossing the ball out of bounds from his own end zone, Marshall gave up a safety.

He was off the hook when the Vikings went home 27–22 winners. "All the guys on the plane asked me to take over as pilot," Marshall said. "They figured I'd land them in Hawaii."

The Dallas Texans' 20–17 victory in double overtime over the Houston Oilers in the 1962 AFL championship game helped put the third-year league on the map. It also made running back Abner Haynes infamous for a slip of the tongue.

Haynes, the Texans captain, went out for the coin toss before the first overtime. A strong wind was blowing toward a clock at one end of Jeppesen Stadium in Houston, and coach Hank Stram told Haynes that he wanted the Oilers moving into the wind. If the Texans won the toss, Stram explained, they would elect to have the wind at their backs. If the Oilers won the toss and elected to receive, the Texans would kick to the clock.

Haynes won the toss but mistakenly said, "We'll kick to the clock." Once he elected to kick, the Oilers could take either end of the field. They got the ball and the wind, but failed to capitalize on Haynes's blunder. The first overtime was scoreless.

"Fortunately for him, it turned out well because we had the wind to our back when the winning field goal was kicked by Tommy Brooker," recalled quarterback Len Dawson, referring to a 25-yarder after seventy-seven minutes and fifty-four seconds.

That was at the time the longest game in pro-football history. For Haynes, you can bet, it seemed even longer.

Chapter 44
Immaculate:
The Famous Reception

It is, unquestionably, the most famous and controversial play in pro-football history. An inspired Pittsburgh Steelers fan gave this play an unforgettable nickname worthy of its improbable outcome. This is, of course, the "Immaculate Reception."

Many mistakenly believe that play in 1972 propelled the Steelers into their first Super Bowl. That actually came two years later. But if any Pittsburghers want to remember rookie running back Franco Harris's unlikely touchdown play against the Oakland Raiders as a harbinger of the Steelers' glory years, who can blame them?

STEELERS FANS HAD waited forty years for a play-off game and were on the brink of more heartbreak. Raiders backup quarterback Ken Stabler scrambled thirty yards for a touchdown and a 7–6 lead with 1:13 left at Three Rivers Stadium. The Steelers started their final drive at the 20 and faced fourth-and-ten at their 40 with twenty-two seconds left.

The Steelers ran the "66 circle post." Despite two pass rushers bearing down, Terry Bradshaw zipped a pass to halfback John "Frenchy" Fuqua, who was twenty-five yards downfield and collided with safety Jack Tatum as the ball arrived. Tatum appeared to spike the ball so hard that it flew toward Harris, who made a shoestring catch at the Oakland 42 and ran into the end zone with five seconds left.

"I knew Brad was in serious trouble, so I went downfield in case he needed me as an outlet receiver," Harris recalled. "I was always taught to go to the ball, so when he threw it, that's what I did. The next thing I knew, the ball was coming right at me.

"The rest has always been a blur. It happened so fast. It was all reaction. My only thought was to get to the end zone. It's amazing to me that this play has stood the test of time."

Bradshaw had been knocked down and never saw the play. Referee Fred Swearingen's crew held a lengthy huddle to determine if Tatum had touched the ball, because at that time, two consecutive Steeler touches would have made the catch illegal.

"I didn't know what happened," Bradshaw recalled. "I just saw a black jersey [Fuqua's] going to the post, gunned the ball, and got waylaid. The next thing, I heard this incredible roar and I knew it wasn't a first-down roar. I know it's a touchdown and I'm wondering, 'Who scored and who did I complete it to?' Then you kind of go, 'That's cool. I put that bad boy in there and I'm a hero to millions.'

"Then there's that humbling part. You walk over and they tell you, 'The ball hit Frenchy and there's a question if Tatum hit it, too.' And I'm going, 'Huh? Come again on all of this?' I had no clue."

The play did not unfold quite the way it was drawn up. "It was a circle by the halfback, who runs a post out of the backfield," Bradshaw said. "The split end runs a post but got cut off. Franco just blocks and drifts out as the safety valve and his alertness is really the key to the whole play. If he stayed and blocked, we never would've had the Immaculate Reception." Bradshaw paused and then needled, "Or if he would've blocked better."

The Raiders are convinced to this day that it was a deception, not a reception. They claimed the ball never hit Tatum and that Harris's catch should have been ruled illegal. "We feel we were taken," Raiders owner Al Davis said. "It was a mistake, but I guess it was an honest mistake."

A lack of conclusive testimony from the players involved or evidence from film merely enhances the play's mystique. Films do show that Raiders linebacker Phil Villapiano, who might have tackled Harris, was clipped by tight end John McMakin.

"I was right with Franco, but after Bradshaw threw the ball, I went over to help out," Villapiano said. "The ball went over my head to Franco. Had I stayed where I was, it would have been right to me. I saw exactly what happened and made a move to cut Franco off. But McMakin dove on the back of my legs. It was a great play, but he never gets any credit."

The Raiders were incensed that the touchdown was signaled belatedly. Swearingen consulted with his crew, then went into the baseball dugout and phoned Art McNally, the NFL's supervisor of officials. Swearingen returned to the field after a few minutes and signaled a touchdown. So many fans swarmed the field that it took fifteen minutes to remove them and allow Roy Gerela to kick the extra point for a 13–7 win.

"If it was a touchdown, why didn't they call it a touchdown right away?" asked John Madden, the Raiders coach before he became TV's top pro-football analyst. "If [Swearingen] didn't know it was a touchdown when it happened, how did he know it was a touchdown after he went and talked on the phone?

"It doesn't go away, so there's never been any closure. I've never gotten over it and I never will. I have seen guys joke about it, but I never have. Just like that, our whole season was over. It's just something you have to live with."

The Raiders are certain that Fuqua is hiding the truth. Fuqua takes special delight in letting them think that.

"Fuqua knows he hit it," Davis insisted.

Raiders tackle Art Shell wrote, "I saw Frenchy Fuqua years later and I said to him, 'Frenchy, why don't you tell the truth? The ball never touched Tatum. It touched you and went into Franco's hands.' And Frenchy smiled and said, 'Art, I'm not saying.'"

Fuqua insists that he never will help resolve the controversy. "I can tell you what happened on that play, but instead I'm going to tell you what happened was truly immaculate," he said, teasingly.

"Don't listen to any of those Raiders. They are still shell-shocked. That's something that happened in their lives they'll never recover from. I don't think any of them have regained their sanity since that play, and that includes John Madden.

"Now I've become obsessed with it. I've been offered money to tell. But there's something about having something you know and no one else in the world knows. Frenchy's going to take it to the grave with him."

A few hours after the victory, Michael Ord, a Steelers season-ticket holder and owner of a local leather shop, was celebrating with friends and family at a local bar. Ord, who received a Catholic education, stood on a chair and announced, "From here on, this day will be forever known as the Feast of the Immaculate Reception."

After the celebration, Ord and Sharon Levosky, his girlfriend and employee, went to her parents' house. They decided to share Ord's nickname for the dramatic play with Myron Cope, the Steelers' radio analyst and local TV sportscaster. Ord didn't want to call, though, because he was worried he might slur his words after too much celebrating. About 11 p.m., when the newscast started, Levosky dialed Cope's station and was startled when Cope picked up the phone.

"I couldn't believe it," she recalled. "When I told him the 'Immaculate Reception,' he was laughing. 'I can't say that on TV,' he said. I said, 'Sure you can.' He said, 'I'll have to think about it.'"

Five minutes later, Cope told his viewers about Levosky's call and the "Immaculate Reception." The play's been known as nothing else ever since.

Chapter 45
Miracle of the Meadowlands:
aka The Fumble

There's no better example of a team snatching
defeat from the jaws of victory than the play
New York Giants fans recall as "The Fumble."
There's no better example of a team snatching
victory from the jaws of defeat than the play
Philadelphia Eagles fans recall as the "Miracle
of the Meadowlands." Both nicknames describe the
same play, which unfolded dramatically at Giants
Stadium on November 19, 1978.

THE GIANTS WERE leading 17–12 with twenty-eight seconds
left and facing third-and-two at their 29-yard line. The Eagles
had no time-outs left, and Giants quarterback Joe Pisarcik could
have sealed the victory simply by taking a knee.

But offensive coordinator Bob Gibson sent in "Pro 65 Up," a
run by fullback Larry Csonka over left guard. Several Giants
yelled at Pisarcik to ignore the play and kneel down. Pisarcik,
though, had been criticized by Gibson for changing a play in the
previous game and didn't want to push his luck. The Giants were
slow to break the huddle and center Jim Clack, watching the

play clock running down, snapped the ball before his quarter-back was ready.

Pisarcik bobbled the snap, then clumsily put the ball on the right hip of Csonka, who never got a grip. The ball bounced loose and took a perfect hop to Eagles cornerback Herman Edwards. He returned the fumble twenty-six yards for a touchdown with twenty seconds left, and the Eagles won, 19–17.

"It was a gift; I was at the right place at the right time," Edwards said. "As a little kid, you always dream about making the play to win the game, and that was one of those deals. I go in the end zone, and Giants Stadium is quiet. I'm looking around going, 'What happened?' and everybody's wondering, 'What happened?'

"Everything got real still. You're almost so afraid, you don't know if it's really true. Did this really happen, or is this a flash to your brain? All of a sudden, we're whooping and hollering."

Eagles coach Dick Vermeil, figuring the game was over, did not bother to watch the play. "The whole team was running by him and he was trying to figure out what happened," Edwards recalled upon succeeding Vermeil as coach of the Kansas City Chiefs in 2006.

Giants coach John McVay must have wished he hadn't seen the play. But he did. "That's the most horrifying ending to a ball game I've ever seen," he said.

For Giants fans, the loss wasn't merely horrifying. It was the last straw, and their long-simmering anger and frustration boiled over. They had been putting up with mediocre-to-inept teams since coach Allie Sherman's last division title in 1963, and a feud between owners Tim and Wellington Mara exacerbated the franchise's bumbling.

Edwards's touchdown was called "the single most ignominious moment in Giants history" by longtime columnist and Giants historian Jerry Izenberg. "The rage that gripped the customers was as ugly as it was passionate," he wrote. "Never before had a crowd turned against a home team like this."

The Maras didn't get their wake-up call for three more weeks, however. The Giants took a six-game losing streak into their final home game, against the St. Louis Cardinals, and some fans burned their tickets in a trash barrel before the game. During the Giants' 17–0 victory, a single-engine plane flew over Giants Stadium, pulling a banner that read FIFTEEN YEARS OF LOUSY FOOTBALL—WE'VE HAD ENOUGH.

NFL commissioner Pete Rozelle realized the Giants' franchise was too important to the league to remain a punching bag. He recommended to the Maras, who didn't speak to each other, that they hire George Young as general manager in 1979. Young had mixed success until he hired Bill Parcells, who went on to win two Super Bowls.

The "Miracle of the Meadowlands" made an immediate impact for the Eagles. It enabled them to have their first winning record since 1966 and first play-off berth since 1960. Vermeil, who in 1976 had taken over a team as bedraggled as the Giants, started a run of four straight play-off seasons, and his Eagles won the NFC championship in 1980.

"The next thing, we're playing in the Super Bowl," Edwards recalled. "You see that in sports. One play gets you feeling like you have confidence. You're not worried about losing anymore. Now you're thinking about how you can win."

After the ball was dropped, the ax dropped. Gibson was fired the next day. He explained that he called the run to avoid a repeat of what happened after Pisarcik kneeled on second down. Middle linebacker Bill Bergey bulldozed Clack and started a fight.

Gibson did not get back in football. McVay's contract was not renewed by the Giants, but he landed on his feet. He got in on the ground floor of the glorious Bill Walsh era when he went to San Francisco as a personnel executive.

Edwards, an undrafted free agent signed by Vermeil, became a fixture in Eagles lore. Yet he said he would've rather been remembered for playing unselfishly and steadily for 135 straight games.

"I guess my mark will be that play," he said. "Fifty years from now, they may still be showing that play."

In a delicious twist of fate, Edwards was hired to coach the New York Jets in 2001. Now he was coaching in the very stadium he once reduced to shocked silence.

Perhaps you've noticed that when a quarterback takes a knee to run out the clock, one offensive player often lines up way behind the quarterback. That formation, thanks to Edwards, was introduced to the NFL the weekend after November 19, 1978. It's designed to prevent another miracle.

Chapter 46
Music City Miracle:
Titans' Super Bowl Run

This play was more inspiring to Nashville than
even the most heartfelt country tune. It means
as much to the Tennessee Titans as the
"Immaculate Reception" means to the Pittsburgh
Steelers. Both plays rank among the most
improbable game-winners in NFL history.

THE BUFFALO BILLS were poised to give the Titans their first
home loss ever at the Coliseum when Steve Christie kicked a 41-
yard field goal for a 16–15 lead in a wild-card play-off game in
January 2000. Only sixteen seconds remained, and the Bills only
had to prevent the Titans from scoring. But they couldn't.

Christie's kickoff, short and high, was caught by running back
Lorenzo Neal. He lateraled to tight end Frank Wycheck, who
passed across the field to wide receiver Kevin Dyson. He
streaked down the left sideline untouched for seventy-five yards,
and the Titans had a 22–16 victory.

This tricky return was "Home Run Throwback," a brainstorm of Titans special-teams coach Alan Lowry. But it wasn't executed quite the way it was drawn up. Wycheck was supposed to take the kick and lateral to Isaac Byrd, who had the option to pitch to a trailing player.

Dyson didn't even know he was going to be on the kick return unit until he heard coach Jeff Fisher call his name. Dyson was replacing Anthony Dorsett, who was out with cramps. Dorsett was supposed to replace Derrick Mason, who was out with a concussion. Fisher was still explaining the razzle-dazzle play to Dyson as he went out on the field.

Lowry was a Dallas Cowboys assistant when he first saw the fateful play. It was used by Southern Methodist for a 91-yard return that beat Texas Tech in 1982.

"I had seen it work one time, so you always hope it will work again like that, but there are no guarantees," Lowry said. "It's a one-shot deal, and it happened to work."

Bills coach Wade Phillips insisted the lateral was an illegal forward pass. However, TV replays and a computerized enhancement showed that Wycheck's pass was thrown perfectly sideways. Officials reviewed the play and pandemonium overtook the Coliseum when the touchdown was upheld.

Maybe the Titans were due for some good fortune after three years of wandering from Houston to Memphis to Nashville. Maybe Fisher was enjoying a home-run payback for his masterful job of keeping a homeless franchise off skid row.

The Houston Oilers opened the 1996 season as a lame-duck franchise. Owner Bud Adams announced the previous November that the team would move to Nashville. Fisher was left with shabby facilities, small crowds, and a situation ripe for a team giving up. The Astrodome, billed as the "Eighth Wonder of the World" when the Oilers moved in for the 1968 season, was not aging gracefully. The Oilers' practice facility, ringed by fences topped by barbed wire, looked more like a minimum-security prison.

Once the Oilers announced they would move, most fans vanished. A crowd of 27,725 showed up for the 1996 home opener. Mostly everybody gave up on the Oilers—except the Oilers. Because of a fast start, they actually drew back-to-back home crowds of more than 50,000 before they faded to their first of three straight 8-8 finishes.

"Coach has been giving us that *Field of Dreams* speech since camp," linebacker Mike Barrow said. "You know, 'If we win, they will come.' Well, they finally came."

Few NFL teams have faced the repeated distractions Fisher's team faced for three years. It played in three cities and three stadiums, yet slowly but surely became the cream of the AFC. Fisher kept the ship afloat by making sure his players always knew where they were sailing.

"That has been the key," he explained during the 1996 season. "Going into this season, we had to paint the picture for them: 'This is what to expect: the fans are extremely frustrated right now—not at you—because they're losing their team. We have to be prepared to play in front of a few people, knowing that if we have some success, we think they'll come back.'

"The challenge wasn't to go in there and play in front of twenty thousand people. The challenge was to play up to our potential. There's no room for excuses here."

For the Oilers' last home game in Houston, the challenge was to play in front of 15,131 people. They lost 21–13 to the Cincinnati Bengals.

Though the Oilers' Astrodome lease extended through 1997, an agreement with Houston officials allowed them to leave early. But the Coliseum in Nashville would not be ready until 1999. So began a comedy of short-term moves.

The Oilers wanted to play at Vanderbilt Stadium in Nashville in 1997, but local residents wanted no part of game-day congestion. The Oilers agreed to play at the Liberty Bowl in Memphis and train in Nashville.

Somebody forget to tell the Oilers that there was no love lost between Memphis and Nashville. Memphians weren't crazy about babysitting their cross-state rival's team, especially when the Oilers dropped by only on weekends. Two of the Oilers' first three Memphis crowds barely topped 17,000. The crowd jumped to 50,677 for the finale against the Pittsburgh Steelers, but much of that crowd was wearing black and gold.

The Oilers were able to use Vanderbilt's 41,000-seat stadium in 1998, though even fans in Nashville were miffed to have a team named the Oilers. Adams finally agreed to rename the team.

Finally, the Titans moved into the Coliseum in 1999 and finished 13-3 to earn a wild-card play-off spot. After beating the Bills, the Titans had to spring upsets at Indianapolis and Jacksonville to reach the Super Bowl. They beat the Jaguars 33–14 in the AFC championship game and broke the game open on—what else?—an 80-yard kickoff return for a touchdown, this time by Mason.

The Titans lost the Super Bowl to the St. Louis Rams, 23–16, and the game ended with Dyson catching a Steve McNair pass and getting tackled at the 1-yard line. There was no miracle or home run this time. The Titans left their last runner of the season stranded on third base.

Chapter 47
Babysitting:
AFL-NFL Signing Wars

Today they'd call it kidnapping. But when the National Football League and American Football League were at each other's throats to sign top college talent in the 1960s, they called it "babysitting."

Draft prospects who'd just finished their college seasons would be spirited away by an NFL or AFL babysitter, sometimes to an exotic locale, until they could be drafted and signed. Both leagues usually held their drafts in late November or the early days of December. Agents weren't yet common and college players were still naive and unspoiled enough to have their heads turned by a free trip.

THE AFL, WHICH began play in 1960, wasn't always taken seriously in the early days. Dallas Texans quarterback Cotton Davidson once threw into the end zone at Boston only to see his pass broken up by a Patriots fan who'd come out of the stands. But by 1963, when the new league received a $36 million TV contract from ABC, the AFL was ready to match the NFL, dollar for dollar, to sign draft choices.

"The AFL was much more aggressive from the standpoint of taking chances and trying to get commitments early—because we needed to be," recalled Lamar Hunt, AFL founder and owner of the Texans before they became the Kansas City Chiefs.

That aggressiveness alarmed NFL owners and commissioner Pete Rozelle. Bert Rose, a former Minnesota Vikings general manager, was hired in 1964 to run Operation Babysitter. He recruited NFL babysitters to watch and woo prospects.

"Each team submitted a list of about fifty players it wanted covered," recalled former Dallas Cowboys player personnel director Gil Brandt.

AFL owners recruited babysitters, too. Both leagues hired ex-coaches, lawyers, politicians, and other professionals who found it exciting to be involved in football. AFL babysitter Ed King couldn't keep University of Massachusetts tight end Milt Morin away from the Cleveland Browns after the 1965 season, but he got enough votes to become governor of Massachusetts in 1978.

Otis Taylor was a star wide receiver at Prairie View A&M in Texas and expected to sign with the Chiefs after the 1964 season. His talent was evident to Lloyd Wells, who scouted black colleges for the Chiefs and who became Taylor's confidant. Taylor met with Chiefs executives in Houston before a game against the Oilers on November 22.

Both leagues held their drafts six days later, and if an NFL team wanted Taylor, it would have to move quickly. So the Cowboys invited Taylor and teammate Seth Cartwright to spend Thanksgiving weekend in Dallas at a party for the region's top draft prospects.

"It's always nice to be wanted, so I figured what the hell, and decided to go," Taylor wrote in his biography. "What I didn't know—didn't even consider—was that the gathering was actually an NFL tactic to keep me and the others away from the AFL."

Wells realized Taylor might be slipping away when Hunt's secretary told him that Taylor was headed for Dallas. Wells was in Nashville to pick up two other Chiefs draft prospects, but quickly changed his plans and went to Dallas to find Taylor. But the Cowboys kept moving him from one hotel to another.

Taylor did not go out except for a dinner date. When Wells phoned Taylor's family, he learned the name of Otis's dinner companion. She told Wells that Taylor was at the Continental Motel in suburban Richardson. Wells, who was also a sportswriter, found Taylor's room and told the babysitter that he was a reporter seeking an interview for *Ebony* magazine.

Though Wells and Taylor were now alone and the Chiefs had a new red Thunderbird waiting for Taylor, he was reluctant to leave. He finally agreed to join Wells in the middle of the night and left through a window to avoid the babysitter in the hall.

"The Cowboys always tried to be very thorough," Brandt said. "We didn't leave a guy alone except to go to the bathroom. Our guy had a few beers and went to sleep."

Taylor was flown to Kansas City and drafted in the fourth round. He led the Chiefs in receptions for five seasons and made a dazzling 46-yard touchdown catch that helped beat the Vikings in the January 1970 Super Bowl. The Chiefs also signed Cartwright, but he didn't make the team.

"We thought Taylor was good," Brandt recalled. "But we had no idea how good."

Memphis State offensive tackle Harry Schuh (pronounced *shoe*) was in the middle of a tug-of-war between the Los Angeles Rams and Oakland Raiders before the 1965 draft. The Raiders flew Schuh, his wife, and infant son to Las Vegas. When NFL babysitter Hampton Pool, a former Rams head coach, got wind of the trip, he convinced Schuh's parents to tell authorities that their son had been kidnapped. The Raiders, however, persuaded Schuh's wife to call authorities and squelch that report.

The Raiders moved Schuh around Las Vegas to get him away from Pool, who, nevertheless, located him at a casino and again at a stage show. The Raiders also drove Schuh around for four hours and finally flew his wife and son to Los Angeles, where they stayed as decoys. Schuh, meanwhile, was taken from Las Vegas to Hawaii until draft day. He signed with the Raiders, who picked him in the first round.

Brandt recalled: "Poole sent a telegram, 'Boo, hoo. I lost my Schuh!'"

The Rams didn't even draft Schuh, and used their first-round pick on halfback Clancy Williams from Washington State. They made sure no AFL team got near Williams.

"The babysitter took him right from the dressing room after his last game and got him on a plane," Brandt recalled. "The kid wanted to go to New York or some place in the East. He still had on jeans or overalls, and for six or seven days, all they did was fly around the country."

All this skullduggery cost Roman Gabriel a pretty penny. A quarterback from North Carolina State, he was taken by the Raiders as the AFL's first overall pick in 1962 and by the Rams as the NFL's second overall pick.

The Rams offered Gabriel $15,000 a year for three years, and the Raiders offered him $12,500 a year. But the Raiders' franchise was in such disarray that it wound up turning over its draft picks to Hunt's Texans just to save them for the AFL.

Hunt was willing to raise the stakes to sign Gabriel. But when he phoned Gabriel, the quarterback was in a hotel room with Elroy Hirsch, the Rams general manager. Hirsch took the call and pretended he was Gabriel. The player never got the message.

"I thought I was talking to Roman Gabriel," Hunt said. "I heard years later that it was Hirsch posing as Gabriel. That was typical. All was fair in love and war and recruiting players."

Gabriel later said he would've jumped at Hunt's offer. "He was offering me one hundred thousand dollars to come play in the AFL," Gabriel recalled. "But I didn't take the call. Elroy Hirsch did. So I ended up going to the Rams."

The babysitting capers, in retrospect, seem like slapstick comedy.

"It sounds incomprehensible today that we would operate that way," Hunt acknowledged. "It definitely was part of the recruiting times. It was sort of guerrilla warfare—every team for itself, every man for himself, whatever it took to keep a player away from the other league. And I think it was effective."

Brandt thinks so, too. "You didn't draft somebody you knew was already signed and committed," he said. "The AFL told guys, 'If someone from the NFL calls, don't tell 'em you've signed. Let 'em draft you and they'll have egg on their face.'"

Chapter 48
A Brave New World:
WFL

Once the American Football League proved it could take on the NFL and survive, it was only a matter of time before another league got in on the act. Pro football was striking gold, and the World Football League was the next prospector.

The WFL started play in 1974, eight years after the AFL-NFL merger, with twelve franchises. It was the brainchild of Gary Davidson, the WFL's first commissioner, who also founded the World Hockey Association. The WFL is best remembered for accumulating a lot of red ink and priceless stories.

THE WFL WAS filled with people trying to make names for themselves or trying to hold on to names they'd already made. Coaching staffs and front offices were mixed bags of the knowledgeable and the neophytes.

Fran Monaco, a fanatical Notre Dame fan who operated a chain of medical labs, owned the Jacksonville Sharks. They opened training camp in Deland, Florida, in the summer of 1974 under coach Bud Asher. He was the former coach at Father Lopez High School in Daytona Beach, where he also owned a resort hotel.

Trainer Brady Greathouse, like Asher, didn't seem to need the Sharks for a paycheck. Greathouse had retired from the University of Florida, thanks to his piece of Gatorade action. Dr. Robert Cade, the physician who developed the sports drink, had Greathouse collect football players' sweat to identify the fluids their bodies needed to have replenished. The university showed no interest in Gatorade until it became a commercial success. Greathouse was fortunate to have gotten in on the ground floor.

Sharks equipment manager Don Butkus was the brother of Dick Butkus, the Chicago Bears Hall of Fame linebacker who then lived in Deland. Don, asked to assess the Sharks' talent, laughed and replied, "They can't be any worse than the Bears."

As Sharks general manager, Bugsy Engelberg turned away scores of WFL wannabes. But one refused to be turned away.

A linebacker from Carson-Newman College in Tennessee showed up in the Stetson University cafeteria and asked for a tryout. Engelberg told him to try minor league football, but the player grabbed a tray, got in line, and ate supper.

When one reporter asked Engelberg why the player he'd turned down was enjoying a meal, Engelberg assumed he was being teased. "Bugsy, he's eating your food," the reporter said as the general manager walked away.

Before the next day's practice, the interloper went to the equipment window and checked out a T-shirt and shorts. He must've thought the linebackers were too talented for him, because he joined the running backs, coached by former University of Miami coach Charlie Tate.

Nobody from the Sharks noticed the imposter until a reporter, prizing a hilarious story more than the player's career, pointed him out to Engelberg. The latter did a double take and told the player to leave. But he got his tryout, after all.

The WFL's best innovation was the action point. After scoring a touchdown, worth seven points, a team could run or pass for a one-point conversion. The WFL's worst innovation was pants that were color-coded for each position group. This idea, meant to help fans who didn't know a tackle from a quarterback, was introduced for the second exhibition season. Players hated the pants. Especially the Memphis Grizzlies.

Wide receiver Paul Warfield's pants were orange with black vertical stripes. "I've spent eleven years in professional football trying to build a serious image," he said. "I'm too far along in my career to begin playing [clown] Emmett Kelly."

Running backs got green pants, which did not sit well with Jim Kiick and Larry Csonka. They joined Warfield in leaving the Miami Dolphins after the 1974 season and gave the WFL its biggest signing coup.

"I'd look like a lime tree—or some kind of fruit," Kiick complained.

Csonka threw his pants on the floor and said, "Sure, and the coaches are going to wear shocking pink suits with high heels and those little lace caps they like so much. Heck, these pants are what the owners wear in their air-conditioned suites when they watch the game. They figure it's only right that we dress as nicely as they do."

The league dropped its pants for lack of cooperation.

The WFL's opening week shocked the skeptics. Attendance for the first six games on July 10 and 11, a Wednesday and Thursday, averaged 43,000.

The most disappointing crowd, 18,625, watched the Florida Blazers open at home in Orlando's Citrus Bowl against the Hawaiians. The Blazers won behind former New York Jets quarterback Bob Davis. During postgame interviews, Davis's hands were stained by the blue and gold dye from the official WFL ball. This was not a good omen.

A night later, the Sharks were hosts to the New York Stars for the WFL's first nationally televised game. The Gator Bowl crowd was announced as 59,110, and long lines of cars were still on the bridge approaching the stadium as the game started. Pregame festivities were elaborate, and few seemed to mind when the game was delayed by a halftime power failure. The Sharks won, 14–7, by returning a fourth-quarter punt for a touchdown, and the entire night appeared an unqualified success.

The WFL's honeymoon was brief. It turned out that the opening-week houses were papered by giveaways. Attendance plummeted in week two and never recovered. The WFL ultimately deteriorated into a circus of bankrupt and transient franchises, dilapidated stadiums, scurrilous owners, and unpaid players and creditors. Monaco met one Sharks payroll by borrowing $27,000 from Asher. Then he fired him.

"It's like investing in an oil well or a mine," Davidson said. "Those who can't afford to lose a million or so fast shouldn't come in. But those who come in early are on the ground floor and stand to make a great deal of money if they succeed."

Davidson was fired before the 1974 season ended, and the league folded twelve weeks into its second season. It didn't take long for the ground floor to fall into the basement.

Chapter 49
The One-Dollar League: USFL

The United States Football League was an upstart to be taken seriously. It mostly avoided the buffoonery that was rampant a decade earlier in the World Football League and that would characterize the XFL. The USFL was sprinkled with NFL-caliber players, coaches, and executives, and was the most credible new pro-football league since the AFL.

Had the USFL attracted more wealthy owners or had better luck in federal court, it might have duplicated the AFL's success. Instead, the USFL played spring seasons from 1983 to 1985 and folded before it could stage its first fall season in 1986.

THE USFL'S MOST offbeat event was a roster swap between the Arizona Wranglers and Chicago Blitz. The Blitz, pushing to compete with Mike Ditka's Bears, initially assembled one of the league's most talented rosters and hired George Allen as coach. The Blitz finished 12-6 in 1983, but average home attendance, announced as 18,133, was disappointing.

In the off-season, Blitz owner Dr. Ted Diethrich, who lived in Phoenix, decided he would rather own the Wranglers. So he bought them and swapped rosters with new Blitz owner Dr. James Hoffman. The teams kept their original names.

The new Blitz coach was Marv Levy, a Chicago native who'd been fired by the Kansas City Chiefs after the 1982 season. Nobody told Levy about the roster swap and he assumed he was inheriting a play-off team. Instead, he took over a team that went 4-14.

"That was a stunner," Levy recalled. "After I got done slapping my forehead with the heel of my hand, I said, 'Let's go.' I was happy to be coaching again. I would've preferred having a stronger team."

Levy also would've preferred a more committed owner. Hoffman abandoned his team shortly before the regular season began and forced the league to take over the Blitz. The league ran the team on such a tight budget that Levy had to buy toilet paper for the rest rooms in the locker room and offices.

The front office included two future NFL executives, however. John Butler was the chief scout and Bill Polian the personnel director. When Polian became general manager in Buffalo, he hired Levy, who coached the Bills to four AFC titles from 1990 to 1993.

The Blitz finished 5-13 in 1984, and home attendance plummeted to 7,455. The team ceased operations and its players were dispersed among other USFL teams.

"I have some great memories; it was a lot of fun," Levy said. "We had a lot of former Bears players, like Doug Plank, Dan Jiggetts, and Vince Evans. It helped me have an association with Bill Polian. It was the first time we worked together on a daily basis."

Levy didn't actually leave the Blitz until it became clear the team wouldn't have a 1985 season. "I kept coming in for a couple of months and finally we were pushed out of our headquarters, an old high school," he recalled. "Apparently, they weren't paying the rent. I'm still waiting for my paycheck."

Many USFL owners buckled under stiff financial losses. J. William Oldenburg, a California real estate investor, bought the Los Angeles Express in 1984 and made a huge splash by signing

Brigham Young quarterback Steve Young. Though Young was the Cincinnati Bengals' top draft choice, he opted for a $40 million USFL deal, which included $5 million up front.

Oldenburg drifted into bankruptcy, however, and his team got so broke that it couldn't afford to replace injured players. So Young, who made pro-football history by passing for 300 yards and running for 100 yards in a 49–29 loss to the Blitz, was switched to running back.

"We had so many injuries, we couldn't field a team," Young recalled. "Frank Seurer was the backup quarterback, and we literally had eleven guys. Frank couldn't play another position, so I figured I'd better play running back."

The Stars, owned by Myles H. Tannenbaum, were the USFL's showpiece franchise. Based in Philadelphia in 1983 and 1984 and Baltimore in 1985, the Stars, under coach Jim Mora and general manager Carl Peterson, played in all three USFL championship games. They won two of them.

The Tampa Bay Bandits, coached by Steve Spurrier, also got off on the right foot. Owner John Bassett had a keen promotional sense, as well as deep pockets. The league took a big hit when he developed terminal cancer and gave up his franchise.

One Bassett promotion was a mortgage burning, in which one lucky ticket holder got his mortgage paid and burned at midfield. Just to generate controversy, Bassett made a public stink over the New York Generals being awarded the rights to running back Herschel Walker. His complaint upset the league office and fellow owners because Bassett had agreed to let the Generals sign the Heisman Trophy winner from Georgia.

"That's the way you sell tickets when you're the little guy in Tampa and you want to build a rivalry," Bassett explained to a miffed league executive. "Herschel is a legend in the Florida and Georgia area. So if I take them on and protest against the big-city New Yorkers, it will help sell tickets."

USFL founder David Dixon considered spring football a good bet because of his experience as a college fan. A New Orleans art and antiques dealer, Dixon recalled that when Tulane was a national power in the 1930s, he would be among some 25,000 fans watching a spring scrimmage.

"It got me to thinking, 'My God, why can't we play games in the spring?'" Dixon said. "I mean, LSU still draws numbers like that to this day. If Princeton and Rutgers had played that first game [in 1869] in the spring instead of the fall, that's when we'd be playing football today."

The USFL's fate, ultimately, was determined in court. On July 29, 1986, a federal jury reached a verdict on an antitrust suit brought by the USFL against the NFL. The USFL sought $1.69 billion, claiming that the NFL had conspired to monopolize pro football and caused the new league to lose about $163 million.

After a twelve-week trial including forty-three witnesses, a jury of five men and one woman found the NFL guilty. But it awarded the USFL just one dollar, which was trebled to three dollars. With interest, the penalty totaled $3.76, and the NFL's check went to USFL executive director Steve Ehrhart. He never cashed the check and declined a collector's offer of $10,000.

"It represents a lot of achievements by a lot of great people," Ehrhart said. "I call it my 'stay humble' check. It's in my top drawer, and just when you think things are going your way, I can open the drawer and be reminded how quickly things can change. It's a color check with two signatures by the NFL and a big ol' red-white-and-blue logo on it. At a certain point in my life, I'm going to donate it to the Hall of Fame. But I haven't gotten there yet."

Chapter 50
World Wrestling Football: XFL

The XFL was part pro football, part pro wrestling, and partly the revenge of NBC. This was not a winning combination, and the league folded after just one season.

When NBC was outbid by CBS for the rights to AFC games, starting in 1998, NBC was left without NFL games for eight years. NBC retaliated by teaming with World Wrestling Federation chief Vince McMahon to start a league of their own. McMahon would merge the violence of pro football with the showmanship and sex appeal of pro wrestling. NBC would be a partner and televise the XFL's "smashmouth football."

PLANS FOR A 2001 winter and spring XFL season were announced on February 3, 2000. Many assumed that XFL stood for "Extreme Football League," but McMahon insisted that the initials stood for nothing at all.

"XFL stands for nothing at all?" asked bewildered Las Vegas mayor Oscar Goodman. "That's amazing. Only Vince McMahon would have something which means nothing stand for something."

Considering that one of the eight league-owned franchises was going into Las Vegas, the mayor's cynicism was not a good omen.

McMahon tried to steal the NFL's thunder by advertising the XFL during a play-off game between the Oakland Raiders and Miami Dolphins on January 6, 2001. A 143-foot blimp, resembling the XFL's black-and-red ball, circled above the Oakland Coliseum, pulling a banner that read XFL—THE TOUGHEST FOOTBALL EVER.

McMahon planned a second flight over the Oakland Coliseum for the next week's AFC championship game. The pilot took the blimp out for a test run between games and was returning to his parking spot at Oakland International Airport when a gust of wind caused him to lose control. The ground crew couldn't hold the blimp, and the pilot and co-pilot jumped out. The 4,000-pound aircraft went off on its own.

It drifted five miles north and climbed as high as 1,600 feet before the gondola got caught on the mast of a sailboat in a marina. The blimp crashed nose first into a fish-and-chips shack, providing an outrageous shot for news photographers.

"No, that wasn't a publicity stunt," McMahon said.

McMahon borrowed the R-rated strategy of the WWF, which later became the WWE. He would feature cheerleaders who'd show more skin and dance more provocatively than their NFL counterparts. McMahon also said the XFL would break from NFL policy by allowing, perhaps even encouraging, cheerleaders to date players.

"We're going to have three or four of them surround our announcers," McMahon promised. "Then when the quarterback fumbles or the wide receiver drops a pass—and we know who he's dating—I want our reporters right back in her face on the sidelines, demanding to know whether the two of them did the wild thing last night."

NBC aired a preseason commercial with shapely young women who were supposed to be XFL cheerleaders. They wore only skimpy towels as they pranced around a locker room. "Don't worry, we'll teach them how to cheer," the announcer said.

For the opening-night telecast, Las Vegas Outlaws quarterback Ryan Clement and cheerleader Crystal Aldershof filmed a skit loaded with double entendres.

"Quarterback Ryan Clement knows how to score," Aldershof purred.

Clement nervously tossed an XFL football from one hand to the other and said, "When the free safety slides over and my receiver gets a nice, free release, [it] causes the defense to collapse, therefore allowing us to penetrate for the touchdown."

The cheerleaders' outfits begged comparisons with exotic dancers. But the outfits weren't designed for winter, and XFL games began February 3, when it was chilly even in Sun Belt cities. In Las Vegas, for instance, the chilly opening-night air forced the cheerleaders to cover up in the second half. They should've been grateful they weren't cheering for the Chicago Enforcers.

Manufactured feuds have always been hits in pro wrestling, so why not in the XFL? Its best-known TV analyst was Minnesota governor Jesse Ventura, a former pro wrestler who needed no primer on how to instigate a feud. On opening night in Las Vegas, he called New York/New Jersey Hitmen coach Rusty Tillman "gutless" for electing to kick a short field goal on fourth down.

Tillman, interviewed on the sideline during the game, responded that Ventura "wouldn't know if a football was pumped or stuffed."

After New York's 19–0 victory, Ventura sought to interview Tillman. When the coach snubbed him, Ventura asked, "Ain't you gonna talk to me?"

As he left the field, Tillman told another announcer, "I got nothing to say to Jesse Ventura."

Ventura, as though back in the ring, looked at the camera and said, "I got him intimidated, there's no doubt about it. The guy couldn't wait to get off the field. He's afraid of me."

Ventura was routinely assigned to Hitmen games in a futile attempt to continue the feud. Tillman ignored him. Tillman, a no-nonsense coach who became the Minnesota Vikings' special-teams assistant in 2003, wanted no part of XFL theatrics. He mistakenly assumed he'd been hired to coach.

"I told Vince McMahon going in that I'm volatile and I didn't want to participate in that kind of stuff, I just wanted to coach football," Tillman said. "They hired Jesse and they wanted to get someone to make me go off. But I wouldn't do it, as much as he tried. It was like a bully in school. They keep bugging you until you ignore them and then they go away. It was like that with him."

Whether viewers enjoyed the Ventura-Tillman repartee or were merely curious, that opening game was watched by about 54 million NBC viewers, plus those watching cable coverage. But the ratings soon fell off a cliff, and one XFL game received the lowest rating ever for a major network program in prime time.

NBC had initially agreed to telecast XFL games for two seasons but pulled the plug after one. The network and WWF lost about $70 million, and McMahon announced on May 10, 2001, that he was folding the league.

The wrestling-football marriage didn't work. Wrestling fans wanted to see more feuding and female flesh. Football fans wanted to see higher-quality play. And maybe, just after the Super Bowl, even the craziest football fans needed a break.

Chapter 51
The Replacements:
The 1987 Strike

You could argue all day over which season was
the NFL's best. But there's no question about
which year was the NFL's worst. For three weeks
in 1987, the owners broke a players' strike by
grabbing guys off the street to play games that
counted in the standings.

THE PUBLIC AND media vilified replacement football. The
temporary teams were given such nicknames as the "Counterfeit
Bills" and "Phoney-Niners." Attendance routinely dropped below
10,000.

But the owners were determined to avoid a repeat of the 1982
strike, which forced seven weeks of games to be canceled. The
owners figured that if they could play the games and collect TV
revenue, they could break the back of another strike. The replacement games, indeed, forced the regulars back. But the
union, led by Gene Upshaw, developed the unity that would
eventually bring the players free agency.

Replacement football inspired a movie called *The Replacements*. Released in 2000, the film was more entertaining than the real thing. The movie portrays a team of misfits and NFL wannabes who replace the regular Washington Sentinels. They're guided by Jimmy McGinty (Gene Hackman), a hard-boiled coach with a heart of gold, and who's brought back by the Sentinels' owner.

The roster includes a safety who is on work release, a wide receiver who can't catch a cold, a psycho linebacker who's as much of a threat to teammates as opponents, a Welsh kicker who gets involved with gamblers, and quarterback Shane Falco (Keanu Reeves), who blew his NFL chances by bombing in the Sugar Bowl.

The replacements get harassed by the regulars and retaliate in a barroom brawl. Falco starts to win games, as well as the team's head cheerleader, Annabelle (Brooke Langton). But he remains full of self-doubt until the final game, when he leads a Hollywood comeback and defeats the Dallas Cowboys.

The movie's climactic game, between the Sentinels and Cowboys, is based upon the final replacement game—Redskins versus Cowboys on a Monday night in Dallas. The Cowboys had eleven veterans who'd crossed the picket line, including quarterback Danny White, running back Tony Dorsett, and defensive linemen Randy White and Ed "Too Tall" Jones. The Redskins had no regulars because coach Joe Gibbs strongly suggested that his players either strike or play as a team. The strike had been settled before the final weekend of replacement games, and Gibbs told his fill-ins, "This is your final audition."

His players made the most of it, sacking White six times in the first half and taking a 3–0 lead on Obed Ariri's field goal. Quarterback Ed Rubbert, cut by the Redskins in 1986, was injured early in the game and replaced by Tony Robinson, who was on work furlough from prison after a drug conviction.

With time running out, the Cowboys trailed 13–7 and faced fourth-and-four at the Washington 13. Safety Skip Lane, who'd left a $175,000-a-year real-estate job, implored the defense to not allow a pass into the end zone. A pass for Kelvin Edwards was broken up at the six and the Redskins celebrated. "It was kind of a miracle," Gibbs said.

The Redskins' replacements went 3-0 and the regulars beat the Broncos in the Super Bowl. Rubbert said he and his fellow stand-ins received Super Bowl tickets and winner's shares of $27,000 apiece. Regulars who'd taunted the replacements and called them the "Scabskins" had a change of heart. "I'd say half the guys called after the strike and thanked us," Rubbert said.

Defensive lineman James Ramey made no pretense about the ability of the replacements in Tampa Bay. "We are the Scabaneers," he said.

The Buccaneers' replacements went 2-1, mainly because many, including Ramey, played for the USFL's Tampa Bay Bandits from 1983 to 1985. The roster included a UPS driver, a freight-dock worker, an aerobics instructor, a real-estate broker, an aluminum salesman, a bill collector, and two deputy sheriffs.

"Some of those guys were horribly out of shape," recalled Buccaneers defensive coordinator Doug Graber. "I remember our first game in Detroit. One of our linemen comes running out in football pants and a half shirt. He's got this huge gut. And I'm thinking, 'Is this really the NFL?'"

For the replacements, though, the ridicule was well worth the chance to wear an NFL uniform. "For most of us, it was another glimmer of glory," Ramey said. "I had no delusions that I was going to make a Warren Sapp-type impact. It was like a dream sequence, just wild stuff.

"I had been out of football for two years. Remember, the USFL dried up and blew away. Many of us couldn't walk away from the game on our own terms. The game walked away from us. It was another chance. It was good money. I know I was out there at practice hitting people, running around, feeling good about myself. The next day I tried to get out of bed and the only thing that didn't hurt on my body was my nose. I knew it was temporary for me. I was a few weeks from getting booted back to reality."

Graber had mostly good memories about the replacements because they gave him everything they had. "Now they're probably sitting across the bar, saying, 'Hey, did you know I used to play for the Bucs?'" he said. "It's a bizarre story."

Happy endings for replacement players were not universal. Ugly incidents abounded as replacements were jeered and insulted. Many found their cars vandalized. The Kansas City Chiefs were one of the strongest pro-union teams and caused some of the strike's most controversial episodes.

Defensive tackle Bill Maas and linebacker Dino Hackett had shotguns in their pickup truck on the picket line one day. The publicity did not help the Chiefs recruit more replacements. They lost all three games, including a 42–0 drubbing at Miami.

Linebacker Jack Del Rio was in his first year with the Chiefs and was sent to picket at the stadium's main entrance. He saw scout Otis Taylor, the Chiefs legendary wide receiver, trying to help a replacement player whose tires had been slashed.

Though Taylor was nearing fifty, Del Rio must've confused Taylor for a replacement player and called him a "dirty scab." Taylor yelled back and Del Rio rushed him, grabbed Taylor in a headlock, and threw him to the ground.

Hackett helped break up the fight and told Del Rio he'd just knocked down Otis Taylor. Del Rio, who became the Jacksonville Jaguars head coach in 2003, said, "Hey, Otis, I used to love watching you. You were a great player."

Replacements were not greeted warmly in Buffalo, either. They were jeered when they arrived at practice and the team hotel and their cars were pelted with eggs. Fans relished the chance to mingle with the regulars and get their autographs on the picket line.

"I hardly knew the names of the players we rushed out onto the field for our game against the Colts," said coach Marv Levy, recalling a 47–6 loss. "Neither did our fans. Only 9,860 of them showed up. I counted them myself."

The Bills' last strike game, against the New York Giants, was the worst replacement game—and possibly the worst pro-football game ever. The teams combined for 258 yards in penalties, five missed field goals, and nine turnovers, including seven by the Bills. The game was most notable for the appearance of Willie Totten, who was Jerry Rice's college quarterback.

The Giants had Lawrence Taylor, one of the greatest linebackers ever, and he was assigned to run over center Will Grant on every down. Grant had retired from the Bills after the 1985 season and was clearly overmatched.

"Will, what in the world is going on out there?" Levy asked during halftime. "You have been called for holding six times in just one half!"

Grant replied: "Hey, coach, that's really good, because I've been holding him on every down."

With the score 3–3 and thirty seconds left, the Giants missed a short field goal. Levy told his quarterback to take a knee and yelled at him not to fumble. He did fumble, but the Giants missed another field goal. Tim Schlopy kicked a 27-yard field goal for the Bills with nineteen seconds left in overtime. The game was sloppy and the hero was Schlopy.

Most coaches were happy to forget the replacement games. Not Philadelphia's Buddy Ryan. It stuck in his craw that coach Tom Landry sent in veterans to stop an Eagles drive during a 41–22 Cowboys victory in a strike game.

When the teams' regulars met two weeks later in Philadelphia, the Eagles led 30–20 with one second left. Ryan had Keith

Byars score from the 1-yard line. "That last touchdown was very satisfying," Ryan said. "I told you, 'What goes around, comes around.'"

Ryan's words struck a nerve for at least one Cowboy. "That's the pathetic ramblings of a pathetic, senile old man," linebacker Steve DeOssie said. "They only did it to pacify Ryan's overinflated ego."

Chapter 52
Shoeless Joe:
Pranksters

Until they take off their uniforms for the last time, pro-football players don't entirely grow up. As busy as coaches try to keep them, players still wind up with too much time on their hands. And in the NFL, idle hands are the prankster's workshop.

REDSKINS LINEBACKER LAVAR Arrington pulled a welcome-to-the-NFL prank on Washington's first-round draft choice, safety Sean Taylor, during a June 2004 minicamp. Arrington shoved a shaving-cream pie in the rookie's face and laughed with delight at Taylor's frantic reaction.

But then Taylor fell to his knees and screamed that he couldn't see. His eyes were inflamed and he spent the next day's practice on the sidelines and wearing sunglasses. "My prank went bad," Arrington said. "He scared the heck out of me. It might be a good thing, because the rest of the rookies are off the hook. I'm not messing around with pranks anymore."

Joe Montana wasn't just the NFL's best quarterback ever. He also was one of the NFL's greatest pranksters ever.

During 1992, Montana's last year in San Francisco, the Tampa Bay Buccaneers came to town with quarterback Steve DeBerg, Montana's old 49ers teammate. DeBerg found his helmet and shoulder pads missing when he got to his locker in Candlestick Park. He didn't need Sherlock Holmes to identify the culprit.

Montana moved to Kansas City in 1993, where DeBerg had started two years earlier. Montana made his Chiefs' debut at Tampa and found his football shoes missing from his locker. In their place was a pair of size-fifteen shoes and a note, which read: "Stop following in my footsteps." He didn't need Sherlock Holmes to identify the culprit that time, either.

Before leading a 27–3 win over the Bucs, Montana retrieved his shoes and chatted with DeBerg. "I wished him well," Montana said, "and thanked him for the size-fifteens."

Montana saved his best pranks for training camp. When the 49ers held camp at Sierra College in Rocklin, California, most players rented mountain bikes to ride the five hundred yards from their dormitories to the practice field. Riding back from practice was often a problem, though, because Montana liked to hide the bicycles.

"Every other day, you'd find your bike up in a tree," said linebacker Jim Fahnhorst. "It was so dark when you came out of our meetings that it took you fifteen to twenty minutes to find a bike and then, when you did find it, you discovered that it wasn't yours."

According to wide receiver Mike Wilson, Montana often waited until the last week of training camp to hide the bikes. He knew players were most tired then. "On the last day of training camp, there must have been ten bikes up in the trees," Wilson said. "Joe had some help from Steve Young."

Montana also hid bikes on the roofs of campus buildings. One year, he got a thirty-foot chain and locked all the bikes together. He didn't have to worry about anybody hiding his bike because he didn't have one. The quarterbacks were always out of evening meetings first, and he'd ride somebody else's bike back to the dorm.

When Montana wearied of hiding bikes, he carried huge water pistols. "I remember Joe and [linebacker] Riki Ellison went wild with squirt guns," Fahnhorst recalled. "Joe's was like an Uzi machine gun. It had a battery pack in it and he could continually hose you down."

Nose tackle Jim Burt got even with Montana by sneaking up on him during a postgame interview in 1989 and dumping ice water on his head. That gave new meaning to the nickname, "Joe Cool."

Kickers are natural prey for pranksters. They're usually among the smallest players on a roster and are often resented because they don't get beat up on Sundays. So they're wise to keep a low profile. The last thing a kicker—or his wife—wants to do is antagonize the animals.

Dena Karlis, wife of Minnesota Vikings kicker Rich Karlis, didn't consider the consequences when she complained to other players' wives at a 1989 baby shower that the offensive linemen were a bad influence on her husband. Since he started hanging out with them, she said, he was getting sloppy in his dress and grooming. Naturally, these remarks got back to the linemen, including Kirk Lowdermilk, a 270-pound center who also was Karlis's brother-in-law.

"She said we were slobs," tackle Gary Zimmerman said.

Revenge was swift. When Karlis, a 180-pounder, came to practice a few days later, the linemen taped his hands and legs together, blindfolded him, gagged him, and hung him by his feet over a crossbar. They pinned to his shirt a note that read HE TALKED ABOUT THE OFFENSIVE LINE.

Karlis looked like a trophy fish displayed on a dock. The linemen got the team photographer to shoot them with their catch before they let him go. "We figured he was too scrawny to keep," Lowdermilk said.

Thanksgiving is pranks-giving day in the NFL. It's a time-honored tradition to tell rookies that free turkeys are reserved for them at a local supermarket. When they show up, they're greeted by confused employees who know nothing about the free turkeys and chortling veterans there to take photos of the gullible rookies.

Coach Marty Schottenheimer was telling Chiefs' rookies where they could pick up their free turkeys after Thanksgiving Day practice in 1990. This seemed dicey because the first-round draft choice, linebacker Percy Snow, could be volatile. It was later reported that he used a handgun to confront a golfer who hit an errant shot into his back yard from the adjoining course.

Tony Dungy, then a Chiefs assistant, was asked if he thought this Thanksgiving prank was a good idea. He replied, "I wouldn't want to be the guy at the Price Chopper to tell Percy Snow he can't have a turkey."

Safety Lyle Blackwood was a notorious prankster during his fourteen NFL seasons. As a Miami Dolphin in the 1980s, he pulled a classic prank on cornerback Robert Sowell. He filled Sowell's jockstrap with deep-heating balm.

"And if Robert hadn't been late for practice, he'd probably never have fallen for it," Blackwood said. "But he came running into the locker room with only a minute to get suited up and make it to a team meeting. He pulled on his jockstrap without checking it first. The instant the balm hit him, he knew what had happened. We were all in the next room, so we heard him go 'Ooowee!'"

Sowell tried to wipe off the balm with a towel but that only worked the ointment in deeper. Then he jumped in the shower but that only intensified the burning. Finally, the team trainer treated Sowell with ice bags and Vaseline.

"Of course, Robert couldn't make it out to practice," Blackwood said, "and when [Don] Shula caught wind of it, the coach really chewed me out."

St. Louis guard Conrad Dobler became famous in the mid-1970s as "the dirtiest man in football." Because of that reputation, glamorous CBS announcer Phyllis George and a camera crew went to the Cardinals' camp in St. Charles, Missouri, to interview Dobler in 1975. He was preparing for his interview as though it were a screen test, much to the disgust of tackle Dan Dierdorf.

"He was lording over the rest of us about Phyllis George coming all the way to St. Louis just to see him," Dierdorf said. "He was really being an insufferable jerk."

Dobler had a new pair of designer jeans for the interview. While tight end Jackie Smith played lookout, Dierdorf cut off the left pants-leg and replaced the jeans on a hanger.

"As luck would have it, Dobler put on the good leg first," Dierdorf recalled. "Then he slid on the snipped leg and when he saw what had happened, he totally lost control. And when Dobler lost control, it was awesome to behold!"

Dobler trashed the locker room and sent everybody running for cover except center Tom Banks, who sat and watched Dobler pound on lockers and toss benches.

"I kind of lost it," Dobler recalled. "I didn't handle it very well. I got kind of crazy. They all ran for their lives. Tom Banks was the only one who didn't. He just sat there and said, 'I told them it would turn out like this.'"

Dobler actually found a use for the ruined jeans when he was invited to Dierdorf's retirement ceremony in 1983. "I kept them forever," Dobler recalled, "and when he retired, I gave them to him as my gift."

Chapter 53
Steve Old:
Steve DeBerg

At age forty-four, Steve DeBerg became the oldest quarterback ever to start an NFL game. It was 1998 and he was near the end of a seventeen-season career that included stops in San Francisco, Denver, Tampa Bay, Kansas City, Miami, and Atlanta. Few NFL players survive so long and even fewer had half as much fun.

STEVE DEBERG COULDN'T outplay some of the greatest quarterbacks of all time, but he outlasted nearly all of them. Wherever DeBerg went, a future Hall of Fame quarterback was sure to follow and send him packing.

But DeBerg didn't pack it in for good until he was forty-five years old. Only George Blanda, at forty-eight, had been older when he ended his playing career.

Though he kept leaving NFL teams once they found better quarterbacks, DeBerg always left them laughing. He met them laughing, too. "I'm not Steve Young," he said when he came back with the Falcons in 1998. "I'm Steve Old."

DeBerg started out like a phenom in San Francisco. He set an NFL record with 347 completions in 1978, Bill Walsh's first rebuilding season with the 49ers. A year later, Walsh drafted Joe Montana, who would lead the 49ers to four Super Bowl wins.

DeBerg moved on to Denver in 1981 and started in 1982. The next year he split time with rookie John Elway, the first overall pick of the 1983 draft. Elway would lead the Broncos to five Super Bowl appearances and two victories.

"I went from this unbelievable organization that was committed to me to, 'Here comes Elway,'" DeBerg recalled.

His next stop was Tampa Bay, where he started for three of four seasons and backed up Steve Young in 1986 as the Buccaneers went 2-14. Young then took the magic dust that came from beating out DeBerg and went to the 49ers. There, he became a Super Bowl winner and the most highly rated passer of all time.

If you want to stretch a point, you could say DeBerg, a tenth-round pick of the Dallas Cowboys in 1977, also backed up Roger Staubach until DeBerg was cut in training camp. And he shared a locker room with Miami's Dan Marino, whose season-ending injury in 1993 prompted DeBerg's signing. That makes five Hall of Fame quarterbacks with whom DeBerg played, or at least rubbed shoulders.

Asked when he last felt as if he really owned the starting quarterback job, DeBerg replied, "Savanna High [in Anaheim, California], really. That was my most secure year of all."

When DeBerg finally got the chance to play for a Super Bowl team, he was forty-four years old, and would turn forty-five by season's end. Falcons coach Dan Reeves went into the 1998 season needing a veteran backup for Chris Chandler, a talented but often-injured quarterback. Mark Rypien, a Super Bowl winner, had been the backup until he was needed at home to stay with his two-year-old son, Andrew, who was dying of brain cancer.

Reeves had coached DeBerg in Denver and brought him to the New York Giants as an assistant coach in 1995. Reeves had seriously considered activating DeBerg in New York and didn't have a better backup in Atlanta.

"I was shocked my arm wasn't sore," DeBerg said, recalling the start of training camp in 1998. "I thought I'd have to ask Dan for a few days off, and that never happened. Normal people couldn't do this, but hey, I'm not normal."

DeBerg's biggest concessions to his age came off the field. "I was forty-four and had curfew and bed checks," he said, smiling. "Sometimes, I'm kind of like a misfit. Players aren't supposed to socialize with coaches, but they're more like my age."

Reeves brought his Giants offense to Atlanta, and DeBerg more than once corrected Falcons quarterbacks coach Jack Burns during meetings.

"I know my knowledge level is as high as maybe anybody who's ever played the game," DeBerg said that year. "I coached with a majority of guys on this staff and tease them all the time: 'I'm working a lot less and getting paid a lot more.'"

DeBerg hadn't played since he led an eight-player, coed flag football team in Tampa in 1997. At the health club where he worked out, DeBerg was asked by some weekend warriors half his age if he'd be their quarterback. "I said, 'I could beat some girls, that would be cool,'" he recalled. "I had a blast."

DeBerg had even more of a blast in 1998. When Chandler was injured in week six against the New Orleans Saints, DeBerg replaced him late in the second quarter and threw a touchdown pass in a 31–23 victory. A week later, DeBerg became the NFL's oldest starting quarterback ever and made all the highlights shows. The highlight, however, was Jets safety Victor Green clobbering DeBerg and forcing a fumble that was returned for a touchdown in a 28–3 romp.

DeBerg remained a valuable backup, though, and his 27-yard touchdown pass helped defeat the St. Louis Rams. The Falcons finished 14-2 and reached the Super Bowl, where they faced the Broncos and Elway in the final game of his career.

"I absolutely thought my opportunity to play in a Super Bowl was over and the only chance I would have would be as a coach," DeBerg said before the 34–19 loss. "It's unbelievable to have this opportunity and get a chance to help us win a few games."

DeBerg had shown his resilience before. With the Kansas City Chiefs in 1989, he was benched twice, in favor of Ron Jaworski and Steve Pelluer. When he regained the job, DeBerg nicknamed himself "Freddy Krueger," after the *Nightmare on Elm Street* character. "I keep coming back to haunt Marty Schottenheimer," DeBerg said, giggling.

The coach didn't feel haunted when DeBerg helped the Chiefs reach the play-offs in 1990 and 1991. Sometimes, though, Schottenheimer became exasperated by his happy-go-lucky quarterback. He once yelled at DeBerg to stop signing autographs for fans near the end of a lopsided home victory. DeBerg kept right on signing.

DeBerg's mischief belied his toughness. He suffered a broken left pinkie late in the 1990 season while the Oilers' Warren Moon was torching the Chiefs for 527 yards. DeBerg was in excruciating pain as his finger was manipulated on the sidelines, yet he returned in the fourth quarter with a splint. He then started two regular-season victories and a one-point play-off loss while wearing a cast to protect a pin in his injured finger.

DeBerg joked that if he were a farmer, he would've just had the pinkie amputated. Rural Chiefs fans jumped off their tractors to make angry responses to talk shows, newspapers, and the Chiefs' public-relations department.

Eight days after the cast on his hand was removed, DeBerg was ice skating for a children's cause. He was just a kid at heart.

Each year before Christmas, DeBerg elaborately decorated his locker, complete with lights. He was an extraordinary play-action passer and also used his sleight of hand as an amateur magician. A *Kansas City Star* reporter asked DeBerg to pose in his magician's garb for a photo. Instead of showing up with just a wand and top hat, DeBerg arrived in full costume, including a tuxedo and cape.

DeBerg was designated by *Sports Illustrated* as the best journeyman quarterback ever. He had the statistics of a Hall of Famer but the itinerary of a traveling salesman.

His 34,241 passing yards rank above Steve Young, Troy Aikman, and Ken Anderson. His 196 touchdown passes rank above Ken Stabler, Joe Namath, and Aikman. His 2,874 completions rank above Johnny Unitas, Young, and Phil Simms. His 57.2 percent completion percentage ranks above Elway, Bob Griese, and Terry Bradshaw.

DeBerg also threw 204 interceptions, however, and is often downgraded by an unverified Walsh quote—that he was "just good enough to get you beat."

DeBerg was also good enough to play 207 games for six teams and eleven head coaches and watched a succession of Hall of Fame quarterbacks blossom. "Yeah, I've seen a lot of quarterbacks come and go," he said. "But I wouldn't trade places with anybody."

Chapter 54
Zebras:
Calls of the Wild

NFL officials are happiest when nobody notices
them, or can't remember them thirty minutes
after a game. That means they haven't made any
messes. If fans remember an official's name on
Monday morning, it's a good bet his name is mud
in some NFL city.

Yet it's becoming tougher and tougher for
officials to remain anonymous even after
well-officiated games. Referees are on camera
to announce every penalty and crews are subject
to second-guessing every time an instant replay
is televised. Though NFL officials are proved
right most of the time, there's often hell to
pay when they're wrong.

REFEREE WALT COLEMAN became infamous for a snowy
play-off game between the Raiders and Patriots at New England
in January 2002. Coleman didn't blow a call. He just enforced a
rule that few fans ever heard of and even fewer knew how to in-
terpret. It's called the "tuck" rule, and Raiders fans were convinced that Coleman made it up on the spot just to put the
screws to them and owner Al Davis.

The Raiders were leading, 13–10, in the last two minutes
when cornerback Charles Woodson stripped the ball from Patriots quarterback Tom Brady, who looked as if he was starting to
scramble. Linebacker Greg Biekert fell on the ball and the

Raiders figured they had just wrapped up their second straight trip to the AFC championship game.

Not so fast. The replay official called for a review, and Coleman ruled that Brady had thrown an incomplete pass. Because he had not brought the ball back to his body, or tucked it, he was legally still in his throwing motion. Five plays later, Adam Vinatieri kicked a 45-yard field goal to force overtime. His 23-yard kick won the game.

NFL director of officiating Mike Pereira said Coleman had properly interpreted the tuck rule. Still, as you might imagine, it took the Raiders and their fans a while to get over the call. That's assuming they've gotten over it yet.

When referee Mike Carey visited the Raiders' training camp for a routine rules orientation the summer after the tuck rule game, most of the team walked out. Veterans, notably wide receiver Tim Brown, instigated the walkout to protest Coleman's call.

"The rule stunk and we let it be known that we didn't like it," running back Charlie Garner said. "It was something Tim and the guys discussed, and we felt it was a good gesture."

Cornerback Terrance Shaw explained, "I was hungry. And they didn't have anything to say. I was told everybody's got to move. It's a team thing." Funny, but Shaw played for the Patriots in the tuck rule game.

Safety Troy Polamalu's non-interception in January 2006 might have become just as infamous in Pittsburgh as the tuck rule became in Oakland—except that the Steelers overcame the call to knock the Indianapolis Colts out of the play-offs on their way to a Super Bowl title. The Steelers led 21–10 with under six minutes left, when Polamalu seemed to seal the Colts' fate with a diving interception of a Peyton Manning pass near midfield.

The safety rolled over with the ball in his hands and fumbled as he was getting up to run, then fell on the ball. Colts Coach Tony Dungy, claiming Polamalu did not complete the catch, challenged the call and was upheld by referee Pete Morelli. The Colts used this second chance to drive to a touchdown and a 2-point conversion and had a chance for a tying field goal near the end.

Morelli explained after the game that Polamalu "never had possession with his leg up off the ground, doing an act common to the game of football."

Outspoken Steelers linebacker Joey Porter went ballistic. "I know they wanted Indy to win this game," he told *The New York Times*. "The whole world loves Peyton Manning, but come on man, don't take the game away from us.

"I felt they were cheating us. When the interception happened, everybody in the world knew that was an interception. Don't cheat us that bad. When they did that, they really want Peyton Manning and these guys to win the Super Bowl. They are just going to straight take it for them. I felt that they were like, 'We don't even care if you know we're cheating. We're cheating for them.'"

Porter also told the *Pittsburgh Post-Gazette*, "The way the refs were going, I wouldn't have trusted them in overtime. If we hadn't won, they would have cheated us in overtime."

Even the Steelers fiery coach, Bill Cowher, called Porter's remarks "ridiculous." Cowher added that he has a 15-minute cooling off period before his players speak with reporters but that, "We've got some guys who could probably use a little longer than that."

Yet, Porter's outrage was vindicated. Pereira said the day after the game that Polamalu maintained possession long enough to establish a catch. He added that Morelli's interpretation would have applied only if another player had forced Polamalu to fumble.

Pereira also had to set the record straight after the 49ers' 39–38 play-off victory over the Giants in January 2003. A key oversight made a wild game and wild ending even wilder. New York blew a twenty-four-point lead at San Francisco but still had a chance to win when Matt Bryant lined up for a 41-yard field goal with six seconds left.

Snapper Trey Junkin, who'd already messed up one field-goal try, skidded the snap. Holder Matt Allen threw a desperate pass for Rich Seubert, a guard lined up as an eligible receiver. Seubert was pulled down by defensive end Chike Okeafor inside the 5-yard line, yet pass interference wasn't called.

Left guard Tam Hopkins also went downfield and was penalized for being an ineligible receiver. The penalty was declined and the game was over. But the league in a statement agreed that pass interference should have been called against Okeafor and offsetting penalties should have given the Giants one more play. "How they missed that, I do not know," Giants coach Jim Fassel said.

Both Okeafor and 49ers coach Steve Mariucci expected a pass-interference call. "I'd have done the same thing again," Okeafor said. "I wasn't going to let him catch it, score, and be over then. I was at least going to make them use another play, give us another chance."

As for Mariucci's reaction to the Giants' misfortune? "Bummer," he said.

Remember that Southwest Airlines ad in 1999 when a referee couldn't find the coin for the pregame toss and is seduced by the message, "Want to Get Away?" Remember *Rat Race*, a 2001 movie in which Cuba Gooding Jr. plays a disgraced NFL referee who can't live down a botched coin toss in a big game?

You can credit—or blame—referee Phil Luckett for making the coin toss part of American pop culture. This happened before overtime with the Steelers and Lions tied 16–16 at Pontiac, Michigan, on Thanksgiving Day, 1998.

Luckett asked Pittsburgh running back Jerome Bettis to make the call. The coin came up tails and Luckett gave the Lions the option. Simple enough? Not by a long shot.

Bettis claimed he'd called tails. Luckett claimed Bettis called "heads-tails," and he was bound to go with the first sound he heard. The Lions received the kickoff and kicked a field goal.

"What happened on the coin toss," Luckett said, "[was that] I talked to number thirty-six Pittsburgh to call it. He first called 'heads.' When it hit the ground it bounced to tails. And I said, 'You called heads, so Detroit has won the toss.'"

Bettis begged to differ. "I did not say, 'heads-tails,'" he said. "That is a lie. That's a bald-faced lie. I've never seen anything like this. This is the most bizarre situation I've been associated with, and I'm sure that I'll take this one to my grave as probably the craziest call that a referee would ever make."

Bettis spoke too soon. Just ten days later, Luckett's head linesman, Earnie Frantz, immediately signaled a touchdown when Jets quarterback Vinny Testaverde sneaked from the five with twenty seconds left in a game at Giants Stadium. That play gave the Jets a 32–31 victory over the Seattle Seahawks. However, as TV replays would confirm, Testaverde actually was a foot short of the goal line.

Critics asked why the call was made so quickly and why Luckett didn't overrule it. "Because he had signaled a touchdown, so far as we're concerned it's over," Luckett said.

Jets coach Bill Parcells didn't follow the winner's etiquette of siding with the officials. "We were very fortunate," he said. "I saw the guy make the call immediately. God was on our side today.

He's telling [Seahawks coach Dennis] Erickson to wait a while and gives Parcells a rabbit's foot."

Testaverde's phantom touchdown helped bring back instant replay the next season by a 28–3 vote of owners. Replay had been gone since 1991, but two weeks of gaffes changed enough minds to give replay the 75 percent majority needed for approval in 1999.

Buffalo owner Ralph Wilson was among those switching sides. He'd complained about a questionable pass-interference call that helped the Patriots beat the Bills, 25–21, on November 30. Wilson described the officiating as "embarrassing to the league," prompting commissioner Paul Tagliabue to say he would fine Wilson $50,000.

"I don't need pompous lectures from the commissioner and I feel the fifty thousand dollars is not only unwarranted, but punitive in nature," Wilson said. "The next time he may ask me to sit in the corner."

Lions owner William Clay Ford Sr. also was told to expect a $50,000 fine for blasting the officiating on Thanksgiving. Ford questioned calls that went against the Lions and even accepted Bettis's version of the coin-toss fiasco.

"The officials screwed everything else up," he said. "Why shouldn't we think they screwed that up, too?"

Pat Haggerty's coin toss before the Redskins' 30–7 victory at Dallas in 1989 was a disaster. Haggerty had a good excuse, though. He was distracted by actress Elizabeth Taylor. She was escorted to the middle of the field as the guest of Cowboys owner Jerry Jones, who asked Haggerty to let her call the toss.

Jones was a star-struck, first-year owner and perhaps oblivious to league rules. Haggerty, though, should have known better than to let anybody besides the visiting team's captain call the toss. He messed up the introductions, too. "Dallas captains, meet the Washington captains," he said. "Washington captains, meet Liz Taylor and Jerry Jones . . . I mean, the Dallas captains."

Taylor called heads and when the coin came up heads, Haggerty gave Dallas the option. Redskins captain Reggie Branch reminded Haggerty that the visitors get to make the call and the referee confessed to Taylor, "You've got me all shook up."

Redskins coach Joe Gibbs was shook up, too, even though his team won the toss on Haggerty's second try. "First time I ever got mad about a coin flip," he said.

Field judge Fred Swearingen had the dubious distinction of making the first big blown call in a Super Bowl.

During the fourth quarter of the Steelers' 35–31 victory over the Cowboys in January 1979, Terry Bradshaw threw a high pop fly from his 44-yard line for Lynn Swann. He was covered by cornerback Benny Barnes and the two collided as the pass fell incomplete. Back judge Pat Knight, the official nearest the play, made no call. Swearingen, however, claimed that Barnes tripped Swann, and the ball was placed at the Dallas 23. The Steelers quickly scored and took a 28–17 lead.

Cowboys coach Tom Landry was livid about the penalty. "He missed it," he said. "[Swann] cut across the back of Benny's legs, tripped, and fell down. Benny was tripped, of course, and fell . . . Swearingen had no idea what happened."

Barnes was even more outspoken. "Swann ran right up my back," he said. "When I saw the flag I knew it was on him. I couldn't believe the call. Maybe Swearingen needs glasses; maybe he's from Pittsburgh."

Swearingen explained, "The Pittsburgh receiver, in trying to get the ball, was tripped by the defender's feet. He interfered with the receiver trying to get to the ball. It was coming to him in that direction and I threw the flag for pass interference."

The league office announced that Swearingen was mistaken. Barnes got vindication. But the Steelers got the ring.

Chapter 55
Gridders Gone Wild:
Pro Wrestlers

Scratch a professional wrestler—if you dare—
and you'll find an NFL wannabe. Scratch an NFL
player near the end of his career and you could
find an aspiring wrestler. Some of pro wrestling's
top personalities first made names for themselves
in pro football.

BROCK LESNAR WAS a big-time pro wrestler when he decided
to try the NFL. Lesnar, the 2000 NCAA heavyweight champion
for Minnesota, was billed in pro wrestling as "The Next Big
Thing." Despite having a seven-year, $45 million contract with
World Wrestling Entertainment, he signed a one-year, $230,000
contract with the Minnesota Vikings in the summer of 2004.

Lesnar already had fans in Vikings defensive tackle Chris
Hovan and tight end Jim Kleinsasser. Hovan showed some of
Lesnar's flair in 2002, when he called Packers quarterback Brett
Favre "the prize," and said he'd be going after him in Green Bay.

Lambeau Field fans threw trash at Hovan and spit on him after the Packers won, 26–22.

"It was fun," Hovan said. "I've watched [pro wrestling] all my life and felt like the villain entering the ring that night. Now I know how all those guys feel. It was cool."

Lesnar hadn't put on pads for nine years and was still acting more like a pro wrestler than a football player when the Vikings held a training-camp practice with the Chiefs. Lesnar hyperextended the throwing elbow of Kansas City reserve quarterback Damon Huard in what was supposed to be a noncontact drill.

Lesnar stayed with the Vikings until late August and was cut. "He gave me a hug," Vikings coach Mike Tice said. "He was very happy for the chance."

If pro wrestlers often lack the technique and experience for the NFL, pro-football players often lack the moves and showmanship for pro wrestling. Former Chicago Bears defensive tackle Steve "Mongo" McMichael appeared a natural-born pro wrestler. He seemed to have just the right size, strength, and craziness.

How crazy was he? McMichael was thrown out of Wrigley Field in 2001 when he was the guest singer for "Take Me Out to the Ball Game" during the seventh-inning stretch. There had been a controversial call in the sixth inning and before he sang, McMichael announced, "I'm going to have a talk with that umpire down there."

Home-plate umpire Angel Hernandez then ordered that McMichael be thrown out of the stadium. McMichael, though, seldom generated that kind of excitement in the ring.

He became involved in wrestling in 1995, when he was invited to help cheer on former New York Giants linebacker Lawrence Taylor against Bam Bam Bigelow. McMichael was hired as a pro-wrestling TV analyst and finally entered the ring as the partner of NFL linebacker Kevin Greene in a match against Ric Flair and Arn Anderson.

According to pro-wrestling critic Mike Stokes, McMichael's career fizzled because he looked "stiff and uncoordinated." His head-turning wife, Debra, acted as his valet. But the couple broke up and she married "Stone Cold" Steve Austin.

Bronko Nagurski, a charter member of the Pro Football Hall of Fame, went from the NFL to the squared circle and back.

Nagurski cemented his place in NFL lore as a Chicago Bears fullback from 1930 to 1937 before spending six years in pro wrestling, a better-paying job. The Bears were strapped for talent during World War II and lured Nagurski, thirty-four, out of retirement in 1943. They made him an offensive tackle and set in motion the NFL's most famous comeback of all time.

In the final game of the season, the Bears needed only to beat the winless Chicago Cardinals to clinch the Western Division title. Yet they trailed 24–14 after three quarters. Nagurski was switched to fullback and gave a performance straight out of a Hollywood movie. He carried sixteen times for 84 yards in the fourth quarter and led a 35–24 victory. That paved the way for a 41–21 victory over the Washington Redskins in the NFL championship game.

Bill Goldberg went from an obscure role with the Atlanta Falcons from 1992 to 1994 to a starring role in pro wrestling. A torn abdominal muscle that forced Goldberg out of the NFL proved a blessing in disguise for him. He's enjoyed a celebrated career, which has included a long winning streak, a feud with Lesnar, and several movie roles.

His shaved head and chiseled six-foot-four, 285-pound physique has made Goldberg an intimidating presence. Using the "spear" and "jackhammer" to finish opponents, he began a streak in 1997 that was estimated to have reached more than 170 straight wins.

The "spear" is the kind of charge a linebacker makes at a ball carrier. The "jackhammer" involves lifting an opponent and slamming him down.

Drafted in the eleventh round by the Los Angeles Rams in 1990, Goldberg was a training-camp roommate of Greene. He kept his career alive in the NFL's developmental league before he finally made the Falcons' roster.

Greene was one of the top pass-rushing linebackers of his era but not a memorable pro wrestler. Goldberg was one of the most forgettable defensive linemen of his era but one of the most popular pro wrestlers in history. Go figure.

Ed "Wahoo" McDaniel was a hot-tempered linebacker who wrestled as "Chief Wahoo." He was a fan favorite in both sports and spent nine years with four AFL teams.

He was at his first training camp in 1961 with the Denver Broncos when McDaniel was ordered by veterans to stand on a dining-room chair and sing his school song. McDaniel, who played at Oklahoma, obliged by singing "Boomer Sooner." He stopped when a teammate hit him in the head with a dinner roll.

McDaniel jumped from his chair and claimed he was going to his room to get his gun and shoot the player who threw the roll. Defensive tackle Bud McFadin chased down McDaniel and convinced him to put the gun away.

Ernie Ladd, six-foot-nine and 310 pounds, was a legendary San Diego Chargers defensive lineman. He began wrestling in the off-season and emerged as a premier villain in the 1970s. His rivals included Andre the Giant, Dick the Bruiser, and Gorilla Monsoon.

Nicknamed "The Big Cat," for his size and quickness, Ladd had a fifty-four-inch chest, twenty-inch biceps, twenty-two-inch thighs, and size 17EEE shoes. He once ate 124 small pancakes in a contest.

Boston Patriots center Jon Morris, recalling a game against Ladd, said: "It was dark. I couldn't see the linebackers. I couldn't see the goalposts. It was like being in a closet."

Dallas Texans quarterback Cotton Davidson recalled: "You couldn't run over him and you didn't want to run away from him because he could run you down from behind. I was scrambling one time and he caught me from behind, clubbed me over the head, and said, 'Don't you know you can't get away from The Big Cat?'"

No former NFL player made a longer-lasting impact upon pro wrestling than Dick "the Bruiser" Afflis. He was a Green Bay Packers guard from 1951 to 1954, then wrestled into the 1970s. He was convinced to try wrestling by Leo Nomellini, a future Hall of Fame defensive tackle with the San Francisco 49ers, who wrestled in the off-season.

Afflis had a ferocious ring presence and gravelly voice and was billed as "The World's Most Dangerous Wrestler." He had one of his most famous matches against Detroit Lions defensive tackle Alex Karras on April 27, 1963, just after Karras was suspended a year for betting on NFL games.

According to wrestling lore, the match was made when Afflis visited Karras's bar in Detroit and they began chatting about wrestling. Afflis challenged Karras to a match and Karras quickly accepted. Afflis, supposedly, wanted to rumble then and there and created such a ruckus that police were summoned.

Their match drew about 16,000 to Detroit's Olympia Stadium. Afflis became enraged after suffering a wide cut above his right eye, bit one of Karras's biceps, and pinned him in about eleven minutes.

"There isn't a man alive I can't lick," boasted Afflis. "No man I've ever wrestled has convinced me I couldn't lick him." Too bad he didn't stay in Green Bay long enough to meet Ray Nitschke.

Chapter 56
Chill of Victory, Agony of the Feet:
Shoe Stories

Imelda Marcos, once the first lady of the Philippines and a woman who owned more shoes than Nike, would have felt right at home in an NFL locker room. There are piles of shoes in every locker so players are prepared for all kinds of playing surfaces and weather.

Don't laugh. Shoes have changed NFL history. When it comes to having the right shoes, nobody wants to get caught flat-footed. Especially not in a big game.

THE WRONG SHOES may have cost the 1934 Chicago Bears the first perfect season in NFL history. They were 13-0 and aiming for their third straight league title when they met the New York Giants in the championship game at the Polo Grounds.

The field was icy, which was nothing new for the Windy City team, and the Bears led 10–3 at halftime. But instead of giving his players a long halftime speech, Giants coach Steve Owen gave them basketball shoes.

The Giants finally found their footing and scored twenty-seven points in the fourth quarter for a 30–13 victory in what's remembered as the "Sneakers Game."

The shoes were on the other feet in 1950, when the Giants found a frozen field in Cleveland for a play-off game to break a tie for the conference title. The Browns wore sneakers and won 8–3 to advance to the title game at home against the Los Angeles Rams. A slight thaw turned the field into a mess and the Browns wore sneakers again.

"If you wore spikes, it was like wearing golf spikes on a marble floor," Browns quarterback Otto Graham said. "There was no traction at all. The rumor going around for years was that [coach] Paul Brown had someone contact all the sporting goods stores in town, saying, 'Don't sell any tennis shoes to the Rams.' I doubt very much it's true, but it's a good rumor."

The Rams, actually, had all the sneakers they needed. But only four Rams wore them, which led to second-guessing after their 30–28 loss. A famous photo from that game shows Graham scrambling in Converse All-Star basketball shoes. His 14-yard run was a key to the winning drive, which ended with a Lou Groza field goal.

The Giants went back to their sneakers trick for the 1956 NFL title game against the Bears at Yankee Stadium. The Giants won 47–7, and were so much stronger than the Bears that they probably could've won this game going barefoot.

The New England Patriots found a better way than footwear to improve their traction in 1982. They and the Miami Dolphins were scoreless during a blizzard at Schaefer Stadium in Foxboro on December 12. Each team had moved into position for a field-goal attempt, but their kickers were helpless trying to overcome a layer of snow.

The Patriots tried another kick when a drive stalled at the Miami 16 with 4:45 left. They called time-out so kicker John Smith could try to clear a spot seven yards behind the line.

Patriots coach Ron Meyer had a better idea. "I saw John Smith on his hands and knees trying to get the snow cleared, and all of a sudden it hit me," he said. "Why not send a snowplow out there?"

A tractor with a broom attached had been clearing the yard lines during time-outs, and Meyer frantically went looking for the operator. By the end of the time-out, he found him. He was Mark Henderson, twenty-four, who was working on the stadium maintenance crew as part of a work-release program from Norfolk State Prison. He was serving fifteen years for burglary.

Henderson ran his tractor along the Miami 20, as though he was just clearing another yard line. Then he made a sharp turn and cleared a patch between the 23- and 25-yard lines. That allowed Smith to make a 33-yard, game-winning kick.

The Dolphins were furious but powerless to do anything except scream at Henderson and the officials. The Dolphins claimed the use of the tractor was illegal but the officials knew of no rule that prohibited it. Such snow jobs became illegal in 1983.

"What were they gonna do?" Henderson asked. "Put me in jail?"

Dolphins owner Joe Robbie later was introduced to Smith by league official Don Weiss. "When I introduced John to Robbie," Weiss recalled, "Joe said, 'That's the only game ever stolen from the Dolphins by a convicted felon.'"

Henderson, who got out of prison in the early 1980s, made a triumphant return to Foxboro in 2001. As part of the ceremonies marking the last regular-season home game at the Patriots' old stadium, Henderson drove his tractor and broom onto the field. As he re-created a classic moment in Patriots history, Henderson received a standing ovation.

Chapter 57
Looks like Tarzan, Plays like Jane: Scouting

Until the 1970s, college scouting by NFL teams was often a joke. Some teams did little more than thumb through college-football preview magazines and phone college coaches for recommendations.

That was before the scouting revolution. Now, NFL prospects are examined as carefully as federal employees who require top-level security clearance.

THE SCOUTING COMBINE in Indianapolis is an annual NFL ritual in which more than three hundred of the nation's top draft prospects are invited for drills, medical exams, interviews, and intelligence and psychological testing. By the time a prospect finishes his seventy-two-hour whirlwind visit, every team knows if he still has his appendix, whether his old knee injury has healed completely, and if he looks buff or flabby in his underwear.

You can credit Los Angeles Rams safety Nolan Cromwell for inspiring the combine's creation. Former Cowboys player personnel director Gil Brandt recalled a weary Cromwell arriving in Dallas before the 1977 draft. The Cowboys were among many teams that wanted to examine a knee injury Cromwell suffered while playing quarterback at Kansas.

"He just got off an all-night flight from Seattle and he was completely worn out," Brandt recalled. "We were the sixteenth team he visited. We said, 'This is ridiculous; a guy flying around the country and missing all this school when you can get all this done at one time and get it done so much better.'"

The Cowboys are credited with leading the NFL into the modern scouting age. Tom Landry was the first head coach to evaluate prospects with an intelligence test. Brandt built a vast network of college coaches and other sources who could tell him as much about a prospect's character as talent.

Prompted by the Cromwell experience, the Cowboys joined five other teams to work out the top 150 prospects before the 1978 draft. "We were probably the first ones who brought players in en masse," Brandt said. "National and Blesto [scouting services] the following year did the same thing."

Cooperation between those two scouting services and NFL teams led to a league-wide combine in 1985. It moved permanently to Indianapolis in 1987.

The lobby of the hotel that houses the combine invitees is jammed with agents, reporters, and hangers-on. The hotel's best efforts to discourage loitering—by removing all lobby chairs and couches—go for naught. The scene may appear hectic, but it's tame compared to how it once was.

"That first year in Indianapolis, there was no security," recalled Dr. Bob Troutwine, a psychologist who's tested draft prospects since 1985. "There were pimps and hookers in the lobby. It was crazy.

"Every player gets asked, 'Do you have an agent.' I saw one guy hand out ten hundred-dollar bills—he fanned them all out. He bought a player for a thousand dollars."

All a scout needs to measure a prospect's skills are a stopwatch, a tape measure, weights, cones, and a sharp set of eyes. To measure what's inside a prospect, however, teams rely on testing. Troutwine administers the Troutwine Athletic Profile, or TAP, for about a half-dozen NFL teams. The test is famous for asking a prospect if he sees himself as a dog or a cat.

"I'm definitely a dog," offensive tackle Chris McIntosh said before the Seattle Seahawks drafted him in the first round in 2000. "I'm allergic to cats."

The question probes a prospect's independence. "At a very subconscious level, you have dogged determination versus your independent cat," Troutwine explained. "They [cat types] might appreciate a coach who gives an explanation for a rule: 'No earrings on game day.' A dog would be fine with that. A cat would at least want to know why."

The TAP asks a prospect if he finds true beauty in a painting he's never seen before or in a classic car. The player who prefers the painting reveals an artistic temperament. "He's more conceptual and thinks outside the box," Troutwine said. "The others are more practical and down to earth."

While the Wonderlic Personnel Test remains the standard predraft intelligence test, the number of psychological tests has grown to about ten. One test question read: "I like tall women. Yes or no?" One player just crossed out the "t."

Troutwine doesn't make draft picks, but his opinions reinforced two draft decisions that proved monumental for one of his clients.

Indianapolis held the first overall pick in 1998 and obviously would select between quarterbacks Peyton Manning and Ryan Leaf. Manning was more polished, though many scouts claimed Leaf's athletic ability made him the better long-term prospect. After listening to Colts president Bill Polian explain that his top pick would be asked to start as a rookie, Troutwine identified Manning as the obvious pick.

"I said he has a low-key type of leadership style, but I felt he would get on a lineman, even a veteran," Troutwine said. "He wasn't passive, he was low-key, and it was important to make that distinction because we needed a leader on that offense.

"His ability to rebound from mistakes and the whole emotional maturity issue, he looked very strong. At that time, we were worried about another three-and-thirteen season. If it was going to be trial by fire, he was somebody who maybe could live through that experience and instead of it leaving him scarred, come out a better player."

The San Diego Chargers traded up to take Leaf with the second pick. His career, dogged by immaturity and injuries, never got off the ground.

"There are things I liked about him," Troutwine said. "He was very competitive. [But] if you are not mature and are very competitive, you really want a lot of attention. His ability to handle frustration just wasn't there."

Manning threw forty-nine touchdown passes, an NFL record, in 2004. Leaf was already out of the league by then.

The Colts went into the 1999 draft holding the fourth overall pick and needed a top running back, preferably one who wouldn't resent Manning's star status. Ricky Williams, the Heisman Trophy winner, generally was considered the marquee back of the draft, and the Colts created a stir by taking Edgerrin James instead.

"My piece of the puzzle was, 'How would they each fit?'" said Troutwine, who spent a day with Williams and briefly visited James. "By then, Manning already was the leader on the offense, and the question came up, 'Would they be satisfied being second fiddle? Or are they going to need star status?' Edgerrin would be grateful if you gave him opportunities, whereas Ricky would have just taken it for granted."

In seven years with the Colts, James helped them reach the play-offs six times. In 2005, he enjoyed his fourth 1,500-yard rushing season while Williams was a backup in Miami.

No matter how scientific scouting becomes, plain talk from scouts will always be helpful. Many a scouting report is spiced with expressions more reminiscent of Mark Twain than Vince Lombardi.

"We try to draw pictures for our coaches," explains Chuck Cook, Kansas City director of college scouting. "You try to have a sense of humor and it comes out on draft day."

Here are some of those pictures, and each is worth a thousand words:

ON PHYSICAL APPEARANCE:

Looks like Tarzan, plays like Jane.

So skinny, he has to jump around in the shower to get wet.

Has such a bad body, he's like a walking water bed.

So fat he takes two loads to haul ass.

So small he could run under a table full speed.

ON RUNNING ABILITY:

Can run the minute in fifty-eight seconds.

So quick he can spit on lightning.

Quicker than a hiccup.

He's like trying to catch a minnow in Lake Michigan.

So quick you couldn't hit him with a handful of rocks.

So clumsy in space, he's like a cow on ice.

ON ARM STRENGTH:

Could throw a ball through a car wash and have it come out dry on the other side.

ON ATTITUDE:

He's so lazy that if his house was on fire and he was lying on the sofa, I doubt that he'd get up.

Dow Jones-type player, up and down.

ON INTELLIGENCE:

Dumber than a houseplant.

Chapter 58
Draft Picks and Draftniks: Draft Day Tales

The NFL all but laughed when ESPN president Chet Simmons asked commissioner Pete Rozelle in late 1979 if the cable network could televise the draft. "Pete thought he was nuts," said longtime draft anchor Chris Berman.

NFL owners thought Simmons was nuts, too, and rejected his proposal, 28–0. Though Rozelle was a visionary, he couldn't envision that potbellied fans in Jets jerseys, arguments over high picks, and draftees baring their joy or despair could turn a mundane administrative procedure into the NFL's springfest in New York.

Rozelle also had no idea how many football fans don't have lives.

EAGLES QUARTERBACK DONOVAN McNabb was accustomed to insults long before teammate Terrell Owens criticized his leadership, or before commentator Rush Limbaugh claimed that he was overrated by white reporters pushing for a black quarterback to succeed. McNabb took more abuse than that at the 1999 draft.

A Philadelphia radio talk-show host took a group of fans to New York with the idea they'd celebrate the selection of Heisman Trophy–winning running back Ricky Williams. The Eagles had the second overall pick and were up after the Cleveland Browns took quarterback Tim Couch. But that wasn't Williams at the podium, being presented with a green jersey. It was McNabb, and the Philly fans booed lustily.

"They're pointing and booing," McNabb recalled. "It pissed me off to the point that my motivation was so high, I couldn't wait to get started."

Andre Sommersell, a Colorado State defensive end, sat in frustration as one team after another passed him over on the second day of the 2004 draft. It never dawned on him that he would end the day as a celebrity. When the Oakland Raiders made him the 255th and last player drafted, Sommersell went from becoming Mr. Nobody to Mr. Irrelevant. There's a tremendous distinction there.

Irrelevant Week was started in 1975 by Paul Salata, to honor the last player drafted. It's a celebration in late June at Newport Beach, California, and Mr. Irrelevant is honored with banquets, a parade, a trip to Disneyland, and the presentation of the Lowsman Trophy. That's the poor man's Heisman.

"When I first got the call from the Raiders," Sommersell said, "I got six other calls from the Irrelevant people."

To be Mel Kiper Jr. is every draftnik's fantasy. Kiper turned his obsession with the NFL draft into a dream job and has been ESPN's chief draft analyst since 1984. Whether because of his shiny pompadour or outspoken opinions, Mel annoys people.

Kiper teed up the Colts during the 1994 draft because they took Nebraska linebacker Trev Alberts with the fifth overall pick. Kiper insisted that Indianapolis should've taken quarterback Trent Dilfer from Fresno State. He said that mistakes like this were the reason the Colts were drafting near the top every year.

Colts general manager Bill Tobin blew his stack. "Who the hell is Mel Kiper?" he asked. "My mailman knows more about the draft than he does." Tobin also asked out loud whether Kiper ever had worn a jockstrap.

Kiper got the last laugh, however. Alberts couldn't crack the starting lineup during three injury-filled seasons with the Colts.

"Say what you will about Dilfer," Kiper said, "but he's been in the Pro Bowl and won a Super Bowl."

Thurman Thomas had a brilliant career at Oklahoma State and wasn't counting on six other running backs going before him in 1988. Buffalo was seeking a first-rate back but had no first-round pick. Just when the Bills assumed they'd be looking at left-overs, offensive backfield coach Elijah Pitts announced in the war room that "the very best running back I worked out on my trip is still on the board."

Thomas was only five-foot-ten and 195, had suffered a severe knee injury in his junior year, and was unproven as a receiver. A quick call from Bills coach Marv Levy to Oklahoma State coach Pat Jones revealed that Thomas hadn't missed a single game or practice since returning from his injury.

With twenty seconds left to make their second-round pick, the Bills took Thomas, who would help them win four straight AFC titles. But the moment was lost on Thomas as he drowsily watched thirty-nine players taken before him. When ESPN showed him waiting for a call, he was sound asleep.

The Tampa Bay Buccaneers demonstrated in 1982 why they misfired on so many picks. Those team representatives you see sitting by the phones in New York are equipment managers or other club employees who aren't involved in draft decisions. They hand in selection cards after hearing instructions from their war rooms. Misunderstandings can result.

The Bucs' man in New York had cards filled out for Penn State guard Sean Farrell and Bethune-Cookman defensive end Booker Reese. The Bucs' brain trust told their man they wanted Reese but he mistakenly turned in the card for Farrell.

As it turned out, their rep was trying to do the Bucs a favor. But they still wanted Reese and got him in the second round after trading their first-round pick for 1983. Farrell made a Pro Bowl for the Bucs. Reese made only seven starts over three years before he was traded to the Los Angeles Rams for a twelfth-round pick.

When the Dallas Cowboys drafted wide receiver David Mc-Daniels in the second round in 1968, it appeared they'd uncovered another diamond in the rough. McDaniels played at tiny Mississippi Valley State, which would produce Jerry Rice, and had an impressive 40-yard dash time of 4.4 seconds.

But defensive backs had no trouble covering McDaniels in training camp and the Cowboys timed him again. He actually ran forty yards in 4.73 seconds, which would've been dandy for a guard. It turned out that Mississippi Valley's 40-yard course was a yard and a half short. That's why NFL scouts always carry tape measures now.

Though McDaniels was a bust, he made the Cowboys' roster in 1968 and they recovered nicely from their oversight. They traded McDaniels to Philadelphia for an aging tight end who'd been injured and was out of favor with Eagles coach Joe Kuharich. That was future Hall of Famer Mike Ditka.

He played four seasons in Dallas and caught thirty passes in 1971. Ditka finished that season with a 7-yard pass from Roger Staubach to score the last touchdown in a 24–3 Super Bowl victory over the Miami Dolphins.

Not every draftee learns right away that he's been picked. Norm Michael, a fullback from Syracuse, learned in 1999, only after reading a newspaper, that he'd been drafted by the Eagles—in 1944.

The Eagles never notified Michael that they had drafted him because they weren't aware that he'd enlisted in the Army before the draft and was stationed in Montgomery, Alabama. Michael must've felt like he was reading his own obituary when he finally spotted his name on a list of every Syracuse player who'd ever been drafted. It was too late for him to get an agent, though.

Chapter 59
Busts:
Worst Picks Ever

When it comes to reminiscing about the NFL
draft, fans are as fascinated with the flops as
with the superstars. Draftniks can tell you the
worst pick their teams ever made as readily as
they can recall the best pick.

Maybe that's because fans invest so much
hope in a first-round pick that a bust stings
them forever. Or maybe they get a sadistic kick
out of seeing scouts caught so far off base. If
you want proof that drafting is not an exact
science, just read on.

TONY MANDARICH, THE second overall pick in 1989, was literally the biggest bust in NFL draft history. A six-foot-six, 315-
pound tackle from Michigan State, he was called the best
offensive line prospect ever by *Sports Illustrated* and featured on
the cover as "The Incredible Bulk."

The Packers took Mandarich after quarterback Troy Aikman
went to the Dallas Cowboys. Taken next were three future
stars—running back Barry Sanders, linebacker Derrick Thomas,
and cornerback Deion Sanders.

Mandarich was a man among boys in college but a child
among adults in the NFL. He staged a training-camp holdout

and claimed he wanted to fight Mike Tyson. Living in Los Angeles, he lifted weights on Venice Beach and affected a rock star persona. Between his attitude and play, Mandarich got off on the wrong foot with nearly everybody in Green Bay.

"It was immaturity, it was arrogance, it was being cocky, it was shooting my mouth off, it was all of those things," he reflected. "I believed my own hype, loved to hear myself talk. I was blind and didn't realize it until one day I woke up and saw I was [nothing]. It was, 'Holy smokes, what did I do?'"

Mandarich started for the Packers without distinction in 1990 and 1991, then sat out 1992 because of a thyroid problem and post-concussion syndrome. He was out of football until 1996, when his former Packers coach, Lindy Infante, gave him a chance in Indianapolis. Mandarich played three seasons for the Colts.

Since retiring from football, Mandarich is more likely to be featured in *Golf Digest* than *Sports Illustrated*. A native of Canada, he became part owner and general manager of Century Pines Golf Club in Flamborough, Ontario, in 2000. "When I retired from football in 1999, I wasn't crazy about getting dressed up in a suit and tie every day," Mandarich said. "So this is the life for me."

The red lights were flashing around Ryan Leaf, but the Chargers drove right through them. Leaf and Peyton Manning were the glamour quarterbacks of the 1998 draft, but were worlds apart in maturity. The Colts had the first pick and coach Jim Mora asked Leaf and Manning how each would react if Indianapolis drafted him.

Mora recalled that Manning replied, "Hey, coach, send me the playbook, get a coach down here, send me videotape so I can start learning the offense. I want to get up to Indianapolis just as soon as I can, start working with the guys."

Leaf's reply, according to Mora, "was something like, 'Oh, man, I'm going to go to Las Vegas with my buddies and we're going to celebrate. Then I'm going to take my girlfriend to Hawaii for a couple of weeks.'"

The Colts, wisely, picked Manning. "You saw right there the difference between the two guys," Mora said. "Not a physical difference, but an inside difference."

The Chargers didn't appreciate Leaf's immaturity until after they made him the second overall pick and paid him an $11.25 million signing bonus. Leaf was shaky in his first two starts but won them both, thanks to his defense. Then, after a 23–7 loss at Kansas City, Leaf threw an obscenity-filled fit at a team-employed photographer. That was the first of several ugly incidents, which included him berating a reporter on camera.

San Diego fans quickly tired of Leaf's boorishness and even booed a public-service message by him. During a bye week, Leaf returned to the Washington State campus to make a charitable donation, yet instead made news for his obnoxious behavior around Pullman.

Leaf's second season, 1999, ended before it began. He skipped part of a voluntary workout in June, then suffered a right-shoulder injury upon his return. He aggravated the injury in training camp and needed surgery.

That August, Leaf had to be led away from a heckler and said, "Maybe it's in the team's best interests to let me go, but I don't want that to be the case. It doesn't seem like there's anything positive around here at all right now."

When general manager Bobby Beathard and strength coach John Hastings tried talking to Leaf about his rehabilitation in midseason, he cursed them and was suspended for four weeks. During his suspension, Leaf was videotaped playing flag football at a local park. In that game, he sprained his ankle.

Leaf's last season in San Diego was hindered by a sprained wrist. After claiming his wrist was too sore for him to practice or play, he was spotted playing golf. The Chargers cut Leaf loose after the 2000 season.

After a final fling at Dallas in 2001, Leaf's career was over. He had fourteen touchdown passes, thirty-six interceptions, and the dubious distinction of being the biggest quarterback bust in the history of the draft.

The Rams would have been better off just skipping the sixth pick of the 1996 draft than drafting running back Lawrence Phillips. He brought to St. Louis a troubled background, which included an arrest for beating his ex-girlfriend at Nebraska.

Phillips was still on probation when, soon after the draft, he was arrested for driving while intoxicated. The Rams wouldn't give Phillips a signing bonus, and his arrest resulted in a jail sentence for violating probation. He served twenty-three days at a Lincoln, Nebraska, jail in March 1997, then was picked up by new coach Dick Vermeil.

Vermeil's compassion was lost on Phillips, who totaled three arrests during his nineteen months with the Rams. He finally was waived in November 1997 because he skipped a meeting and a practice after Vermeil told him he wouldn't start the next game. Phillips then joined the Miami Dolphins but was gone the next summer after he allegedly punched a woman in the face at a nightclub.

Phillips revived his career by starring in NFL Europe during the summer of 1999 and immediately joined the San Francisco 49ers. He was suspended for repeated insubordination. The last straw came when Phillips laughed as coach Steve Mariucci lectured the offense for allowing a sack during a drill.

Phillips drifted to the Florida Bobcats of the Arena League and Montreal and Calgary of the Canadian Football League. He quit or had disciplinary problems everywhere. It's hard to find another player who wore out his welcome so often.

As NFL prospects, most Penn State running backs have been cursed. Ki-Jana Carter, the top overall pick by the Bengals in 1995, and Blair Thomas, the second overall pick by the Jets in 1990, fizzled as pros. Curtis Enis fizzled, too, but not before some bizarre fireworks.

The Bears had the fifth overall pick in 1998 and brought Enis and Marshall wide receiver Randy Moss to Chicago for interviews. Moss seemed unrepentant for having a criminal record and a questionable attitude and overslept for a meeting with the Bears. Enis came across as a model citizen, though he'd been ruled ineligible for Penn State's bowl game because he took a free suit from an agent.

Enis rushed for 2,573 yards and thirty-two touchdowns in his last two college seasons and came out after his junior year. A month after the draft, a woman in Dallas accused him of raping her, though a grand jury declined to indict him.

Enis said that experience, a drinking problem, and frequent womanizing led him to a Bible study session held by Greg Ball, head of Champions for Christ in Austin, Texas. Enis replaced veteran agent Vann McElroy with an agent close to Ball.

In July 1998, Enis married his pregnant fiancée, Tiffanie, a former exotic dancer. Enis announced at the reception that he and his wife had been saved by a religious awakening and that any guests who didn't follow their example were condemned to eternal damnation.

"It was the most inappropriate moment I've ever experienced," one guest told *Sports Illustrated*. "Here was a guy marrying a three-months-pregnant stripper telling a roomful of family that they were going to hell."

That's pretty much where Enis's career went. He spent three disappointing seasons with the Bears before they let him go. And Moss? Character issues knocked him down to the twenty-first spot of the first round, but he's well on his way to one of the best receiving careers in NFL history. And maybe the curse on Penn State running backs was finally lifted when the Chiefs' Larry Johnson had a Pro Bowl season in 2005.

Here's our all-time bust team. Only first-round picks are included.

OFFENSE

Wide Receivers: Clyde Duncan, Tennessee, 17, Cardinals, 1984. Desmond Howard, Michigan, 4, Redskins, 1992.

Tackles: Tony Mandarich, Michigan, 2, Packers, 1989. Brian Jozwiak, West Virginia, 8, Chiefs, 1986

Guards: Eugene Chung, Virginia Tech, 13, Patriots, 1992. Rod Walters, Iowa, 14, Chiefs, 1976.

Center: Robert Shaw, Tennessee, 27, Cowboys, 1979.

Tight End: Ken McAfee, Notre Dame, 7, 49ers, 1978.

Quarterback: Ryan Leaf, 2, Washington State, Chargers, 1998.

Running Backs: Ki-Jana Carter, Penn State, 1, Bengals, 1995. Blair Thomas, Penn State, 2, Jets, 1990.

DEFENSE

Defensive Ends: Eric Curry, Alabama, 6, Buccaneers, 1993. Andre Wadsworth, Florida State, 3, Cardinals, 1998.

Defensive Tackles: Steve Emtman, Washington, 1, Colts, 1992. Dan Wilkinson, Ohio State, 1, Bengals, 1994.

Linebackers: Tom Cousineau, Ohio State, 1, Bills, 1979. Mike Junkin, Duke, 5, Browns, 1987. Trev Alberts, Nebraska, 5, Colts, 1994.

Cornerbacks: Bruce Pickens, Nebraska, 3, Falcons, 1991. Michael Booker, Nebraska, 11, Falcons, 1997.

Safeties: Patrick Bates, Texas A&M, 12, Raiders, 1993. Rickey Dixon, Oklahoma, 5, Bengals, 1988.

SPECIAL TEAMS

Kicker and Punter: Russell Erxleben, Texas, 11, Saints, 1979.

Acknowledgments

When I told some sportswriting friends that I was writing a humor book about pro football, they reacted as if I were writing a humor book about the bubonic plague.

But there really is humor in pro football. You just have to know where to look. I started at the Pro Football Hall of Fame, where Chad Reese and his library staff had a pile of the funniest books ever written about pro football waiting for me.

The Football Hall of Shame volumes by Bruce Nash and Allan Zullo, and *The Pro Football Chronicle*, by Dan Daly and Bob O'Donnell were on top of the pile. These were just the right books to put me in laugh mode, though not all the stories in this book are laughing matters.

I've been laughing at and with the crazy characters in pro football for a long time, and want to thank all the players, coaches, and front office executives who've been willing to share their reminiscences. I've been privileged to have spent at least some time around most of the characters in this book during the past thirty-five years.

This book wouldn't have been published without encouragement from two editors at The Lyons Press. Gene Brissie helped me to submit the manuscript, and Rob Kirkpatrick became its advocate, then provided invaluable guidance. Jessie Shiers and Melissa Hayes gave the manuscript meticulous and exceptional care. I want to thank Ed Claflin, my literary agent, for his role in negotiations.

I especially want to thank my wife, Barbara, and son, Steven, for laughing when they peeked over my shoulder at what I was writing. There's always the fear that you may be the only one who thinks your material is funny. I also want to thank my older children, David and Danielle, for their sustained support of my writing.

Bibliography

Attner, Paul. *The Complete Handbook of Pro Football*. New York: New American Library, 1982.

Attner, Paul. "Steel-willed—Pittsburgh Steeler coach Bill Cowher." *The Sporting News*, July 27, 1998.

Attner, Paul. "Here's Johnny." *The Sporting News*, December 7, 1998.

Bayless, Skip. *The Boys*. New York: Simon & Schuster, 1993.

Bosworth, Brian and Rick Reilly. *The Boz: Confessions of a Modern Anti-Hero*. New York: Doubleday, 1988.

Byrne, Jim. *The $1 League: The Rise and Fall of the USFL*. New York: Prentice Hall Press, 1986.

Campbell, Jim. "Rules of the Name." *The Coffin Corner*, Volume XXI, 1999.

Daly, Dan and Bob O'Donnell. *The Pro Football Chronicle*. New York: Collier Books, 1990.

Day, Chuck and Don Weiss. *The Making of the Super Bowl*. New York: Contemporary Books, 2003.

Delsohn, Steve and John Matuszak. *Cruisin' with the Tooz*. New York: Franklin Watts, 1987.

Dienhart, Tom, Joe Hoppel, and Dave Sloan, editors. *Complete Super Bowl Book*. St. Louis: The Sporting News Publishing, 1994.

Favre, Brett and Chris Havel. *Favre: For the Record*. New York: Doubleday, 1997.

Forrest, Brett. *Long Bomb: How the XFL Became TV's Biggest Fiasco*. New York: Crown Publishers, 2002.

Hubbard, Steve. *Shark among Dolphins: Inside Jimmy Johnson's Transformation of the Miami Dolphins*. New York: Ballantine Books, 1997.

Izenberg, Jerry. *No Medals for Trying*. New York: Ballantine Books, 1990.

Jenkins, Dan. "The Sweet Life of Swinging Joe." *Sports Illustrated*, reprinted October 31, 1994.

Kaspris, Ron. "First and 10: former football star Tony Mandarich finds new life on the fairways." *Golf Digest*, August 2003.

Keim, John. *Legends by the Lake*. Akron, Ohio: University of Akron Press, 1999.

Knox, Chuck and Bill Plaschke. *Hard Knox*. New York: Harcourt Brace Jovanovich, 1988.

Levy, Marv. *Where Else Would You Rather Be?* Champaign, Illinois: Sports Publishing, 2004.

Littwin, Mike. "Game Breakers." *ESPN The Magazine*, January 20, 1999.

Maraniss, David. *When Pride Still Mattered: A Life of Vince Lombardi*. New York: Simon & Schuster, 1999.

Mullin, John. *Tales from the Chicago Bears Sideline*. Champaign, Illinois: Sports Publishing, 2003.

Nash, Bruce and Allen Zullo. *The Football Hall of Shame*. New York: Pocket Books, 1986.

Nash, Bruce and Allen Zullo. *The Football Hall of Shame, Volume 2*. New York: Pocket Books, 1990.

Ryczek, Bill. *Crash of the Titans: The Early Years of the New York Jets and the AFL*. New York: Total Sports, 2000.

Silver, Michael. "Passing Marks." *Sports Illustrated*, December 20, 2004.

Silver, Michael and Don Yaeger. "Leap of Faith." *Sports Illustrated*, August 24, 1998.

Stabler, Ken and Barry Stainback. *Snake*. New York: Doubleday, 1986.

Stallard, Mark and Otis Taylor. *The Need to Win*. Champaign, Illinois: Sports Publishing, 2003.

Tandler, Rich. *The Redskins from A to Z, Volume 1*. Midlothian, Virginia: Walking Encyclopedia Publications, 2002.

Underwood, John. "He's Burning to be a Success." *Sports Illustrated*, September, 20, 1971.

Walsh, Bill and Glenn Dickey. *Building a Champion: On Football and the Making of the 49ers*. New York: St. Martins Press, 1992.

Whittingham, Richard. *The Bears*. Dallas: Taylor Publishing, 1994.

Williamson, Bill. *Tales from the Vikings Locker Room: A Collection of the Greatest Stories Ever Told*. Champaign, Illinois: Sports Publishing, 2003.

Wyatt, Jim. *Tales from the Titans Sidelines*. Champaign, Illinois: Sports Publishing, 2004.

Zimmerman, Paul. *The New Thinking Man's Guide to Pro Football*. New York: Simon & Schuster, 1984.

Index